D0204126

Steroids and Doping in Sports

Recent Titles in the

CONTEMPORARY WORLD ISSUES
Series

Books in the **Contemporary World Issues** series address vital issues in today's society such as genetic engineering, pollution, and biodiversity. Written by professional writers, scholars, and nonacademic experts, these books are authoritative, clearly written, up-to-date, and objective. They provide a good starting point for research by high school and college students, scholars, and general readers as well as by legislators, businesspeople, activists, and others.

Each book, carefully organized and easy to use, contains an overview of the subject, a detailed chronology, biographical sketches, facts and data and/or documents and other primary source material, a forum of authoritative perspective essays, annotated lists of print and nonprint resources, and an index.

Readers of books in the Contemporary World Issues series will find the information they need in order to have a better understanding of the social, political, environmental, and economic issues facing the world today.

Steroids and Doping in Sports

A REFERENCE HANDBOOK

Second Edition

David E. Newton

An Imprint of ABC-CLIO, LLC

Santa Barbara, California • Denver, Colorado

Library of Congress Cataloging-in-Publication Data

Names: Newton, David E., author.
Title: Steroids and doping in sports : a reference handbook / David E. Newton.
Description: Second edition. | Santa Barbara, California : ABC-CLIO, LLC, [2018] | Series: Contemporary world issues | Includes bibliographical references and index.
Identifiers: LCCN 2017030028 (print) | LCCN 2017030589 (ebook) | ISBN 9781440854828 (ebook) | ISBN 9781440854811 (alk. paper)
Subjects: LCSH: Doping in sports—Handbooks, manuals, etc. | Anabolic steroids—Health aspects—Handbooks, manuals, etc. | Steroid drugs—Handbooks, manuals, etc.
Classification: LCC RC1230 (ebook) | LCC RC1230 .N48 2018 (print) | DDC 362.29/088796—dc23
LC record available at https://lccn.loc.gov/2017030028

ISBN: 978-1-4408-5481-1
EISBN: 978-1-4408-5482-8

22 21 20 19 18   1 2 3 4 5

This book is also available as an eBook.

ABC-CLIO
An Imprint of ABC-CLIO, LLC

ABC-CLIO, LLC
130 Cremona Drive, P.O. Box 1911
Santa Barbara, California 93116-1911
www.abc-clio.com

This book is printed on acid-free paper ∞

Manufactured in the United States of America

vii

4   Profiles, 165

In 2014, a German film company produced a documentary motion picture called *Secret Doping—How Russia Makes Its Winners*. The film brought to public view an issue that had been lingering at the edges of professional and amateur sports worldwide for more than a century. When, where, how, and to what extent were individual athletes and athletic teams using illegal sports to gain an unfair advantage in competition? Specific, individual acts of cheating in sports had been known since the time of the ancient Greeks. But were such events simply uncommon and relatively minor deviations from the wide field of sports? Or did they extend to a wider field of individuals and events?

The German film seemed to suggest that the latter might be the case: that a nation's entire sports program had been permeated by formal programs developed and approved at the highest levels to allow its competitors to gain an advantage in a broad range of athletic endeavors. Before long, evidence began flooding in that cheating was a common part of most professional and amateur sports worldwide. The leader of the Russian anti-doping program, Grigory Rodchenkov, confirmed in 2016 that "secret doping" was essentially correct, and that the Russian government had been at least complicit, and perhaps even active, in efforts to evade international prohibitions on the use of illegal substances and procedures in sporting events. A number of international athletic agencies, such as the International Olympic Committee (IOC), the International Association of Athletic Federations, and the World Anti-Doping Agency (WADA), began to appoint committees and organize efforts to learn more about this trend. Three reports from WADA in 2015 and 2016 in particular focused the world's attention on the use of performance-enhancing drugs and procedures in national, regional, and international athletic competitions. In December of 2017, the IOC voted to ban Russia from competing in the 2018 Winter Olympics in PyeongChang, South Korea; however, individual athletes who tested cleanly were allowed to compete under the designation "Olympic Athletes from Russia" (OAR), carrying a neutral Olympic flag. Several athletes tested positive for doping at the 2018 Olympics and were suspended or stripped of their medals.

Among the most commonly mentioned of these drugs were the anabolic asteroids, a group of compounds designed to make an individual "faster, higher, stronger," to borrow from the IOC motto. Numerous studies and reports confirmed that individual athletes had for many decades been seeking and using such compounds to gain an unfair advantage in sporting events. At the same time, sporting officials were looking for and tagging most such compounds in an ever-growing effort to identify and prohibit the use of such compounds.

This book is an effort to provide readers with a general introduction to this centuries-long cat-and-mouse game between competitors and sporting agencies, dating at least to the time of the ancient Greeks. It discusses the history of anabolic steroids, their productive use in the treatment of adverse human conditions, their applications in athletic competition, and their growing use by boys and girls and men of women of all ages in all parts of the world to improve their own body image.

The first edition of this book was published just prior to the release of the most serious revelations about the use of performance-enhancing drugs in amateur and professional sports. It has seemed appropriate, therefore, to bring that story up to date with a review of the events of 2014 and later. In addition to this new information, presented in Chapters 1 and 2, the book also has an updated chronology (Chapter 7), new information about important individuals and organizations (Chapter 4), updated statistical information about steroids and the use of performance-enhancing drugs (Chapter 5), a more current list of print and electronic resources (Chapter 6), and new essays by individuals with special and important perspectives on steroid-related issues (Chapter 3).

Steroids and Doping in Sports

Taylor seemed abnormally upset. His parents could not understand how their normally happy, optimistic 16-year-old athlete-son could have become so depressed. And his health had taken a turn for the worst. He complained of aches and pains much of the time, although he otherwise seemed in the best of health. Perhaps it was just the pressure of trying to become the high school baseball team's number one pitcher. When the symptoms did not pass, they convinced Taylor to see a psychiatrist. There he confessed the probable source of his unhappiness and distress: steroids. Believing that he probably had to become physically stronger, Taylor had started injecting himself with anabolic steroids (sometimes abbreviated as AS). Now there seemed to be only one way out: he had to give up on the drugs.

Taylor's parents were hopeful that the problem had been solved. Then, about six weeks later, they discovered how wrong they were. When Taylor failed to come down from his bedroom one morning, his parents found that he had hung himself. The

---

Don Hooton sits in a room with remembrances of his late son, Taylor Hooton, at his home in McKinney, Texas, March 17, 2015. Texas is ready to dump its high school steroids testing program. Hooton, who started the Taylor Hooton Foundation for steroid abuse education after his 17-year-old son's 2003 suicide was linked to steroid use, was one of the key advocates in creating the Texas program. Hooton believes the low number of positive tests doesn't mean Texas athletes are clean, only that they're not getting caught because of inadequate testing and loopholes that allow them to cheat the test. (AP Photo/LM Otero)

probable cause of Taylor's suicide was found to be a deep depression caused by his withdrawal from steroid use. (The true story of Taylor Hooton's death is chronicled at a number of websites. See, for example, Willey 2008.)

When Taylor Hooton died in Plano, Texas, in 2003, concerns about the use of AS for the enhancement of athletic performance were just reaching their peak. During the decade, a number of the world's greatest athletes would see their fame diminished or destroyed by evidence or suspicion that their accomplishments were not solely the result of their own natural skill and dedicated training programs but also the consequence of synthetic chemicals that artificially increased their muscle mass, strength, endurance, speed, and other physical attributes. Where, how, and when did this movement to enhance physical performance with synthetic chemicals begin? How did it develop? Where does it stand today? And what does it foretell for the future of amateur and professional sports, as well as for the physical and psychological well-being of those who choose to use AS? These are some of the questions posed and—to some extent—answered in this book.

The History of Performance-Enhancing Drugs

It is probably impossible to say precisely when competitive sports first appeared among humans. Some observers have argued that competition is an innate human characteristic, so it should hardly be surprising that competitive athletic events were common as far back as the earliest stages of human civilization (Potter 2012). Certainly, there is abundant archaeological evidence for the existence of competitive sports dating to at least the second millennium BCE (Carroll 1988). One of the oldest (and fastest) of all European sports, hurling, for example, dates to at least 1400 BCE in Ireland (Phelan 2017).

Dating to at least the same period in Mesoamerica was a group of games played with balls and, sometimes, sticks in large open or enclosed arenas that sometimes resulted in the deaths of members of the losing teams. One well-documented discovery traced a still-extant ball field to about 1400 BCE near Chiapas, Mexico (Hill, Blake, and Clark 1998). A primitive form of football was also played in ancient China in the pre-Christian era. The game, called cuju, was first mentioned in a first-century-BCE document, the *Shi Ji* ("Historical Record"), as being a very popular sport played by both men and women (a bit unusual in and of itself in a predominantly male-oriented era) (Speak 1999, 32–33; Timm 2015).

One might like to believe that there was once a time in human history when competition was pure and simple, when races were won by the swiftest of competitors and wrestling awards went to the strongest of participants. But that view seems somewhat unlikely. A number of observers have commented on the fact that men and women who engage in competition do so because they want to win; they want to be the best among their peers. As one historian of the use of performance-enhancing substances in sports has written:

> When humans compete against one another, either in war, in business, or in sport, the competitors, by definition, seek to achieve an advantage over their opponent. Frequently they use drugs and other substances to gain the upper hand. In sport such conduct . . . has existed for as long as sport has been organised. (Yesalis and Bahrke 2002, 42)

Still, reliable reports of the specific ways in which athletes can cheat to win a competition are essentially nonexistent until the first millennium BCE in Greece. During that period, historians began to record a number of strategies by which competitors unfairly took advantage of their opponents, most commonly perhaps by simply bribing an opponent to run more slowly, fall down during a boxing match, or intentionally drive a chariot less quickly than possible ([Hsu, Li-Hong] 2002). It was also about this time that what is apparently the first specific reference to the use of performance-enhancing substances was mentioned. A prescription widely attributed to perhaps the most famous of all classical physicians, Galen, called for a mixture consisting of "the rear hooves of an Abyssinian ass, ground up, boiled in oil, and flavored with rose hips and rose petals." This preparation, Galen said, was likely to improve an athlete's performance in any sport. (This prescription is cited in many sources. See, for example, Buti and Fridman, 2001, 27, citing the International Olympic Committee multimedia presentation Olympic Gold: A 100 Year History of the Summer Olympic Games.)

Many classical athletes also adopted a vaguely homeopathic (or, more properly, an organotherapeutic) approach to substance use. In preparation for a competition, they were likely to adopt a diet that included specific items that were related to strength, endurance, speed, and other desirable physical traits in other animals. The assumption was that the consumption of an animal's testicles, as an example, would confer upon a person the manly qualities that they gave to a bull, ram, stallion, or other male animal. Similarly, one might consume animal brains to improve one's own intelligence or animal hearts to improve one's courage.

Athletes relied on performance-enhancing substances other than animal organs. Charmis, the winner of the stade race in the Olympic Games of 668 BCE, for example, existed almost entirely on a diet of figs in preparation for the competition. Another champion, Dromeus of Stymphalos, attributed his success in winning seven Olympic races to a diet consisting almost entirely of meat (a very unusual diet for the times). Other athletes relied on cheese, wheat meal, brandy and wine mixtures, sesame seeds, or hallucinogenic mushrooms for the special boost they needed in a competition (Yesalis and Bahrke 2002, 44–45).

These practices were by no means limited to the ancient Greek civilization. As early as about 1400 BCE, for example, the Indian physician Sushruta recommended the consumption of testicular tissue as a means of curing impotence and improving one's masculinity. Athletes from a number of cultures also relied on plant materials to produce enhanced physical characteristics. The legendary Berserkers from the ancient Norse tradition are known to have consumed the drug bufotenin obtained from the *Amanita muscaria* mushroom to increase their fighting strength "12-fold." Under the influence of the drug, they became such fierce warriors that their behavior is preserved in the modern word *berserk*. Similar use of plant-based drugs to improve an individual's physical skills has been traced to early cultures throughout Europe, Africa, and Mesoamerica (Bøje, 1939; Prokop, 1970; Yesalis and Bahrke, 2002).

Doping in the Modern Era

The rise of Christianity in Europe during the late Roman Empire, according to some observers, had the consequence of eliminating or reducing sports competitions, largely because they were viewed as pagan events that distracted a person's attention from more important religious activities. Among the events most commonly cited by such observers was the banning of the Olympic Games by Emperor Theodosius in 393 CE, apparently for just that reason (Gertz 2008).

It was not, therefore, until the 18th century that sports competitions again became widely popular and, perhaps as an inevitable consequence, the use of performance-enhancing substances once more became common. An event that is sometimes cited as the first documented case of doping in the modern era occurred in 1865, when some contestants in a swimming competition at an Amsterdam (Netherlands) canal were suspected of having taken an "unknown" substance (now thought to have been caffeine) to improve their performances (Prokop 1970). (Other writers tell a somewhat different story, claiming that the 1865 doping event actually involved swimmers at a race in the English Channel; see Müller 2010, 3.)

Over the next seven decades, there were isolated reports of drug use in athletic competitions, sometimes with terrible consequences. In 1886, for example, the first death attributed to the use of performance-enhancing drugs was recorded when a European cyclist (reported to have been either Dutch or French) died after using a combination of heroin and cocaine, a mixture known as a "speedball" (Lee 2006; von Deutsch, Abukhalaf, and Socci 2012, 493). One of the most notorious individuals involved with doping at the time was the English cyclist and trainer Choppy Warburton. Warburton was a highly successful runner who won more than 500 races in his career. When he retired from track and field, he began a second career as a cycling coach. He achieved notable success in that field also, at least partly because of the infamous "little black bottle" that he shared with his athletes. Although the bottle supposedly contained magical powers, no one knows what the bottle actually contained. But judging from its effects on the cyclists who used it, the contents may have been something more dangerous, perhaps cocaine, heroin, trimethyl, or strychnine, all common performance enhancers of the time. In any case, at least three cyclists are thought to have died after having taken a draft of the little black bottle, and Warburton is now widely thought to have been the first coach or trainer to have systematically supplied performance-enhancing drugs to his charges (Moore and Ritchie 2011; Rosen 2008, 5–7).

The first known case of doping in the Olympics Games occurred in the 1904 St. Louis event. During the marathon, American runner Thomas Hicks appeared to be so tired that his assistants gave him a dose of strychnine in brandy to "perk him up." When that treatment didn't have much effect, they gave him a second dose of the same mixture. Hicks quickly regained his stride and won the gold medal. (Hicks actually finished second to Fred Lorz, who was disqualified for having ridden in a car for more than half of the race distance.) Hicks collapsed after crossing the finish line as a result of the doping experience. Medical experts later pointed out that one more dose of strychnine would almost certainly have killed him (Cronin 2010).

One of the sports in which performance-enhancing drugs took root early and widely was cycling. The demands of long-distance races, such as the Tour de France, place enormous stress on a person's physical body, and it is easy to see how competitors would constantly search for any means by which they can survive and win such contests. One of the most famous doping cases of the first quarter of the 20th century occurred in connection with the 1924 Tour de France. Three French brothers who participated in the race, Henri, Francis, and Charles Pélissier, gave a somewhat unusual interview to journalist Albert Londres, a reporter for the newspaper *Le Petit Parisien*. The Pélissier brothers told Londres that the only way they could keep going was with drugs, and they showed him their "stash," consisting of aspirin, chloroform, strychnine, cocaine, "horse ointment," and other drugs. Londres published the results of this interview in *Le Petit Parisien* under the headline "Les Forçats de la Route" ("The Convicts of the Road") (Langeron 2012).

The Pélissier brothers later said that they were just kidding around when they spoke with Londres. But other evidence suggests that they were probably describing the situation more accurately than they were willing to admit. By 1930, for example, tour organizer Henri Desgrange found it necessary to make note in the tour rule book that race officials would not supply drugs to contestants and that they would be responsible for those substances themselves (Heijmans and Mallon 2011, xxi).

In spite of a few dramatic incidents like these, there are relatively few known cases of doping in sports until almost the middle of the 20th century, especially in comparison with the number of such cases that have been uncovered since that time. One observer of the topic has suggested that reports of the disastrous consequences of using drugs may have scared off many competitors from using such substances. On the contrary, he suggests, such reports may simply have made athletes far more secretive about their activities, resulting in many fewer reports of drug use than was actually the case (Lee 2006, 9).

In any case, the story of drug use by athletes after the 1930s underwent a dramatic change from anything that occurred prior to that time. The turning point in that history was the discovery and synthesis of testosterone and its analogs. (Drug analogs are chemical compounds that are structurally similar to some parent compound, such as testosterone, but that have relatively modest molecular modifications that change their properties slightly or substantially from those of the parent compound.) Prior to the discovery of testosterone, the purpose of taking a performance-enhancing drug was to activate or inactivate body systems that contribute to success in sporting events. For example, strychnine has the tendency to stimulate the nervous and muscular system, increasing the efficiency with which the body functions. It seemed a reasonable decision, then, to give athletes very small doses of the substances to enhance their performance. Indeed, some sports authorities at the time thought that athletes probably could not compete successfully in some endurance sports, like the marathon, without using a drug like strychnine (de Mondenard 2000).

Other drugs were used to reduce the pain and discomfort associated with athletic events, just as modern-day professional athletes may (usually illegally) receive an injection of a narcotic analgesic, such as heroin, morphine, or oxycodone, that will allow them to return to competition with a sore arm, a twisted ankle, or a broken bone. Testosterone and its chemical cousins have a totally different effect: they actually initiate the production of new cells and tissue in the body, resulting in an increase in body muscle mass. This change, in turn, increases a person's strength, speed, endurance, and other physical traits. Testosterone and related compounds not only help a person become better at what he or she does with his or her body but fundamentally alter that body to raise the bar as to what one's maximum achievement can be.

Testosterone

The Early Years

The first inklings that animals might possess some sort of material responsible for primary and secondary sexual characteristics date to at least the fourth millennium BCE. At some point in time, farmers discovered that castration of a male animal alters (often dramatically) many of that animal's behaviors, such as aggressiveness, interest in sexual mating, vocalization, and display. The first scientific research designed to study this phenomenon was conducted in 1767 by the famous English physician and surgeon John Hunter. Hunter removed the testes from two male chickens and transferred the tissue taken from these organs to the abdominal cavity of two other roosters, who were otherwise not altered. Hunter found that the roosters who received the testicular tissue experienced no behavioral changes, while the two roosters from whom the tissue was taken lost many of their natural male characteristics. In a word, they "grew fat and lazy" (Martin 1970). Hunter was actually not very interested in the demasculinization effects produced in the experiment, as he was primarily interested in learning more about the process of tissue transplantation (Freeman, Bloom, and McGuire 2000, 371).

Hunter's experiment was repeated and refined some eight decades later by the German physiologist Arnold Berthold. In 1849, Berthold castrated six young chickens. From four of the chickens, he removed both testes; from the other two, he removed only one of each pair of testes. He noted that castration had observable effects on all six birds, reducing their aggressiveness toward other birds and their sexual interest in females. Their combs and wattles (both sexual organs in chickens) both continued to grow, although at a much slower rate than normal and with virtually no color.

Berthold next transplanted the testes removed from the young chickens into the abdominal cavities of two of the castrated birds, a procedure similar to that of Hunter. He found that this procedure caused a reappearance of male sexual characteristics in the birds that had received the transplantations. When these birds were sacrificed, he found that new connections had developed between the transplanted testes and the animal's circulatory system. He concluded from this research that the testes provided some substance that circulated in the bloodstream and evoked male sexual characteristics in an animal (Berthold 1849).

Perhaps the first experiment of this type performed on humans was reported in 1889 by the French neurologist and physiologist Charles E. Brown-Séquard. In a letter to the British scientific journal *The Lancet*, Brown-Séquard told how he had injected himself (he was 72 at the time) with extracts taken from the testes of dogs and guinea pigs. He reported that

> a radical change took place in me. . . . I had regained at least all the strength I possessed a good many years ago. . . . My limbs, tested with a dynamometer, for a week before my trial and during the month following the first injection, showed a decided gain of strength. . . . With regard to the facility of intellectual labour, which had diminished within the last few years, a return to my previous ordinary condition became quite manifest. (quoted in Cussons et al. 2002, 678)

Brown-Séquard said that he had achieved similar results with three additional subjects, aged 54, 56, and 68 years, and he found no such results in two elderly men injected with pure water as a placebo.

(Brown-Séquard's research has long been the subject of some debate, with many authorities questioning whether the results he reported were the result of the injections or were, in fact, themselves placebo effects. In 2002, a group of Australian researchers reported a study that suggests that the amount of testosterone injected by Brown-Séquard was far less than needed to produce the effects of which he wrote [Cussons, et al. 2002, 679].)

Regardless of whether Brown-Séquard's reports represented true phenomena or whether they were merely artifacts based on the placebo effect, they soon had a profound effect on medical practice worldwide. Men of all ages saw in his research a way of regaining or enhancing the masculine qualities that were seemingly never great enough for most men. The new field that arose from Brown-Séquard's research was called *organotherapy*, the improvement of life by using organ extracts. Before long, medical entrepreneurs were offering such extracts taken not only from the sex organs but from almost every part of the body. These extracts were being recommended for the cure of an almost endless list of diseases, including epilepsy, tuberculosis, diabetes, paralysis, gangrene, anemia, arteriosclerosis, influenza, Addison's disease, hysteria, and migraine (Hoberman and Yesalis 1995, 78). Within a year of Brown-Séquard's *Lancet* article, more than 12,000 medical practitioners were producing and selling some version of his rejuvenating fluid, soon given the name Elixir of Life (Tatteresall 2009, 730).

Reports about experiments with the Elixir of Life soon began to pour in from around the world. Some observers reported remarkable changes in men who received injections from dogs, rats, guinea pigs, lambs, and other animals. Others saw no improvement in subjects' conditions. But, in a not-unexpected reaction, men around the world concerned about the (natural) loss of their masculine powers thronged to medical practitioners who promised to solve this problem for them with a simple injection or two (or three or more) (Lefler 2017). For an interesting contemporary description of the state of affairs, see "Elixir of Life—A Brief History of Testosterone" 1889; for Brown-Séquard's own account of the discovery and benefits of the elixir, see Dunbar 1889.

Demand for the Elixir of Life was so great that a new problem arose: a deficiency of testicular tissue needed for making the extracts from which the elixir was made. In the early 1920s, Viennese physiologist Eugen Steinach suggested a solution for this program. Based on an extended series of experiments on guinea pigs, rats, and other laboratory animals, Steinach argued that vasoligation of the vas deferens (tying off the tubes through which sperm is released) would allow the materials responsible for male sex characteristics to be retained in the body, permitting a rejuvenation of the male body. (The so-called

Steinach operation is generally similar to the procedure used in a vasectomy today.) As with the Elixir of Life, Steinach's operation soon became widely popular, with such famous figures as Sigmund Freud and William Butler Yeats receiving the treatment (Lock 1983; Turner 2008).

The Search for Testosterone

Even as practicing physicians were putting to use the empirical discoveries of Brown-Séquard, his predecessors, and his successors, another line of research was directed in a more mechanistic direction: the effort to discover and characterize the specific material responsible for the observable changes caused by "testicular fluids." The key introductory step in that search occurred in 1902, when English physiologists William Maddock Bayliss and Ernest Henry Starling discovered a substance (which they called *secretin*) that causes the pancreas to secrete water and bicarbonate even after all nerve connections to the organ have been severed. They concluded that the action of the pancreas was controlled not by messages from the nervous systems but by some type of material, which they called a "chemical messenger." Some years later, British physiologist William B. Hardy suggested the name *hormone* for these chemical messengers. It became apparent to medical researchers at that point that both male and female sex organs produce their effects on the human body by releasing one or more hormones into the body. These hormones then travel throughout the body, where they act on other organs that are responsible for primary and secondary sexual characteristics.

Interest in the discovery of sex hormones was of considerable interest to a number of major pharmaceutical companies. The raging success of the Elixir of Life formulas and the Steinach operation made it clear to such companies that, even when treatment effectiveness was somewhat in question, there was great demand for these products and procedures. Thus, companies such as Organon, in the Netherlands, Ciba, in Switzerland, and Schering, in Germany, began to pour money into research on the still-mysterious sex-giving hormones. The first breakthrough in this race occurred in 1929, when a team of researchers led by American biochemist Edward Adelbart Doisy isolated the hormone responsible for female sex traits from hundreds of liters of female urine. Doisy called the hormone *theelin*. Only a few months later, an identical discovery was announced by German chemist Adolf Butenandt. Butenandt suggested the name *oestron* (now, *estrone*) for the hormone, a name that has been retained. For this and later discoveries, Butenandt was awarded a share of the 1939 Nobel Prize in Chemistry.

Butenandt then turned his attention to the comparable male sex hormone, which he first isolated in 1931. He called that hormone *androsterone* (based on the terms *andro-*, for "male," *-ster-*, for the chemical structure of the molecule, and *-one*, the suffix used for ketones, the chemical family to which the compound belongs). It is now known that androsterone is a metabolite of testosterone with no androgenic or anabolic properties of its own. (A metabolite is a substance formed as the result of the breakdown of some other substance, as when testosterone breaks down in the body to produce androsterone [and other products]. The term *androgen* [or *androgenic*] refers to any substance that promotes the development of masculine physical properties, such as the growth of body and facial hair, deepening of the voice, enlargement of the larynx, increase in muscle mass and strength, and broadening of the shoulders in humans.) Butenandt's success in isolating androsterone is rather remarkable since it involved the collection of anywhere from 15,000 to 25,000 liters (authorities differ with regard to the exact number) of urine from local policemen (Dotson and Brown 2007, 764).

The final step in this phase of the testosterone story occurred in 1934, when Croatian biochemist Leopold Ružička, starting with readily available relatively simple organic compounds, synthesized androsterone. For the first time, scientists had an essentially complete knowledge of a single sex hormone, androsterone. At the same time, they had extensive evidence to suggest that androsterone was not the hormone responsible for male sexual characteristics.

The discovery of that substance was actually well under way by the time Doisy, Butenandt, and Ružička had completed their studies. As early as 1926, two researchers at the University of Chicago, Fred Koch and Lemeul C. McGee, had begun their own search for the male sex hormone. They were fortunate in the fact that, residing in Chicago, they had access to one of the world's largest supplies of the raw product needed for such studies, the testicles of domestic bulls headed for the slaughterhouse. They began by purchasing 40 pounds of bull testicles from the Chicago stockyards and then developing processes for extracting the hormone found in the testicles. They obtained a minuscule sample of 20 milligrams of the substance that when injected into capons (neutered roosters) restored the bird's normal masculine characteristics, such as a pronounced comb and wattles. They then expanded their experiment by starting with an even larger supply of bull testicles—more than 1,000 pounds—from which they were able to extract a much larger amount of the male sex hormone. Again, they tested this hormone on experimental animals and, eventually, on a male eunuch (a castrated male). In all cases, they found that the hormone produced the masculinizing effects for which they had been searching. They had clearly demonstrated that some type of a male sex hormone exists.

Determination as to the precise nature of that hormone was resolved by another group of researchers at the Organo pharmaceutical firm, in Oss, Netherlands, led by Ernst Laqueur, a founder of the firm. In 1935, the Organo research team announced that they had isolated a new substance with powerful androgenic properties. They reported their results in a now-classic paper in endocrinology, "Über krystallinisches mannliches Hormon aus Hoden (Testosteron) wirksamer als aus harn oder aus Cholesterin bereitetes Androsteron" ("On Crystalline Male Hormone from Testicles [Testosterone] Effective as from Urine or from Cholesterol") (see David et al. 1935 for the original paper).

The search was almost over. The male sex hormone had been found, its physiological properties had been demonstrated, it had been named, and it had been prepared in crystalline form. All that remained was for someone to synthesize the substance in the laboratory, and testosterone could be said to be completely understood. That final step occurred in 1935, when Butenandt and Ružička independently synthesized testosterone, the former completing his work only a week before the latter. This achievement was at least partially responsible for the joint award of the 1939 Nobel Prize in Chemistry to these two researchers.

What Is Testosterone?

Testosterone is an anabolic, androgenic steroid found in mammals, reptiles, amphibians, birds, fish (in a slightly different form), and other vertebrates. The term *anabolic* is derived from the word *anabolism*, which refers to the process by which living cells convert relatively simple chemical compounds, such as sugars and amino acids, to more complex organic compounds, such as carbohydrates and proteins.

Derivatives of Testosterone

The most widely prescribed testosterone derivative is testosterone enanthate, an oil-based injectable drug that is very effective at building muscle tissue and is legally used to treat hypogonadism and other disorders of androgen deficiency. (Hypogonadism is a condition in which a person's sex glands produce a deficient quantity of sex hormones. It is often treated with pure testosterone or a testosterone derivative.)

Another common class of testosterone derivatives consists of the alkyl testosterones, a compound that is used with individuals who do not have adequate levels of testosterone in their blood. It is marketed under the trade names Android, Testred, and Virilon.

Two other close relatives of testosterone are also used to make testosterone derivatives: dihydrotestosterone (DHT) and nortestosterone. DHT has two more hydrogen atoms than does testosterone, and nortestosterone has one carbon atom less than testosterone. So the three compounds are all quite similar structurally.

These derivatives have slightly different physical, chemical, physiological, and pharmacological properties from pure testosterone itself. They may have stronger or weaker anabolic or androgenic properties; they may have more severe, less severe, or just different side effects; they may be absorbed by the body more or less easily; they may be more or less soluble in water; they may cause more or less irritation at the injection site; they may be more or less easily detectable in standard doping tests; and they may differ from pure testosterone in some other way.

Some of the most commonly used of the hundreds of testosterone derivatives currently available are the following:

- Testosterone cypionate takes a long time to completely metabolize (about two weeks), allowing it to produce its effects on the body over a long period of time.

- Testosterone heptylate is currently produced by only one pharmaceutical firm in France, under the trade name Theramex. Although effective as an anabolic product, it also has the disadvantage of producing somewhat excessive androgenic effects.

- Testosterone undecanoate was developed by Organon in the 1980s. Compared to other testosterone derivatives, it has relatively mild anabolic and androgenic effects and can, therefore, be expensive to use in order to achieve significant muscle-mass-building effects.

- Fluoxymesterone is sold by the Upjohn pharmaceutical company under the trade name Halotestin. It has strong strength and endurance properties but is not very effective at building muscle tissue. It is also toxic to the liver, so it can be used in only small quantities at a time.

- Oxandrolone was first developed by Searle Laboratories, but it is now produced by Savient Pharmaceuticals and sold under the trade name of Oxandrin. It is prescribed for weight gain for patients who have lost weight as the result of surgery, injury, or disease. Its androgenic and anabolic effects are both relatively mild, but it tends to be effective at reducing fat content in the body.

- Trenbolone enthanate is on almost everyone's list of *best of* and *worst of* anabolic steroids. It is the best because it has powerful anabolic effects, producing up to five times the muscle-building capacity of testosterone itself. But it is also the worst because of its serious side effects, such as damage to the liver and heart.

- Stanozolol, also known as Winstrol, is a derivative of DHT. It is more stable in the body, capable of remaining longer in the bloodstream. It also cannot be converted into a female sex hormone, eliminating the possibility of gynecomastia.

- Oxymetholone is another derivative of DHT. It is currently regarded as the most powerful of all anabolic steroids with the most pronounced androgenic effects. It is the only anabolic androgenic steroid (sometimes represented as AAS) to have been classified as a possible carcinogen (cancer-causing agent). It is sold commercially as Anadrol-50.

- Trenbolone is a derivative of nortestosterone with a strong tendency to promote nitrogen retention in muscle tissue, a key to the development of new muscle tissue. It is also thought to act as an anticatabolic substance that blocks the action of glucocorticoids, such as cortisol. Finally, it is thought to promote the action of the growth-promoting substance, insulin growth factor 1 (IGF-1).

- Deca-durabolin, widely known simply as "Deca," has been used successfully to treat wasting in patients with HIV/AIDS infection and is very popular with weight lifters and bodybuilders as a reliable substance for weight gain.

In conclusion, researchers have synthesized hundreds of derivatives of testosterone, DHT, and nortestosterone over the past century. In general, the most important objective of this research has been to find testosterone derivatives that have greater anabolic effects and reduced androgenic effects. To a considerable extent, that search has been successful, and the medical profession now has an arsenal of products that can be used for a wide variety of medical disorders, ranging from muscle-wasting disorders, damaged myocardium in heart disorders, and growth retardation to bone marrow failure disorders, end-stage renal disease, and deficient plasma protein production. (For an excellent review of the history of testosterone derivative development and current applications, see Shahidi 2001. Also see Husayn 2008.)

How Testosterone Works in the Human Body

The human body grows and develops as the result of a complex network of chemical reactions made possible by a number of specialized substances known as *enzymes*. The processes by which testosterone is produced in the body and by which it exerts its effects on the body are an example of that pattern of events. Testosterone is produced in males almost exclusively in *Leydig cells* (also called *interstitial cells*) of the testes and in the ovaries in females. Very small amounts (usually less than 5 percent) of the testosterone in the male body come from other sources, such as the breakdown of other androgens.

The amount of testosterone produced by the male body is many times greater than that produced in the female body: an average of 300–1,000 nanograms per deciliter, or 3–7 milligrams per day in the average male. In females, the rate of testosterone production is about 25–90 nanograms per deciliter, or 0.1–0.4 milligrams per day (Kicman 2010, 28–29; Virtual Muscle 2015.) Testosterone production is very much a function of age, with an early peak occurring in the first six months of life, followed by a decline and a second peak at the onset of puberty. As males age, their level of testosterone production declines continuously. Testosterone production is also a diurnal function, meaning that the amount of testosterone produced varies cyclically throughout a 24-hour period (Winters 2017).

Testosterone is synthesized in Leydig cells through a series of chemical reactions that begin with another familiar steroid, cholesterol. Each step involves a small discrete change in a molecule, adding or removing a single hydrogen atom, for example. Overall, the series of reactions illustrates the way in which the body makes important biochemical changes one step at a time.

A number of substances are involved in the synthesis of testosterone. These substances are known as *precursors*, compounds that "go before" the final product itself; if the final product is a hormone, they are called *prohormones*. Prohormones that lead to the formation of testosterone generally have weak or no androgenic or anabolic effects themselves. They may still be desirable as performance-enhancing drugs, however, because they increase the amount of testosterone that forms in the body.

The amount of testosterone produced by the body is ultimately a function of the number of Leydig cells available in the testes. That number, in turn, is determined by the action of two hormones, luteinizing hormone and follicle-stimulating hormone, produced by the hypothalamus and pituitary glands. Genetic disorders, diseases, or injuries that affect the production of these hormones, then, can result in a reduction in the number of Leydig cells produced and, hence, the rate of testosterone production. In such cases, and the disorder known as *hypogonadism* is one, testosterone can be supplied externally (*exogenously*) to compensate for the loss of natural (*endogenous*) testosterone.

A very great majority of the testosterone produced in the testes is converted to a bound form with albumin and globulin proteins. This reaction is a simple one, in which testosterone essentially becomes biologically inactive. These reactions appear to serve a number of important functions in the body, such as protecting testosterone from degradation by enzymes produced in the liver or increasing the solubility of testosterone, improving the ease with which it is transported in the bloodstream. Less than 5 percent of all the testosterone synthesized each day, then, exists in a "free" form in the blood, so-called *serum testosterone*. When a test is performed to determine the amount of testosterone in a person's blood, it is generally a test for serum testosterone.

Testosterone produces its physiological effects when it is delivered to individual cells. Testosterone molecules pass through the membrane of a cell and enter the cytoplasm. Then, in some cases, the testosterone is converted by the enzyme 5-alpha-reductase to a closely related androgen, DHT, which is many times more potent as an androgenic substance than is testosterone itself. In cells that lack 5-alpha-reductase, testosterone remains in its original form. Next, either testosterone or DHT attaches itself to a protein molecule that contains a special "recognition site" called an *androgen receptor*. The binding of the testosterone or DHT to the receptor site of the molecule initiates a cascade of reactions in which genes in DNA in the nucleus of the cell are activated to begin producing amino acids that, in turn, are used to synthesize new protein in the cell. (For an excellent technical review of this subject, see Kishner 2015. For a visual explanation of this overall process, see Testosterone Production 2011.)

The precise proteins produced depend on the specific cells involved. In the skin, scalp, and prostate, for example, it is the action of DHT on DNA that is thought to be responsible for the production of both primary and secondary male sexual characteristics. In muscle cells, protein synthesis results in the formation of new actin and myosin molecules, the substrates from which muscle tissue is formed. It is precisely this series of reactions that bodybuilders, weight lifters, and other athletes are hoping for when they take anabolic steroids to improve their performance.

One of the practical issues with which athletes have to deal is that, in a normal, healthy male, a very large fraction of androgen receptor sites are already engaged by endogenous testosterone or other anabolic steroids. In such a case, the addition of exogenous anabolic steroid may have little or no effect, since there are few or no binding sites remaining on androgen receptors. Anabolic effects of the exogenous steroids occur, then, only because of other biochemical changes, such as reducing catabolic changes that may be taking place within cells (Calfee and Fadale 2006).

Another chemical reaction of considerable interest and importance involving testosterone occurs in cells that contain the enzyme aromatase. Aromatase is an enzyme that converts androgens (male sex hormones) to estrogens (female sex hormones). Specifically, it converts testosterone to estradiol and androstenedione to estrone.

This action of aromatase poses a problem for athletes who choose to use AASs in their training programs. With an increase in the amount of testosterone in the bloodstream, the likelihood of aromatization occurring significantly increases. As that process becomes more common, more and more female sex hormones are produced within the body, and a person's body begins to take on more feminine characteristics, such as a reduction in body hair, increase in voice pitch, narrower shoulders and broader hips, and increase in breast size. The last of these changes is probably of greatest concern to athletes who use steroid supplements, because it clearly distracts from the characteristically masculine body that most men strive for. The condition is given the name of *gynecomastia*, from the two Greek words for "breast" and "woman."

One of the most common complaints among athletes who use steroid supplements is that they do not achieve the results promised by the product. There are a number of reasons for this situation. One is that many of those who complain about the problem do not realize that improvement on body muscle mass, strength, endurance, and other properties is a process that actually has two components. One, around which this discussion has centered so far, is anabolism, the processes by which the body converts simple chemical compounds into more complex compounds needed to build new tissue. The second component is catabolism, the normal bodily function by which bodily tissue and the complex compounds of which it is made are degraded to simple compounds, which are then eliminated from the body. Catabolism, then, is the process by which body tissues "wear out" and break down. Taking supplements to increase anabolic reactions in the body are of little or no value if catabolic reactions result in a loss of comparable or more body tissue.

For this reason, experts in sports medicine sometimes recommend the addition of anticatabolic supplements to a person's diet to reduce the amount of muscle tissue lost by catabolism. Sometimes, these supplements are chemicals that actually block or disrupt the function of enzymes that cause catabolism. Perhaps the best example of the action of anabolic steroids as anticatabolites is in their action on cortisol. Cortisol is a hormone that belongs to the class of compounds known as the corticosteroids, steroids that are produced in the adrenal gland of vertebrates. They are, more specifically, members of the family of glucocorticoids, corticosteroids that contain a sugar-like component. Cortisol has a number of important functions in the body, one of which is the catabolism of proteins in tissue to release amino acids, which are then available for anabolic reactions that result in the formation of new protein and new tissue. Anabolic steroids can interfere with the action of cortisol because it can displace cortisol from its position on cortisol receptors, preventing it from producing its catabolic functions.

Anabolic steroids have a number of other effects on the body by which they increase the concentration of substances that contribute to the growth of body tissue. For example, they may increase the amount of the enzyme creatine phosphokinase, which increases the rate of muscle tissue growth, and IGF-1, which also regulates the growth of cells (Kishner 2015). Given the fact that, as noted earlier, androgen receptor sites are often full, or nearly full, in a healthy adult male, these anticatabolic and metabolic functions may actually be more important in increasing body muscle mass than the anabolic reactions discussed earlier in this chapter. (For an extended discussion of the anticatabolic effects of anabolic steroids, see Kicman 2008.)

Effects of Anabolic Steroids on the Human Body

Perhaps the most fundamental question one might ask about anabolic steroids is, "how effective are these substances in accomplishing the purposes for which people take them?" That is, do they increase muscle mass, strength, endurance, speed, balance, and other physical traits for which they are supposedly designed? Do athletes who use anabolic steroids actually perform better in their sports than do those who do not use drugs?

Over the past half century, hundreds of studies have been conducted in an attempt to answer these questions. At first, those studies focused on performance. What evidence was there that people who use anabolic steroids are more successful in athletic competitions than are those who do not? Over time, the focus of research shifted to asking questions as to how the use of anabolic steroids affects a person's body composition. Do these drugs increase a person's muscle tissue, nervous response, metabolic rate, or other physiological characteristics? Over the last two decades or so, the research emphasis has shifted once again, this time to the potential adverse effects associated with prolonged use of anabolic steroids.

In addition to the many individual research studies that have been conducted, other researchers have attempted to review large groups of such studies and glean general conclusions from them, studies that are classified as *metaresearch*. A handful of those reviews, published since the 1980s, provides a summary of the information that researchers have obtained about the way in which anabolic steroids affect the human body (and the bodies of other animals) and performance in physical exercises and athletic events.

One of the interesting conclusions to be drawn from all these studies and reviews with regard to the efficacy of anabolic steroids on body composition and performance is *it's hard to say*. Every review of research on anabolic steroids emphasizes the ongoing problems associated with such research. Here are some of the problems with research design and execution that are commonly mentioned in reviews:

- Subjects of many research studies are not typical of the type of individuals who use anabolic steroids for performance enhancement on an everyday basis. A college professor might select, for example, a group of men and women who work out at a local gym and who also take anabolic steroids to improve their athletic skills. These individuals are unlikely to have the same characteristics as the Mark McGwires, Barry Bonds, and Arnold Schwarzeneggers who might consider the use of anabolic steroids to improve performances that are already among the highest in the world.

- Much of the research on anabolic steroid effects, in fact, is not even conducted with humans but, instead, with experimental animals, such as laboratory rats, mice, guinea pigs, and frogs. The reason for this kind of research is obvious. The researcher can sacrifice an animal at the end of an experiment and actually examine anatomical changes that have taken place in the animal's brain or other organs. But it is generally not clear how or to what extent the discoveries made in this kind of research apply to comparable changes in the human body that has been exposed to anabolic steroids.

- Research that is conducted with professional athletes must somehow take into consideration the fact that such athletes are already participating in intense training programs that include the most effective training schedules and nutritional programs known to sports science. Separating the gains from such programs from those derived from the use of anabolic steroids is sometimes difficult.

- Most research is hampered by the fact that researchers cannot or do not use the level of anabolic steroids that athletes themselves use. It is not unusual in controlled experiments on anabolic steroid use for subjects to be provided with less than 10 percent the dose used by practicing weight lifters, bodybuilders, or other professional athletes. Doses that exceed levels that occur naturally in the body are known as *supraphysiological* or *suprapharmacological doses*. One of the main reasons that researchers cannot and do not use supraphysiological doses in their experiments is that the practice would almost certainly violate university and other rules that guide the design of experiments with humans (Lin and Erinoff 1990, Chapter 1).

- Some observers have even suggested that the very idea that one is taking an anabolic steroid causes changes in a person's mental state, producing a "psychosomatic" condition that contributes to bodily change that might include gains in muscle mass. This effect is also described as a *placebo* effect, in which real changes in a person's body or behavior may come about because of his or her beliefs about the process that is occurring rather than anything that anabolic steroids themselves have done (Fahey 1998).

- Another common problem with anabolic steroid research is selection criteria. Researchers pretty much have to use people who volunteer to take part in their studies, people who perhaps are highly motivated to improve their body image or performance or individuals who may be strongly opposed to the concept of using performance-enhancing drugs. Researchers may not know very much about their subjects' motivations for participating in a study, although that factor might have an important effect on the study outcome. (For an excellent review of problems with research design and execution for anabolic steroid research, see Hartgens and Kuipers 2004, 517–518.)

So, are there any conclusions that can be drawn from the available research on anabolic steroids, changes in the body, and athletic performance? As noted here, one theme that runs through most, if not all, review articles is the uncertainty of much of the results from such studies. A 1988 review, for example, noted that "although a large number of studies of the effects of anabolic steroids on athletic performance have been completed, there are very few that have been well controlled and randomized" (Rogol 1988, 7). A later review of the research reached a similar conclusion. "The majority of 'evidence' concerning the efficacy of anabolic steroids as performance enhancing agents," it said, "is anecdotal. In the main, experimental investigations have been poorly designed scientifically, clinically and statistically" (Mottram and George 2000, 55). A still later report came to the conclusion that "[a]t this time, scientific support for the ergogenic or anabolic use of steroid precursors does not exist" (Powers 2002, 305). A 2008 article about the use of anabolic steroids also reaches a somewhat similar conclusion, in which the author says that, while anabolic steroids have found a number of useful applications in treating medical conditions, "their efficacy still needs to be demonstrated in terms of improved physical function and quality of life" (Kicman 2008, 502).

(It should be noted that questions about the efficacy of anabolic steroids among scientific and medical professionals have not prevented enthusiasts for these drugs from publishing their own lists of the "most effective" anabolic steroids and the categories in which they are especially effective. See, for example,

Steroid Effectiveness Chart 2017 for one of the more thought-ful of such efforts.)

Given these research results, how do scientists explain what appear to be the fairly massive changes in women and men who "bulk up" after use of anabolic steroids? Some authorities suggest, as noted here, that a well-designed training and nutri-tion program can be credited with significant improvement in muscle mass, strength, endurance, speed, and other physical properties. Some researchers, however, have come to a some-what different conclusion, namely that evidence *does* exist for the presumption that the use of anabolic steroids does, indeed, contribute significantly to the growth of new muscle tissue and can be a real factor in the "bulking up" that occurs among in-dividuals who use anabolic steroids.

One of the best expressions of this position can be found in a paper by Cynthia M. Kuhn, at the Duke University Medi-cal Center. In a 2002 review of research on anabolic steroids, Kuhn begins by acknowledging long-standing concerns about the research design and execution of research on anabolic ste-roids. She also notes that "[t]he anabolic effects of restoring normal physiologic levels of testosterone in hypogonadal men are uncontested" (Kuhn 2002). Hypogonadal men are men who have much-lower-than-normal levels of testosterone in their bodies, so the additional exogenous testosterone (or other anabolic steroids) would be expected to have observable and measurable effects on physical properties attributable to the ac-tion of testosterone (such as muscle mass). The same statement can be made for women in general who, of course, have a much lower level of testosterone in their blood than do men. Stud-ies are relatively clear that supraphysiological doses of anabolic steroids can significantly increase a woman's muscle mass and athletic performance.

Kuhn then goes on, however, to challenge the traditional view among scientists that anabolic steroids are really not very effective in improving muscle mass and athletic performance among men who are eugonadal, that is, men who have normal levels of testosterone in their bodies. She cites a number of studies that appear to show that the use of supraphysiological doses of anabolic steroids can have measurable and observable effects on body structure and athletic performance in eugonadal men. She concludes her review with the observation that

> Studies in AAS [anabolic androgenic steroid]-using human subjects as well as experimental model systems have refuted the decades-old assertion that suprapharmacologic dose regimens of AAS are not anabolic in normal men or are only anabolic due to the impact of their CNS effects on motivation to train. The physiopathology of suprapharmacologic doses of AAS is clearly demonstrated and predicted by the beneficial effects on the same systems when AAS are used in hypogonadal men. (Kuhn 2002, 432)

Kuhn then concludes her review with the observation that perhaps the most interesting point about this whole debate is that there has been so little research on the anatomical, biochemical, pharmacological, and physiological changes produced by anabolic steroids on the human brain. (An excellent source of the most recent research news about anabolic steroids is "Anabolic Steroid News and Research" 2017.)

It should be noted that the individuals who are probably most interested in getting accurate, up-to-date information about the efficacy of anabolic steroids are men and women who have committed substantial amounts of time to weight lifting, bodybuilding, and related sports. The Internet is now flooded with websites advertising such products for sale and, not so incidentally, often provides surprisingly accurate and useful information about steroids. These websites are often very helpful for men and women trying to decide which anabolic steroid to purchase and use, in what amounts the product should be taken, by what means it should be taken, whether it should be taken alone or with other steroids and, if so, in what pattern, and so on. In many cases, the advice available at these sites is accurate and reliable, although the efficacy of the advice provided is always, and inherently, somewhat limited. (See, for example, websites such as anabolicsteroids-hormoneknowledge-bigmuscles-drugs.com, EliteFitness.com, isteroids.com, Steroid.com, and SteroidAbuse.com. For a particularly good example of this phenomenon, see Shugarman 2017.)

Therapeutic Uses of Anabolic Steroids

Using anabolic steroids for increasing body mass, strength, and other physical attributes is important in fields other than sports and athletics. For nearly a century, researchers have been looking for ways in which such substances can be used to treat and cure a wide variety of physical disorders. The medical applications of anabolic steroids can be classified into one of three general categories: treatment of hypogonadism in males, treatment of other disease conditions in eugonadal males, and treatment of non-hypogonadal elderly males. The first of these applications is generally known as *androgen replacement therapy* (ART) because it is used with individuals whose serum testosterone levels are significantly lower than those found in a normal male. A number of conditions are responsible for hypogonadism, including the genetic disorder known as Klinefelter's syndrome, castration, diseases of the testes (such as testicular cancer), medical treatments that affect testicular function (such as chemotherapy or radiation therapy), and the action of certain drugs such as cytotoxins and spironolactone. Hypogonadism may also be caused by a number of other medical conditions, such as tumors of or surgery to the pituitary or hypothalamus gland, morbid obesity, the use of illicit drugs or anabolic steroids, and certain genetic disorders. ART has been used with hypogonadal males since the 1950s with generally good success. According to one source, treated individuals can expect to gain about 1.7 kilograms (3.7 pounds) of body mass, often with a corresponding increase in strength and decrease in body fat mass (Bagatell and Bremner 2003).

A decrease in serum testosterone also tends to occur in association with certain diseases and injuries, such as HIV infection, chronic obstructive pulmonary disease, burns, renal failure, cancer, liver failure, and postoperative recovery. Treatment of such conditions with testosterone and its derivatives is called *pharmacological androgen therapy* (PAT) and, like ART, has been quite successful for well over a century in raising serum testosterone levels of individuals with these conditions. Weight gain, increased bone mass and bone density, improved strength, and other advances are commonly associated with the use of PAT. One study has noted, however, that the use of anabolic steroids in PAT has become somewhat less popular not because of its poor track record but because it is so inexpensive that drug companies prefer to offer more expensive (and, thus, more profitable) options for achieving the same results (Handelsman 2006, 436).

The third application of testosterone therapy is used with aging males who have normal serum testosterone levels for individuals of their age but who may be candidates for the treatment for a variety of physical and mental reasons. For example, males who are recovering from surgery may benefit from increased muscle mass and body strength provided by anabolic steroid treatments. At this point, the use of anabolic steroids for such purposes is somewhat controversial. It is also, according to some experts, hampered by an inadequate level of research that, in turn, results from the unfavorable view of illegal anabolic steroid use by bodybuilders, weight lifters, and other athletes (Navar 2008).

Risks Associated with the Use of Anabolic Steroids

As noted in the preceding section, the emphasis of research on anabolic steroids in the recent past has shifted to a considerable extent to the question of the adverse effects of steroid use on the human body. The implicit argument behind at least some of that research seems to be that, whether or not anabolic steroids have positive effects on the human body, such as increasing muscle mass and strength, it also is responsible for a number of negative physiological and psychological effects. This recent line of research has produced a number of findings that seem to suggest that the deleterious effects of anabolic steroid use are great enough to be of concern to anyone who chooses to use those substances and to the parents of young people who might consider their use.

One of the strongest official statements along this line is one provided by the New York State Department of Health. On its website ("Anabolic Steroids and Sports: Winning at Any Cost 2008"), the department lists more than three dozen adverse effects associated with the use of anabolic steroids, ranging from increased blood pressure, impaired liver function, and liver tumors to male pattern baldness, striae (stretch marks), and HIV infection to mood swings, aggression, and depression. (Other websites and publications with similar themes include "DrugFacts—Anabolic Steroids" 2016, "Anabolic Steroids: A Dangerous and Illegal Way to Seek Athletic Dominance and Better Appearance" 2004, "Dangers of Anabolic Steroids" 2017, and "Are Steroids Worth the Risk?" 2013.)

Although documents such as those found on the Internet may sometimes seem overly melodramatic or unduly cautionary, there is probably little doubt that misuse of anabolic steroids can have a host of deleterious physical effects on users, including cardiovascular, reproductive, nervous, hormonal, hepatic, and orthopedic complications. Perhaps even more troublesome are a number of psychological and psychiatric problems that include aggression, violence, depression, and suicide. Among the best known of these problems may be the so-called *'roid rage* (from "android rage"), a condition of unusual violence and aggression associated with the use of supraphysiological amounts of anabolic steroids. Some authorities suspect that the murder-suicide of professional wrestler Chris Benoit's family in 2007 was the result of Benoit's having gone on a 'roid rage, killing his wife and son and then committing suicide (Hitti 2007). Depictions of 'roid rage events are available on the Internet (see, for example, http://www.youtube .com/watch?v=gfJTXDppVNA, accessed on March 13, 2017), although they are sometimes age restricted because of their violent nature. Other observers suggest that 'roid rage and other psychological effects of anabolic steroids are either exaggerated or completely incorrect and that the use of anabolic steroids is essentially never associated with psychopathic or sociopathic behavior. David Handelsman, at the University of Sydney's Concord Clinical School of Medicine, for example, has called the theory of 'roid rage "street folklore" that serves "mostly as an excuse for bad behavior" (Handelsman 2001; see also Lundholm et al. 2014). Those who doubt that 'roid rage really exists argue instead that the phenomenon occurs not because of anabolic steroids but because people who were combative and aggressive before they started using supplements simply have a new excuse for venting their antisocial feelings.

More generally, some researchers have suggested that the risks posed by use of anabolic steroids by athletes may have been exaggerated in the past. In one of the best available presentations of this viewpoint, Jay R. Hoffman and Nicholas A. Ratamess at the College of New Jersey have identified a number of factors that may have resulted in a disconnect between medical researchers studying the effects of anabolic steroids on the human body and actual practices of amateur and professional athletes. One factor that Hoffman and Ratamess identify is differences in dosage and patterns of usage between athletes and medical researchers. As noted earlier, athletes typically use much larger doses of anabolic steroids than researchers do or can use in their own research. Athletes also use steroids in a variety of distinctive ways, such as in various forms of cycling, pyramiding, and stacking. Also, researchers tend to study steroid effects on relatively short-term bases, while athletes are more likely to use such drugs for extended periods of time. Time factors may also account for the fact that researchers limit their observations to periods of use only and do not follow up on long-term effects of steroid use. As a result, Hoffman and Ratamess say, researchers miss the fact that most of the side effects that are reported are transit and that long-term studies would probably show many fewer and less severe consequences of steroid use (Hoffman and Ratamess 2006, 189).

Overall, Hoffman and Ratamess suggest that actual users of anabolic steroids are probably well ahead of most medical researchers in their knowledge of the products available and the effects of those products on the human body. As a result, athletes often use performance-enhancing drugs for which researchers have no data and, indeed, about which they may not even know.

Finally, existing research often does not distinguish between correlations and cause and effect. For example, assume that the data show that coronary problems are more common among athletes who use anabolic steroids than those who do not. That finding expresses a correlation between two variables: coronary problems and steroid abuse. But those data do not necessarily show a cause-and-effect relationship. It is entirely possible that the athletes involved in this study had coronary problems before they began using steroids, and steroid use is unrelated to such problems.

This disconnect between medical research and actual practice among athletes is not an entirely benign phenomenon. One consequence of the disconnect, according to Hoffman and Ratamess, is that steroid-using athletes tend to ignore the advice of medical professionals, relying instead on gym trainers, training partners, other athletes in the field, and other nonprofessional sources (perhaps another reason for the glut of blogs about steroids on the Internet). This problem is unfortunate, Hoffman and Ratamess say, because athletes who use anabolic steroids on a regular basis can benefit from monitoring by medical professionals, which neither they nor the professionals themselves are inclined to provide.

Some support exists for the concerns raised by Hoffman and Ratamess. A 2004 study by researchers from the Harvard Medical School and the Duke University Medical Center asked

80 weight lifters how they assessed the expertise of their own physicians both in the field of medicine in general and with regard to anabolic steroids in particular. A majority of respondents rated their physicians' overall knowledge of medicine highly but trusted their knowledge about anabolic steroids no more highly than they trusted that of their trainer, friends, sources of drugs, or Internet sites. Four out of 10 respondents trusted their drug supplier at least as much, and usually more, than they did any physician they had ever seen. Indeed, more than half of all respondents (56 percent) had never informed their own physician of their use of steroids. Researchers concluded from these results that such attitudes "compromise physicians' ability to educate or treat anabolic steroids users" and that physicians can be of greater help to their possible anabolic steroids-using patients "by learning more about these substances" (Pope et al. 2004, 1193).

Appearance- and Performance-Enhancing Drug Use

The discussion of anabolic steroid use thus far has focused almost entirely on therapeutic applications and the use of anabolic steroids to improve athletic performance. Yet there is another, relatively new and rapidly growing use for anabolic steroids: in the improvement of a person's overall physical appearance. For a variety of reasons, many children and adolescents today are dissatisfied with their own bodily appearance and would like to be more physically attractive. While gaining strength, endurance, speed, and other athletic attributes may be part of this effort, they are secondary to the goal of simply matching more closely the cultural norm as to what the "good-looking" boy or girl, or man or woman, is "supposed" to look like. The use of anabolic steroids to "burn fat," add muscle, and improve strength and stamina is central to such an effort.

Research directed at a better understanding of the causes, features, and treatment of appearance- and performance-enhancing drugs (APEDs) is still quite limited. The evidence produced so far suggests that three factors are associated with the condition. First, those who are concerned about APEDs tend to be individuals who are significantly more dissatisfied with their bodily appearance than are most children and adolescents. Given that many or most adolescents are somewhat unhappy with the way they look to others, APED use is an issue primarily with those who have unusually strong feelings in this regard. Second, those who fall into this category are likely to rely heavily not only on anabolic steroids but also on a number of other substances that they believe will help alter their physical appearance, substances such as insulin and insulin-like products, human growth hormone, xanthines (caffeine-like substances), sympathomimetics (such as ephedrine and ephedra), and thyroid hormones. Finally, those with concerns about their physical appearance generally commit themselves to a relatively intense program of physical exercise and nutritional diet to go along with the use of anabolic steroids (Hildebrandt 2013; Hildebrandt et al. 2011b). As of early 2017, the medical and psychiatric communities are just beginning to recognize the seriousness of the APED syndrome and starting to develop diagnostic tools and programs for treatment of the condition (Hildebrandt et al. 2011a).

One of the most interesting pieces of data about APED may be its prevalence. From the fact that so little is known about it and so little research has been conducted on the topic, one might assume that APED use is only a modest contributing factor to the general problem of anabolic steroid abuse. One review of the literature published in 2010 suggests that such is almost certainly not the case. In that review, P. A. Hammer, of Willamette University, in Oregon, found that appearance enhancement is actually a more common cause of steroid use among high school students in the United States and other parts of the world than is athletic motivation. He summarizes the results of his research by noting that recent research indicates that "the risk of AAS use is lower for those involved in organized sport than for the general adolescent population and that AAS use is more like part of a broader syndrome of problem behaviours than a response to situation-specific goals such as success in sport" (Hammer 2010, 31; see also O'Dea and Cinelli 2016; Ricciardelli and Williams 2016).

Prevalence of Anabolic Steroid Use

Beginning in the 1950s, a number of studies were conducted to determine the prevalence and, sometimes, incidence of anabolic steroid use in the United States and other parts of the world. (The term *prevalence* refers to the number of individuals involved in an activity at the present time, and the term *incidence* means the number of individuals who took part in that activity for the first time within some period of time, usually the last year.) The vast majority of these studies have focused on children and young adults. There are at least two reasons for that fact. One is that it is often easier to collect data from youngsters than it is from adults. Most children attend school, so questionnaires and interviews are relatively easy to distribute, collect, and analyze. Also, adults tend to be concerned about steroid use (and other illegal and undesirable behavior) among children and adolescents, so they may want to know how widespread the problem is.

One of the most important single sources of information available about anabolic steroid use among youngsters can be found in the article by P. A. Hammer mentioned earlier. In that article, Hammer relied on two important surveys, by Charles E. Yesalis and Michael S. Bahrke and by Patrick Laure for pre-2000 data. Those surveys covered more than two dozen discrete research studies of teenagers in the United States and 10 more in other countries of the world, including Australia, Canada, South Africa, Sweden, and the United Kingdom. As one might expect because of differing research design, the number of anabolic steroid users as reported in these surveys varied considerably, with the one general finding that steroid use was almost without exception higher among males than among females.

The prevalence rate in the approximately three dozen individual surveys ranged from a low of about 1.5 percent to a high of about 4.5 percent for males. Based on these percentages, other researchers have estimated that anywhere from 500,000 to 700,000 high school students were using anabolic steroids in the United States during the 1990s. (These data are presented in Hammer 2010, 26, as compiled from Yesalis and Bahrke 2000 and Laure 2000. The prevalence estimate comes from Foley and Schydlower 1993.)

Hammer also reviewed 19 additional studies between 2000 and 2008 conducted in the United States, Brazil, France, Germany, Norway, Poland, Sweden, and other European countries. The U.S. surveys were conducted nationally, regionally, and within individual states. These 19 surveys reported on anabolic steroid use by grade level and gender from populations overall. They found prevalence rates very much within the range reported by other studies. For males, those rates ranged from a low of 0.5 percent (Germany) to a high of 14.3 percent (Poland), with an average within the 3–5 percent range. For females, they ranged from a low of 0.1 percent (Oregon and Washington) to a high of 11.1 percent (Poland), with an average within the 1–2 percent range (Hammer 2010, 26).

Arguably the best single source of data about steroid use among high school students in the United States over the past four decades is the Monitoring the Future (MTF) study conducted by the Institute for Social Research at the University of Michigan. That study has been conducted annually since 1975 among high school seniors and, since 1991, among eighth- and tenth-grade students also. The MTF has asked students since 1991 about their own use of steroids at any time in their lifetime, during the year preceding the survey, and during the 30-day period before the survey. It also asks students about their attitudes regarding the use of steroids and about the availability of steroids in their own environment.

The most recent MTF report indicates that the prevalence of lifetime use of steroids among twelfth graders increased from 2.1 percent in 1991 to a high of 4.0 percent in 2002. It then dropped off to about 2.0 percent in 2010, a point around which it has remained since that time. The 2015 prevalence rate among twelfth graders was 2.3 percent. Similar patterns held for eighth and tenth graders. For the former, the rate was 1.9 percent in 1991, 3.0 percent in 2000, and 1.0 percent in 2015; for the latter, it was 1.8 percent in 1991, 3.5 percent in 2000 through 2002, and 1.2 percent in 2015 (Johnston et al. 2016, Table 5). More detailed lifetime rates, along with annual and 30-day rates, are shown in Table 1.1.

Table 1.1   Steroid Use by U.S. High School Students, 1991–2015 (Percentage)

Lifetime Use

Grade	1991	1992	1993	1994	1995	1996	1997	1998	1999
Eighth	1.9	1.7	1.6	2.0	2.0	1.8	1.8	2.3	2.7
Tenth	1.8	1.7	1.7	1.8	2.0	1.8	2.0	2.0	2.7
Twelfth	2.1	2.1	2.0	2.4	2.3	1.9	2.4	2.7	2.9

Grade	2000	2001	2002	2003	2004	2005	2006	2007	2008
Eighth	3.0	2.8	2.5	2.5	1.9	1.7	1.6	1.5	1.4
Tenth	3.5	3.5	3.5	3.0	2.4	2.0	1.8	1.8	1.4
Twelfth	2.5	3.7	4.0	3.5	3.4	2.6	2.7	2.2	2.2

Grade	2009	2010	2011	2012	2013	2014	2015
Eighth	1.3	1.1	1.2	1.2	1.1	1.0	1.0
–							
–							

Past Year Use

Grade	1991	1992	1993	1994	1995	1996	1997	1998	1999
Eighth	1.0	1.1	0.9	1.2	1.0	0.9	1.0	1.2	1.7
Tenth	1.1	1.1	1.0	1.1	1.2	1.2	1.2	1.2	1.7
Twelfth	1.4	1.1	1.2	1.3	1.5	1.4	1.4	1.7	1.8

Past Year Use

Grade	2000	2001	2002	2003	2004	2005	2006	2007	2008
Eighth	1.7	1.6	1.5	1.4	1.1	1.1	0.9	0.8	0.9
Tenth	2.2	2.1	2.2	1.7	1.5	1.3	1.2	1.1	0.9
Twelfth	1.7	2.4	2.5	2.1	2.5	1.5	1.8	1.4	1.5

Grade	2009	2010	2011	2012	2013	2014	2015
Eighth	0.8	0.5	0.7	0.6	0.6	0.6	0.5
–							
–							

30-Day Use

Grade	1991	1992	1993	1994	1995	1996	1997	1998	1999
Eighth	0.4	0.5	0.5	0.5	0.6	0.4	0.5	0.5	0.7
Tenth	0.6	0.6	0.5	0.6	0.6	0.5	0.7	0.6	0.9
Twelfth	0.8	0.6	0.7	0.9	0.7	0.7	1.0	1.1	0.9

Grade	2000	2001	2002	2003	2004	2005	2006	2007	2008
Eighth	0.8	0.7	0.8	0.7	0.5	0.5	0.5	0.4	0.5
Tenth	1.0	0.9	1.0	0.8	0.8	0.6	0.6	0.5	0.5
Twelfth	0.8	1.3	1.4	1.3	1.6	0.9	1.1	1.0	1.0

Grade	2009	2010	2011	2012	2013	2014	2015
Eighth	0.4	0.3	0.4	0.3	0.3	0.2	0.3
–							
–							

Source: Johnston, Lloyd D., et al. 2016. "Monitoring the Future: National Survey Results on Drug Use, 1975–2015: Overview, Key Findings on Adolescent Drug Use." Ann Arbor, MI: Institute for Social Research, The University of Michigan. Available at http://www.monitoringthefuture.org/pubs/monographs/mtf-overview 2015.pdf. Accessed on March 10, 2017, Tables 5, 6, 7.

Prevalence surveys among adults are much less common, and they tend to provide somewhat less useful information. Most commonly, these surveys have focused on specific nations, such as Nigeria, Poland, South Africa, Sweden, and the United

Kingdom, and on specific groups, such as athletes training for the Olympic Games. The results of these surveys vary widely depending on a number of factors, including the nationality of the population, the sport for which individuals are training, their professional versus amateur status, and the mode by which data were collected. Prevalence rates for these studies range from a low of about 1 percent for both men and women in Nigeria training for the Olympic Games to more than 50 percent for active weight lifters training for national or international competitions. As an example, a survey conducted in 1997 of 21 gymnasia in England, Scotland, and Wales found an average rate of anabolic steroid use of 9.1 percent among men and 2.3 percent among women. That rate ranged wildly, however, from site to site, with a low of zero percent at three gymnasia and a maximum of 46 percent of all respondents at another location (Korkia and Stimson 1997). (An excellent and comprehensive review of studies on the prevalence of anabolic steroid use by men, women, elite athletes, and adolescents and children is available from Lenehan 2003, 12–20.)

One of the most recent studies on the prevalence of AAS users in the United States confirmed the evolving view that concerns for physical attractiveness are a greater motivating force for the use of steroids than is athletic competitiveness. In a survey of 1,955 male adult nonmedical anabolic steroid users culled from the Internet, researchers found that the typical AAS user was a "Caucasian, highly-educated, gainfully employed professional approximately 30 years of age, who was earning an above-average income, was not active in organized sports, and whose use was motivated by increases in skeletal muscle mass, strength, and physical attractiveness." Such a finding, the researchers noted, suggests a reconsideration of conventional views about the motivations that drive individuals to use anabolic steroids (Cohen, et al. 2007).

Finally, a 2011 study raised a new issue about the use of anabolic steroids for purposes of physical enhancement. In this study, researchers asked a group of physicians how they feel about prescribing steroids to individuals who want the products primarily or exclusively for the purposes of improving their physical appearance. Physicians who participated in the study provided a range of views, extending from the belief that individuals should have the right to use such products if they feel they need them to questions about providing some individuals an advantage with pills that might not be available to other individuals (Hotze et al. 2011).

This study illustrates some of the many social, ethical, legal, and other issues that exist in connection with the use of anabolic steroids by athletes and nonathletes. Should such drugs be readily available to anyone who wants them? What kinds of regulations, if any, should be imposed on their athletic use and on their non-athletic use? Are special policies and practices needed for adolescents and children who want to use anabolic steroids for performance enhancement or improvement of physical appearance? Should standards be different for those who want to use the drugs solely for athletic purposes or solely for the purpose of appearance enhancement? These are some of the issues to be considered in Chapter 2 of this book.

References

"Anabolic Steroid News and Research." 2017. News Medical Life Sciences. http://www.news-medical.net/?tag=/Anabolic-Steroid. Accessed on February 13, 2017.

"Anabolic Steroids: A Dangerous and Illegal Way to Seek Athletic Dominance and Better Appearance." 2004. Drug Enforcement Administration, U.S. Department of Justice. http://www.deadiversion.usdoj.gov/pubs/brochures/steroids/public/public.pdf. Accessed on February 13, 2017.

"Anabolic Steroids and Sports: Winning at Any Cost." 2008. New York State Department of Health. http://www.health.ny.gov/publications/1210/. Accessed on February 13, 2017.

"Are Steroids Worth the Risk?" 2013. TeensHealth. http://kidshealth.org/teen/drug_alcohol/drugs/steroids.html#a_Dangers_of_Steroids. Accessed on February 13, 2017.

Bagatell, Carrie J., and William J. Bremner, eds. 2003. *Androgens in Health and Disease*. Totowa, NJ: Humana Press.

Berthold, Arnold A. 1849. "Transplantation der Hoden," *Archiv für Anatomie, Physiologie und Wissenschaftliche Medicin*. 42–46. Trans. D. P. Quiring. 1944, "Transplantation of Testis," *Bulletin of the History of Medicine*. 16: 399–401. http://labs.bio.unc.edu/Goldstein/Berthold1849.pdf. Accessed on February 11, 2017.

Bøje, Ove. 1939. "Doping: A Study of the Means Employed to Raise the Level of Performance in Sport." *Bulletin of the Health Organization of the League of Nations*. 8: 439–469.

Buti, Antonio, and Saul Fridman. 2001. *Drugs, Sport and the Law*. Mudgeeraba, QLD: Scribblers.

Calfee, Ryan, and Paul Fadale. 2006. "Popular Ergogenic Drugs and Supplements in Young Athletes." *Pediatrics*. 117(3): e577–e589. http://pediatrics.aappublications.org/content/117/3/e577. Accessed on February 12, 2017.

Carroll, Scott T. 1988. "Wrestling in Ancient Nubia." *Journal of Sport History*. 15(2): 121–137.

Cohen, Jason, et al. 2007. "A League of Their Own: Demographics, Motivations and Patterns of Use of 1,955 Male Adult Non-Medical Anabolic Steroid Users in the United States." *Journal of the International Society of Sports Nutrition*. 4: 12. doi: 10.1186/1550-2783-4-12. PMCID: PMC2131752. https://www.ncbi.nlm.nih.gov/pmc/articles/PMC2131752/. Accessed on February 10, 2017.

Cronin, Brian. 2010. "Sports Legend Revealed: A Marathon Runner Nearly Died Because of Drugs He Took to Help

Him Win." *Los Angeles Times*. http://latimesblogs.latimes
.com/sports_blog/2010/08/sports-legend-revealed-a-mara
thon-runner-nearly-died-because-of-drugs-he-took-to-help-
him-win.html. Accessed on February 10, 2017.

Cussons, Andrea J., et al. 2002. "Brown–Séquard Revisited:
A Lesson from History on the Placebo Effect of Androgen
Treatment." *Medical Journal of Australia*. 177(11):
678–679.

"Dangers of Anabolic Steroids." 2017. Taylor Hooton
Foundation. http://taylorhooton.org/dangers-of-anabolic-
steroids/. Accessed on February 17, 2017.

David, K., et al. 1935. "Über krystallinisches männliches
Hormon aus Hoden (Testosteron), wirksamer als aus Harn
oder aus Cholesterin bereitetes Androsteron." *Hoppe–seyler's
Zeitschrift Für Physiologische Chemie*. 233(5–6): 281–283.

de Mondenard, Jean-Pierre. 2000. "History and Evolution of
Doping." *Annals of Analytical Toxicology*. 12(1): 5–18.

Dotson, Jennifer L., and Robert T. Brown. 2007. "The
History of the Development of Anabolic–Androgenic
Steroids." *Pediatric Clinics of North America*. 54(4):
761–769.

"DrugFacts—Anabolic Steroids." 2016. National Institute
on Drug Abuse. https://www.drugabuse.gov/publications/
drugfacts/anabolic-steroids. Accessed on February 13,
2017.

Dunbar, Newell. 1889. "The Elixir of Life." Internet Archive.
http://www.archive.org/stream/elixiroflifedrbr00dunbuoft/
elixiroflifedrbr00dunbuoft_djvu.txt. Accessed on February 11,
2017.

"Elixir of Life—A Brief History of Testosterone." 1889.
Te Aroha News. 7(405): 25. https://paperspast.natlib
.govt.nz/newspapers/TAN18890925.2.17. Accessed on
February 11, 2017.

Fahey, Thomas D. 1998. "Anabolic–Androgenic Steroids: Mechanism of Action and Effects on Performance." Encyclopedia of Sports Medicine and Science. http://www.sportsci.org/encyc/anabster/anabster.html. Accessed on February 13, 2017.

Foley, John D., and Manuel Schydlower. 1993. "Anabolic Steroid and Ergogenic Drug Use by Adolescents." *Adolescent Medicine*. 4(2): 341–352.

Freeman, Erica R., David A. Bloom, and Edward J. McGuire. 2001. "A Brief History of Testosterone." *The Journal of Urology*. 165(2): 371–373.

Gertz, Stephen. 2008. "Revisiting the Pagan Olympic Games." *Christian History*. http://www.christianitytoday.com/ch/news/2004/aug19.html. Accessed on February 10, 2017.

Hammer, P. A. 2010. "Anabolic–Androgenic Steroid Use among Young Male and Female Athletes: Is the Game to Blame?" *British Journal of Sports Medicine*. 44(1): 26–31.

Handelsman, David. 2001. "Book Review: Adonis Complex: The Secret Crisis of Body Obsession." *New England Journal of Medicine*. 344(2): 146–147.

Handelsman, David J. 2006. "Testosterone: Use, Misuse and Abuse." *Medical Journal of Australia*. 185(8): 436–439.

Hartgens, Fred, and Harm Kuipers. 2004. "Effects of Androgenic–Anabolic Steroids in Athletes." *Sports Medicine*. 34(8): 513–554. http://www.afboard.com/library/Effects%20of%20Androgenic-Anabolic%20Steroids%20in%20Athletes.pdf. Accessed on February 13, 2017.

Heijmans, Jeroen, and Bill Mallon. 2011. *Historical Dictionary of Cycling*. Lanham, MD: Scarecrow Press.

Hildebrandt, Tom. 2013. "Abuse of Performance-Enhancing Drugs." In Donald W. Pfaff, ed. *Neuroscience in the 21st Century: From Basic to Clinical*. New York: Springer, 2813–2832.

Hildebrandt, Tom, et al. 2011a. "Development and Validation of the Appearance and Performance Enhancing Drug Use Schedule." *Addictive Behaviors*. 36(10): 949–958.

Hildebrandt, Tom, et al. 2011b. "The Diagnostic Dilemma of Pathological Appearance and Performance Enhancing Drug Use." *Drug and Alcohol Dependence*. 114(1): 1–11.

Hill, Warren D., Michael Blake, and John E. Clark. 1998. "Ball Court Design Dates Back 3,400 Years." *Nature*. 392(6679): 878–879.

Hitti, Miranda. 2007. "Chris Benoit: Was Roid Rage to Blame?" WebMD. http://www.webmd.com/mental-health/features/roid-rage-14-questions-and-answers. Accessed on February 13, 2017.

Hoberman, John M., and Charles E. Yesalis. 1995. "The History of Synthetic Testosterone." *Scientific American*. 272(2): 76–81.

Hoffman, Jay R., and Nicholas A. Ratamess. 2006. "Medical Issues Associated with Anabolic Steroid Use: Are They Exaggerated?" *Journal of Sports Science and Medicine*. 5(2): 182–193.

Hotze, Steven F., et al. 2011. "'Doctor, Would You Prescribe a Pill to Help Me . . .?' A National Survey of Physicians on Using Medicine for Human Enhancement." *American Journal of Bioethics*. 11(1): 3–13.

[Hsu, Li-Hong]. 2002. Appendix 1: Case Analysis: Instances of Cheating in the Olympic Movement. Ethics and Sports Rules. Dissertation. https://doc.rero.ch/record/12703/files/HSU_Leo_-_5_-_Appendix_1-_Case_study_of_cheating.pdf. Accessed on February 9, 2017.

Husayn. 2008. "Steroid Profiles." T Nation. https://forums.t-nation.com/t/steroid-profiles/111256. Accessed on February 11, 2017.

Johnston, Lloyd D., et al. 2016. "Monitoring the Future: National Survey Results on Drug Use, 1975–2015: Overview,

Key Findings on Adolescent Drug Use." Ann Arbor, MI: Institute for Social Research, the University of Michigan. http://www.monitoringthefuture.org/pubs/monographs/mtf-overview2015.pdf. Accessed on February 10, 2017.

Kicman, Andrew T. 2008. "Pharmacology of Anabolic Steroids." *British Journal of Pharmacology*. 154(3): 502–521. https://www.ncbi.nlm.nih.gov/pmc/articles/PMC2439524/. Accessed on February 12, 2017.

Kicman, Andrew T. 2010. "Biochemical and Physiological Aspects of Endogenous Androgens." In Detlef Thieme and Peter Hemmersbach, eds. *Doping in Sports*. Heidelberg; New York: Springer, 25–64.

Kishner, Stephen. 2015. "Anabolic Steroid Use and Abuse." Medscape. http://emedicine.medscape.com/article/128655-overview. Accessed on February 12, 2017.

Korkia, Pirkko, and Gerry Vivian Stimson. 1997. "Indications of Prevalence, Practice, and Effects of Anabolic Steroid Use in Great Britain." *International Journal of Sport Medicine*. 18(7): 557–562.

Kuhn, Cynthia M. 2002. "Anabolic Steroids." *Recent Progress in Hormone Research*. 56: 411–434.

Langeron, Jean-Luc. 2012. "Albert Londres (1884–1932)." Cholet Velo Sport. http://choletvelosport.free.fr/histoir_velo/londre.htm. Accessed on February 10, 2017.

Laure, Patrick. 2000. "Le Dopage: Données Épidémiologiques." *La Presse Médicale*. 29(24): 1365–1371. In French.

Lee, Yu-Hsuan. 2006. "Performance Enhancing Drugs: History, Medical Effects & Policy." https://dash.harvard.edu/bitstream/handle/1/8848241/LeeY06.pdf?sequence=1. Accessed on February 10, 2017.

Lefler, Leah. 2017. "The Elixir of Life: A Brief History of Testosterone." http://leahlefler.hubpages.com/hub/

The-Elixir-of-Life-A-Brief-History-of-Testosterone. Accessed on February 11, 2017.

Lenehan, Pat. 2003. *Anabolic Steroids and Other Performance-Enhancing Drugs*. London; New York: Taylor & Francis.

Lin, Geraline C., and Lynda Erinoff, eds. 1990. Anabolic Steroid Abuse. Rockville, MD: U.S. Department of Health and Human Services, Public Health Service, Alcohol, Drug Abuse, and Mental Health Administration, National Institute on Drug Abuse. https://ia902705.us.archive.org/35/items/bub_gb_DXTysiS5ndQC/bub_gb_DXTysiS5ndQC.pdf. Accessed on February 13, 2017.

Lock, Stephen. 1983. "'O That I Were Young Again': Yeats and the Steinach Operation." *British Medical Journal*. 287(6409): 1964–1968.

Lundholm, Lena, et al. 2014. "Anabolic Androgenic Steroids and Violent Offending: Confounding by Polysubstance Abuse among 10 365 General Population Men." *Addiction*. 110(1): 100–108.

Martin, C. E. 1970. "John Hunter and Tissue Transplantation." *Surgery, Gynecology & Obstetrics*. 131(2): 306–310.

Moore, Gerry, and Andrew Ritchie. 2011. *The Little Black Bottle: Choppy Warburton, His Mysterious Potion, and the Deaths of His Bicycle Racers*. San Francisco, CA: Cycle Publishing.

Mottram, David R., and Alan J. George. 2000. "Anabolic Steroids." *Clinical Endocrinology and Metabolism*. 14(1): 55–69.

Müller, Rudhard Klaus. 2010. "History of Doping and Doping Control." In Detlef Thieme and Peter Hemmersbach, eds. *Doping in Sports*. Heidelberg; New York: Springer, 1–23.

Navar, Paul D. 2008. "Optimizing Testosterone Levels in Aging Men." LifeExtension. http://www.lifeextension.com/magazine/2008/7/optimizing-testosterone-levels-in-aging-men/Page-01. Accessed on February 14, 2017.

O'Dea, Jennifer, and Renata Leah Cinelli. 2016. "Use of Drugs to Change Appearance in Girls and Female Adolescents." In Matthew Hall, Sarah Grogan, and Brendan Gough, eds. *Chemically Modified Bodies: The Use of Diverse Substances for Appearance Enhancement.* London: Palgrave Macmillan, 51–76.

Phelan, Kate. 2017. "A Brief History of Hurling in Ireland." Culture Trip. https://theculturetrip.com/europe/ireland/ articles/a-brief-history-of-hurling-in-ireland/. Accessed on February 9, 2017.

Pope, Harrison G., et al. 2004. "Anabolic Steroid Users' Attitudes towards Physicians." *Addiction.* 99(9): 1189–1194.

Potter, David. 2012. *The Victor's Crown.* Oxford, UK; New York: Oxford University Press.

Powers, Michael E. 2002. "The Safety and Efficacy of Anabolic Steroid Precursors: What Is the Scientific Evidence?" *Journal of Athletic Training.* 37(3): 300–305.

Prokop, Luxembourg. 1970. "The Struggle against Doping and Its History." *The Journal of Sports Medicine and Physical Fitness.* 10(1): 45–48.

Ricciardelli, Lina A., and Robert J. Williams. 2016. "Use of Supplements and Drugs to Change Body Image and Appearance among Boys and Male Adolescents." In Matthew Hall, Sarah Grogan, and Brendan Gough, eds. *Chemically Modified Bodies: The Use of Diverse Substances for Appearance Enhancement.* London: Palgrave Macmillan.

Rogol, Alan D. 1988. "Anabolic Steroid Hormones for Athletes: Efficacy or Fantasy?" *Growth, Genetics, and Hormones.* 4(4): 2–3.

Rosen, Daniel M. 2008. *Dope: A History of Performance Enhancement in Sports from the Nineteenth Century to Today.* Westport, CT: Praeger.

Shahidi, Nasrollah T. 2001. "A Review of the Chemistry, Biological Action, and Clinical Applications of

Anabolic–Androgenic Steroids." *Clinical Therapeutics.* 23(9): 1355–1390.

Shugarman, Alan E. 2017. "Muscle Building Supplement Guide." http://www.nutritionexpress.com/article index/ authors/alaneshugarman ms rd/showarticle.aspx?articleid= 793. Accessed on February 13, 2017.

Speak, Mike. 1999. "Recreation and Sport in Ancient China: Primitive Society to AD 960." In James Riordan and Robin Jones, eds. *Sport and Physical Education in China.* London; New York: International Society for Competitive Physical Education and Sport, 20–44.

"Steroid Effectiveness Chart." 2017. isteroids. http://www .isteroids.com/steroids/Steroid%20Effectiveness%20Chart .html. Accessed on February 13, 2017.

Tatteresall, R. B. 2009. "Charles-Edouard Brown-Séquard: Double-Hyphenated Neurologist and Forgotten Father of Endocrinology." *Diabetic Medicine.* 11(8): 728–731.

"Testosterone Production." 2011. Mechanisms in Medicine. YouTube. https://www.youtube.com/watch?v=djqqao2Uebo. Accessed on February 12, 2017.

Timm, Leo. 2015. "Cuju: 2,000 Years of Ancient Chinese Soccer." *Epoch Times.* http://www.theepochtimes.com/n3/ 1745118-cuju-2000-years-of-ancient-chinese-soccer/. Accessed on February 9, 2017.

Turner, Christopher. 2008. "Vasectomania, and Other Cures for Sloth." *Cabinet.* http://www.cabinetmagazine.org/ issues/29/turner.php. Accessed on February 11, 2017.

Virtual Muscle. 2015. "All about Testosterone." Body Building.com. http://www.bodybuilding.com/fun/vm12 .htm. Accessed on February 12, 2017.

von Deutsch, Daniel A., Imad K. Abukhalaf, and Robin R. Socci. 2012. "Anabolic Doping Agents." In Ashraf Mozayani and Lionel P. Raymon, eds. *Handbook of Drug Interactions*, 2nd ed. Totowa, NJ: Humana Press.

Willey, Jessica. 2008. "Man Crusades to Save Kids from Steroids." ABC13 Eyewitness News. http://abclocal.go.com/ktrk/story?section=news/local&id=5903834. Accessed on February 9, 2017.

Winters, Stephen J. 2017. "Laboratory Assessment of Testicular Function." Endotext. https://www.ncbi.nlm.nih.gov/books/NBK279145/. Accessed on February 12, 2017.

Yesalis, Charles E., and Michael S. Bahrke. 2000. "Doping among Adolescent Athletes." *Baillieres Best Practice and Research. Clinical Endocrinology and Metabolism.* 14(1): 25–35.

Yesalis, Charles E., and Michael S. Bahrke. 2002. "History of Doping in Sports." In Michael S. Bahrke and Charles Yesalis, eds. *Performance-Enhancing Substances in Sport and Exercise.* Champaign, IL: Human Kinetics, 42–76.

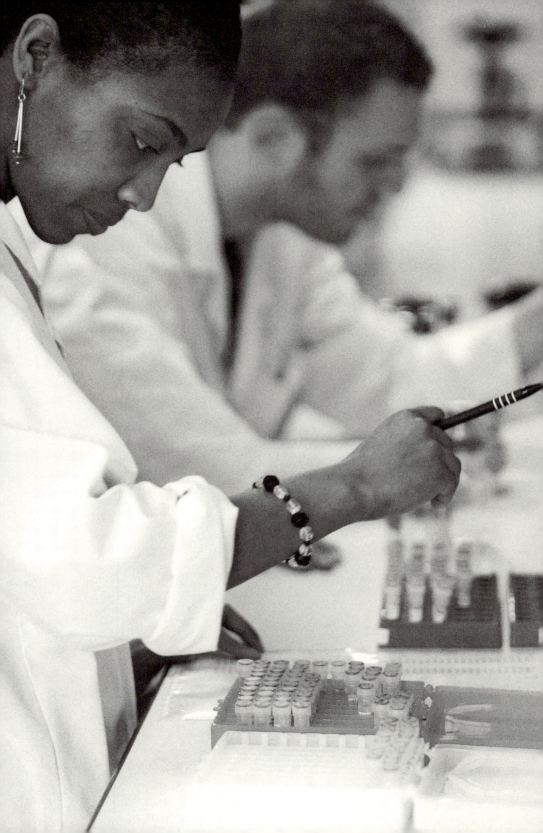

In the 1932 Olympic Games held in Los Angeles, the United States won the largest number of medals of any nation: 110 medals, of which 44 were gold, 36 silver, and 30 bronze. Germany ranked ninth among all nations, winning a total of 20 medals: 3 gold, 12 silver, and 5 bronze. Four years later, at the 1936 Games in Berlin, this result was reversed, with Germany bringing home the greatest number of medals of any nation: 89 medals, of which 33 were gold, 26 silver, and 30 bronze. The United States was placed second behind Germany, with a total of 56 medals, 24 gold, 20 silver, and 12 bronze. How does one explain this remarkable change in results ("1932 Los Angeles Medal Tally" 2017; "1936 Berlin Medal Tally" 2017)?

For many decades, some historians have pondered the question as to whether steroids played a part in this dramatic reversal of athletic fortunes. They point out that testosterone had first been synthesized only two years before the 1936 Games, in 1934, and it was already in commercial production by the time those Games were under way. With their almost manic desire to prove that the Aryan civilization was inherently superior to all other forms of human life, would it not have been a

---

Laboratory technicians prepare samples of urine for doping tests during a media open day, ahead of the Vancouver Winter Olympics, at the King's College London Drug Control Centre in London, February 5, 2010. The drug control center is the UK's only World Anti-Doping Agency (WADA) accredited laboratory to carry out doping tests on sports competitors. (AP Photo/Sang Tan)

great temptation for the Nazi party to provide steroids to German competitors in the Olympic Games, some observers have asked. Indeed, abundant evidence is now available that Adolf Hitler himself was almost certainly a regular user of steroids, and he may have encouraged the use of such products among German military and athletic groups (Reinold and Hoberman 2014).

Little other than rumors, anecdotal evidence, hearsay, and comments from other questionable sources exists to support these speculations. What is clear, however, is that the discovery, synthesis, and commercial production of anabolic steroids that began in the 1930s marked a turning point in the history of the use of illegal steroids in sports. If the Germans did not, in fact, supply steroids to their Olympic athletes in 1936, it was all but inevitable that Germany or some other nation would soon set out on a similar campaign to make their athletes "the greatest in the world."

Doping in Athletic Competition, 1950–1970

The debate over the use of testosterone and other performance-enhancing drugs in athletics aside, the fact remains that some such phenomenon now seems to have been inevitable at some point in time. Research on testosterone and its derivatives was moving along in at least three major pharmaceutical firms in Europe: Ciba, in Switzerland, Schering, in Germany, and Organon, in the Netherlands. It seems inconceivable that news of the apparently wondrous physical effects of these substances on the human body would not eventually become known—and probably common knowledge—among athletes before very long.

Perhaps the first instance in which testosterone was used to improve athletic competition in a formal event occurred in 1950, when Dr. Axel Mathiesen, trainer for the Danish rowing team at the European championships held in Milan, was accused of providing his crew with "hormone pills" to improve their performance. When the matter was referred to the International Olympic Committee (IOC) for adjudication, Dr. Mathiesen readily admitted the practice of which he was accused. His defense was that giving his rowers "hormone pills" (identified by the committee as Androstin) did not provide them with extraordinary skills, but only helped them to achieve the highest level of performance of which they were capable. In any case, the committee decided that it was not yet clear what constituted "doping" in an athletic competition and, therefore, was not competent to make a decision about the 1950 rowing incident (Mullegg and Montandon 1951).

Only two years after the Danish rowing incident, the issue of steroid doping was at the fore of international sports debates again. This time, the occasion was the amazing success of the Soviet Union's weight lifting contingent at the 1952 Helsinki Olympic Games. Those Games were the first occasion in which the Soviet Union participated in the Olympics, and they made a concerted effort to put their best foot forward in Helsinki. They had begun four years earlier by sending a group of observers to the 1948 London Games with the task of determining, not whether they could compete in the Games at all but whether they could be clear winners and, if so, in what sports (Riordan 1993).

The London observers concluded that the Soviet Union could compete most successfully in various strength sports, such as weight lifting and wrestling. The evidence suggests that they thought success in these fields could come not only from the natural skills of their athletes but also from the availability and use of certain supplements—steroids—that could produce the muscle bulk and strength needed to win in these competitions.

They turned out to be correct. In 1952, in the first Olympic Games in which the Soviets ever competed, they won the greatest number of weight lifting medals—seven—of any nation, three gold, three silver, and one bronze. By contrast, the United States won six medals overall, and no other nation won more than two medals in the sport. In addition, the Soviets won 9 medals in Greco-Roman and freestyle wrestling and 43 medals in gymnastics. Overall, the Soviet Union won 71 medals at the Helsinki Games, just behind the United States (76 medals) and well ahead of any other nation (Hungary was third with 42 medals) ("1952 Helsinki Medal Tally" 2017).

A number of observers were surprised and puzzled by the Soviets' success. Bob Hoffman, who had been assistant coach of the U.S. weight lifting team at the 1948 and 1952 Games and head coach for the 1956 and 1960 Games, expressed the view in Helsinki that "I know they're taking that hormone stuff to increase their strength" (as quoted in Almond, Cart, and Harvey 1984 and cited in Hunt 2011, 8). He later told a reporter that he felt certain that Soviet lifters were "taking injections of some kind." "They would come out [for the competition] glassy-eyed, like wild men, and lift like crazy" (quoted in Fair 1993, 4).

Confirmation of this suspicion came in 1954 during the World Weightlifting Championships being held in Vienna, Austria. One evening, over a friendly glass of beer, a Soviet sports physician told Dr. John Ziegler that Soviet weight lifters had been so successful because they had been receiving injections of pure testosterone. Ziegler, a consultant to the U.S. weight lifting team, was familiar with testosterone. In addition to being an avid fitness proponent, he worked on weekends at the Ciba Pharmaceutical Company near his home in Maryland. The company had been providing Ziegler with samples of testosterone with which to carry out his own research on the compound's anabolic properties. Ziegler had queried the Soviet doctor in Vienna at least partly because he was struck by the unusual appearance and behavior of the Soviet weight lifters, unusual to the point that some of them required catheterization in order to urinate, so much had their bodies changed as a result of testosterone use.

That "friendly glass of beer" may have been one of the most momentous social events in the history of sports. Upon his return home, Ziegler decided to seek out a product that could produce the same results he had seen in Soviet weight lifters but without the grotesque side effects he also observed as a result of the practice. He was looking, that is, for a substance that had the desirable anabolic (muscle-building) properties of testosterone without the undesirable androgenic (masculinizing) properties of the hormone.

Historians of sport differ somewhat as to Ziegler's involvement in the development of the testosterone derivative for which he was looking. Ziegler's background included both a medical degree and research on hormone structure and function (see his biographical sketch in Chapter 4). That background would have allowed him to understand the principles and technology involved in the development of such a product. Ziegler's training and experience, then, would certainly justify the title of "father of Dianabol," the derivative of testosterone eventually developed by Ciba that some historians have given to him (Dvorchak 2012; Goldman and Goldman 1980, 5, cited in Fair 1993, 2).

But it is somewhat unlikely that he had the time, materials, and other resources needed to develop a new product. In fact, the more likely story is that Ciba researchers were already working on analogs of testosterone in their own laboratories and that one eventually became available that met the requirements set out by Ziegler (Yesalis, et al. 1990, 97). That compound was (8S,9S,10S,13S,14S,17S)-17-hydroxy-10, 13,17-trimethyl-7,8, 9,11,12,14,15,16-octahydro-6H-cyclopenta[a]phenanthren-3-one, better known (for obvious reasons) as *methandrostenolone* and sold commercially as *Dianabol*. Although Ciba researchers originally developed Dianabol as a treatment for burn victims, they also knew of Ziegler's interest in modified forms of testosterone for other applications. So they provided him with samples of their new product.

At the time, Ziegler had the ideal setting in which to test Dianabol. He was a member of the York Barbell Club, in York, Pennsylvania, where he himself worked out and where he knew a number of leading weight lifters of the time. When some of those weight lifters came to Ziegler for advice about improving their performance, he suggested that they try Dianabol pills. The results of this experiment were mixed. One of the first York members to try the new drug was Bill March, a devoted but run-of-the-mill lifter at the time. Within a short period of time, March's muscle mass and strength began to improve dramatically. After a year of working out and taking Dianabol, March had moved to the forefront of U.S. weight lifters. He gained 20 pounds in 11 months and by March 1963 set a new world record for standing bench press at 354 pounds. He attributed his success not only to the new muscle he had gained from using Dianabol but also to the sense of euphoria he felt after taking the drug (Dvorchak 2005).

Other weight lifters had less remarkable success. One of these was John Grimek, one of the greatest weight lifters of his time, winner of both the Mr. America and Mr. Universe titles. At Ziegler's suggestion, Grimek also began taking Dianabol to increase his weight and strength. He soon decided that he was getting no results from the product and decided to give them up. As he told an interviewer some years later, "after six weeks I gave it up. I got no results" (Fair 1993, 5).

Ziegler's experiment with Dianabol was made even more difficult by the fact that York members were also trying out a new system of training at the time, a system known as *functional isometric contraction*. A number of athletes and trainers had become convinced that isometrics were the training system of the future, a way of increasing one's muscle mass and strength (the same qualities expected from taking a testosterone derivative). Thus, when athletes found that they were gaining weight and strength while using isometric exercises and taking Dianabol, it was not clear to which practice their success could be attributed to or, more likely, how much success to each of the two practices. (For an extended discussion of this point, see Fair 1993, passim.) In any case, it appears that Ziegler eventually lost interest in continuing his experiments with Dianabol for the rest of the 1950s. One observer has suggested that he had become too involved in his own medical practice to spend time on Dianabol experiments (Todd 1965, as quoted in Fair 1993, 5).

Regardless of Ziegler's personal involvement, news of the success of steroids in promoting weight and strength gain began to spread throughout the sports community. By the early 1960s, steroid use had become widespread and common in weight lifting, power lifting, competitive bodybuilding, professional football, a number of track-and-field events, and, according to some reports, even swimming and long-distance running (Yesalis, et al. 1990, 98). For example, U.S. hammer thrower and gold medal winner in the event in the 1956 Olympic Games Harold Connolly testified before a U.S. Senate subcommittee in 1973 that steroid use had become widespread in track and field by the mid-1960s. "By 1968," he said, "athletes in every event were using anabolic steroids and stimulants. I knew any number of athletes on the 1968 Olympic team who had so much scar tissue and so many puncture holes in their backsides that it was difficult to find a fresh spot to give them a new shot" (Schudel 2010). Dr. Tom Waddell, who finished sixth in the decathlon at the 1968 Summer Olympic Games, confirmed Connolly's view. He said that more than a third of the athletes at the Lake Tahoe training site for the 1968 Games were taking steroids (Scott 1971, 40).

Professional football was another fertile field for the spread of anabolic steroid use. Perhaps the most famous instance of steroid use by an entire football team was that of the 1963 San Diego Chargers. The 1962 season had been a disaster for the Chargers, who won only 4 games in a 14-game schedule. During the winter months following that season, however, head coach Sid Gillman vowed to do whatever was necessary to turn that record around. One of those steps was the introduction of intensive weight training, accompanied by the use of Dianabol pills. As one player later recounted, those pills were provided for players in cereal bowls after every meal at the training camp (Quinn 2009). The pills obviously had their intended effect. San Diego won the American Football League (AFL) West Division championship with an 11–3 record and then went on to demolish the Boston Patriots in the AFL championship game by a score of 51–10. (The 1963 championship was the only professional football championship won by the franchise.)

By the time the 1964 Olympic Games were held in Tokyo, rumors were rife about the possible use of steroids among competitors. Many athletes, coaches, and trainers simply assumed by that point in time that the majority of weight lifters almost certainly used drugs to improve their performance. Athletes in other sports, especially those from the Soviet Bloc, also came under suspicion. For example, the Press sisters, Irina and Tamara, were track-and-field competitors from Ukraine who, during the first half of the 1960s, set 26 world records in their sports: shot put, discus, hurdles, and pentathlon. The bodily appearance of the two sisters was so strongly masculine that most observers assumed that they were (1) taking steroids, (2) taking hermaphrodites, or (3) actually men. Since no drug testing was available for their sports in the 1964 Games, this question was never answered, and when testing programs were introduced soon after the Tokyo Games, the sisters retired from sports competition (Transgender and Intersex Olympians 2011).

Banning the Use of Anabolic Steroids

Concerns about the use of illegal performance-enhancing substances in athletic competitions go back almost a hundred years. Even before the discovery of testosterone, a handful of sporting organizations had been discussing the problem of doping in their sports and devising methods for reducing this problem. The first organization to adopt such a ban was the International Amateur Athletic Federation (IAAF), which produced a list of substances that were not permitted to be used in competitions under their sponsorship. In the 1928 version of its handbook, the IAAF said that

> Doping is the use of any stimulant not normally employed to increase the power of action in athletic competition above the average. Any person knowingly acting or assisting as explained above shall be excluded from any place where these rules are in force or, if he is a competitor, be suspended for a time or otherwise from further participation in amateur athletics under the jurisdiction of this Federation. ("A Piece of Anti-doping History: IAAF Handbook 1927–1928" 2006)

The IAAF action was, to a large extent, symbolic because tests were not yet available for the detection of the vast majority of potential doping agents. About the only way a person could be convicted of violating the IAAF rule was for the person to admit to the use of an illegal substance, an unlikely event.

In fact, little or no effective action against the use of illegal performance-enhancing drugs occurred until the mid-1960s, when two organizations, the Union Cycliste Internationale (International Cycling Union) (ICU) and the Fédération Internationale de Football Association (International Federation of International Association Football Associations) (FIFA), took the lead in establishing anti-doping regulations for their sports. The ICU, for example, first included an article on "doping" in the 1960 edition of its rules book. It then added a similar article to its Technical Guide in 1966. A year later, it published a list of prohibited substances and a list of sanctions against riders who violated the association's anti-doping rules ("40 Years of Fighting against Doping" 2001). The FIFA also introduced an anti-doping regulation in 1966 ("Regulations: Doping Control for FIFA Competitions and Out of Competition" [2004]).

Anti-doping regulations were also being considered by the IOC in the 1960s. The IOC's concerns over the issue had a long history. It had received confirmation that a German male named Herman Ratjen had competed in the 1936 Games (and placed fourth in the high jump) as a female with the name "Dora" (Hunt 2011, 40). The IOC's problem only became worse in the early 1960s amid rumors that drugs capable of changing a person's sex (androgenic steroids) had become available to athletes. In a 1961 issue of the IOC bulletin, one writer warned of "a particularly revolting form of doping: that of women athletes who take male hormones which lead to castration of the functional cycle of women and amount sometimes to an atrophy of the ovaries which may cause a chronic disease in the long run" and, not accidentally, also vastly improve their athletic prowess.

The use of such drugs, the writer warned, "may bring success in the immediate present but at what a cost!" (Eyquem 1961, 50).

The one organization that might have been expected to take the lead against performance-enhancing drugs was probably the IOC. The committee not only had control over the most important athletic events in the world, the Summer and Winter Games, but also served as an example to national Olympic committees and both national and international sports associations. Yet, the IOC dithered about the illegal drug problem both in its own events and in those of other associations.

As early as 1960, the IOC had been confronted with the issue of drug use in an Olympic event. On August 26 of that year, Danish cyclist Knud Jensen collapsed and died during a trial run for the Rome Games. Officials eventually determined that his death was the result of having taken a drug called Roniacol, which enhances blood circulation. Earlier attempts by the IOC to simply ignore "rumors" of illegal drug use were not sufficient this time, and President Avery Brundage was forced to consider how the IOC would respond to Jensen's death. Brundage was in something of an awkward position because of the IOC's traditional views about illegal drug use. That position was based on two presumptions: first, that drug use was a relatively minor problem that was probably rare enough simply to ignore; second, that any drug problem that did exist should probably be dealt with by national organizations, rather than the parent international group. In this regard, Brundage wrote in early 1960 that "[t]he initial responsibility is in the hands of the National Federations of a score or more sports in more than ninety countries . . . [among whom] there may be some who are unscrupulous" (Hunt 2007, 8–9). (By "National Federations," Brundage meant the groups that controlled individuals sports worldwide, such as the IAAF [track and field], Fédération Internationale de Natation [swimming], International Archery Federation, Fédération Internationale d'Escrime [fencing], and Fédération Internationale de Gymnastique [gymnastics].)

Pressure on the IOC continued to mount, however, and in January 1962, Brundage announced that he would appoint a scientific committee to help the IOC determine exactly what constituted doping. That committee was appointed two months later, with Dr. Arthur Porritt of the Royal College of Surgeons as its chair. The choice of Porritt sent a message about the IOC's attitude about doping, since he had long argued that the IOC had no business becoming involved in medical and scientific issues about doping in sports. His tenure as chair only confirmed that view as he failed to carry out some of the most fundamental responsibilities associated with his position, such as attending meetings at which his committee was supposed to give a report (Hunt 2007, 17–19).

While the IOC doping subcommittee made essentially no progress in its mission of defining the problem for which it had been created to study, pressures continued to mount from other sources. In November 1963, for example, the European Council on Doping and the Biological Preparation of the Athlete Taking Part in Competitive Sports called for the establishment of an international commission that would develop rules dealing with the use of illegal substances in athletic competitions. The obvious organization to take on that task, the IOC, however, continued to deflect any responsibility for such a task, and, as a result, the 1964 Summer Games in Tokyo came and went with essentially no progress in the problem of dealing with doping (Todd and Todd 2001, 67).

The period between the 1964 and 1968 Games witnessed an increase of pressure on the IOC and other national and international agencies to resolve the doping problem. The point was fast approaching when decisions had to be made as to what these agencies would do, if anything, about the continuing increase in the popularity of performance-enhancing drugs, perhaps most spectacularly, the anabolic steroids. One of the first post–1964 Games elements influencing this debate came with a report that unofficial random tests during the 1964 Games had found that a number of participants had received injections of substances designed to improve their performance. With this information in hand, the IOC Executive Board concluded that the IOC "ought to have a rule obliging the athletes to submit to a medical examination," and if the results of those tests show that performance-enhancing drugs have been used, "the athlete or the team should be disqualified" (Hunt 2007, 31).

The Board finally acted on this recommendation at a meeting in Teheran in May 1967. It established a Medical Commission, under the leadership of Prince Alexandre of Mérode of the Belgian royal house. The Board also drew up a list of prohibited substances, which included alcohol, cocaine, cannabis, amphetamines, and ephedra, but not anabolic steroids. The fact that the Board already had in hand a report on the dangerous side effects of steroids when they made that decision was, according to a leading historian of doping in sports, "quite damning" (Hunt 2007, 35).

At its first meeting in September 1967, the Medical Commission (which still exists today) laid out its plan for testing at the 1968 Winter Games in Grenoble. Participants would have to promise to submit to medical examinations, agree to random drug testing, and arrange for suitable conditions under which to supply urine or blood samples, an agenda much the same as that the IOC had proposed in the past. At the same time, the debate continued between the IOC and the international federations as to who was to be responsible for the actual testing of athletes and what penalties were to be assessed for those who failed the test.

In any case, the debate turned out to be somewhat moot. Of the 86 athletes tested during the Grenoble Winter Games, none failed; among the 667 athletes tested at the Mexico City Summer Games, only one participant failed, pentathlon contestant Hans-Gunnar Liljenwall, who had ethanol in his blood. Table 2.1 shows the results of drug testing for other Olympic Games since testing originated in 1968 to the 2012 Games in London. Data after 2008 are now highly questionable as a result of research released in 2016 about widespread doping at least and primarily by the Soviet Union and Russia throughout at least the 2000s.

Table 2.1 **Number of Cases of Confirmed Doping at Summer and Winter Olympic Games, 1968–2012**

Year	Site (S/W)	Tests Performed	Positive Results*	Percentage Positive**
1968	Mexico City (S)	667	1	0.15
1968	Grenoble (W)	86	0	0.00
1972	Munich (S)	2,079	7	0.34
1972	Sapporo (W)	211	1	0.47
1976	Montreal (S)	2,054	11	0.54
1976	Innsbruck (W)	390	2	0.51
1980	Moscow (S)	645	0	0.00
1980	Lake Placid (W)	440	0	0.00
1984	Los Angeles (S)	1,507	12	0.80
1984	Sarajevo (W)	424	1	0.24
1988	Seoul (S)	1,598	10	0.62
1988	Calgary (W)	492	1	0.20

(continued)

Table 2.1   (continued)

Year	Site (S/W)	Tests Performed	Positive Results*	Percentage Positive**
1992	Barcelona (S)	1,848	5	0.27
1992	Albertville (W)	522	0	0.00
1994	Lillehammer (W)	529	0	0.00
1996	Atlanta (S)	1,923	2	0.10
1998	Nagano (W)	621	0	0.00
2000	Sydney (S)	2,359	11	0.47
2002	Salt Lake City (W)	700	7	1.00
2006	Turin (W)	1,200	7	0.58
2008	Beijing (S)	4,770	27	0.57
2010	Vancouver (W)	2,149	3	0.14
2012	London (S)	5,051	24	0.48
2014	Sochi (W)	2,453	8	0.33

*Includes tests conducted during the Games as well as reanalyses conducted after completion of the Games.

**Calculated from table data.

S, Summer Games; W, Winter Games.

Source: "Factsheet: The Fight against Doping and Promotion of Athletes' Health Update—September 2016." International Olympic Committee. https://stillmed. olympic.org/media/Document%20Library/OlympicOrg/Factsheets-Reference-Documents/Medical/Fight-against-Doping/Factsheet-The-Fight-against-Doping-and-Promotion-of-Athletes-Health.pdf#_ga=1.255298568.1868910684.1481307 880. Accessed on February 20, 2017.

The considerable success of the testing program conducted by the Medical Commission at the Grenoble and Mexico City Games did not bring to an end the conflict among the three entities involved in this issue: the IOC, the international federations, and the national Olympic committees. Indeed, each of these three entities appeared to be eager to pass on the responsibility for testing, and only the Medical Commission was ready and willing to take on that challenge. The problem, of course, was that the Medical Commission was a division of the IOC, which was one of those groups eschewing the opportunity to run a testing program. (For a superb discussion of this history, see Hunt 2007, 45–51.)

The aura of confusion surrounding drug testing in the 1960s has not completely disappeared today. A number of different agencies are responsible for drug testing at various levels of competition in a great range of sports. For example, a runner who has qualified for the Olympic Games might expect to be tested by the United States Olympic Committee through the United States Anti-Doping Agency (USADA); by USA Track and Field, the controlling body for the sport in the United States; by the IAAF, the controlling group for all amateur athletics worldwide; and/or by other local, regional, national, and international organizations that have an interest in track and field at the national or international levels. Indeed, sorting out this maze of drugging regulations may demand the advice of someone trained in sports law. (See, for example, Pilgrim and Betz 2008).

One of the most serious deficiencies in the 1967 actions by the IOC in Teheran was the omission of anabolic steroids from the list of banned substances. Even when it was aware of the serious health consequences of taking anabolic steroids, the IOC Board and Medical Commission weren't really quite sure what to do about the problem of their use in sports competitions. Testing issues were at the core of this uncertainty. One IOC official noted that tests conducted at the 1964 Olympics showed up a number of substances that were chemically similar to, but not identical to, substances on the banned list. The explanation for this observation is twofold. In the first place, any substance that is ingested in the human body is not likely to remain in its original form throughout its period of time in the body. It is broken down, producing a number of so-called *metabolites*, the products of digestion. What drug tests must measure, then, is not only the banned substance itself but also all possible metabolites of that substance. For many chemicals, that information simply was not available in the 1960s, so test analysts could not be certain whether they had really detected drug use or not.

The second problem is that chemists in many parts of the world were synthesizing new performance-enhancing drugs even as the Olympic Committee was trying to develop fool-proof methods for testing for the older products. As noted earlier, Ciba had already produced one such product, Dianabol, in the late 1950s, well in advance of the IOC's efforts to develop a drug-testing program. From the time Dianabol was released in 1958 (and probably even earlier), weight lifters and other athletes around the world had access to an anabolic steroid about which the IOC and other governing agencies knew relatively little and about which they could do even less. A similar story was being played out in the Soviet Union, where researchers had developed a derivative of testosterone, nandrolone decanoate, sold commercially in the Soviet Bloc as Retabolil and now available in the West as Deca Durabolin. And in East Germany, researchers had produced yet another testosterone derivative, 4-chlorodehydromethyltestosterone, marketed under the trade name of Oral Turinabol. Each of these new compounds found an eager and accepting market among competitive and amateur athletes (Baker 2011; Mantell 2011).

And this was just the beginning. One anonymous weight lifter who competed in the 1968 Games explained the challenge facing drug testers. When asked if he was concerned about the IOC ban on drugs, he responded:

> What ban? Everyone used a new one [performance-enhancing drug] from West Germany. They [the IOC] couldn't pick it up in the test they were using. When they get a test for that one, we'll find something else. It's like cops and robbers. (Gilbert 1969, 66)

This "game" of cat and mouse between drug users and drug-ban enforcers continues today, not only in the field of athletics and sports but also in the everyday life of substance abusers around the world. (For an interesting discussion of this phenomenon, see Werner and Hatton 2011, especially p. 37.)

In spite of its concerns about the bad publicity that would almost certainly be associated with drug testing and the consequent banning of competitors, the IOC continued to find a way of adding anabolic steroids to the list of prohibited substances first announced in 1967. For example, President Brundage wrote to Prince de Merode, chair of the Medical Commission, in 1971, asking if it had found any way of testing reliably for the presence of "hormones." De Merode responded that such testing was very difficult since all trace of hormones disappeared from the body within a matter of weeks, so it would be easy for an athlete to use drugs during training without hope of detection (Hunt 2011).

Even as this exchange of letters was taking place, researchers were making significant progress in finding ways to test efficiently for anabolic steroids in the blood and urine. Between 1970 and 1975, researchers developed methods for using radioimmunoassay, gas chromatography-mass spectrometry (GC-MS), and other methods for reliably detecting anabolic steroids and their metabolites in body fluids. (See, for example, Brooks, Firth, and Sumner 1975; Sumner 1974; Van Eenoo and Delbeke 2006; Ward, Shackleton, and Lawson 1975.) And this progress prompted the IOC to consider adding anabolic steroids to its list of prohibited substances. As a trial for the proposed policy, the new testing procedures for steroids were used at the Commonwealth Games held in Christchurch, New Zealand, in January 1974. At those Games, nine competitors failed the initial immunoassay test, of whom seven also failed the confirmatory GC-MS test (Kicman and Gower 2003, 323).

This progress in testing technology was sufficient to convince the IOC Medical Commission that testing should be adopted for future Olympic events. It announced in April 1974 that random testing for anabolic steroids would begin at the 1976 Games in Montréal. At its next meeting, in October 1974, the Committee announced changes in Rule 26, the Eligibility Code for competitors in the Games. Those changes specified the following:

- The use of illegal substances was forbidden in Olympic competition, and the IOC would create a list of prohibited substances covered by this rule.
- Any competitor who refused to take a test or who failed a test was to be disqualified from competition.
- If the person who failed a drug test was a member of a team, the entire team was to be disqualified.
- Anyone who participates in a sport designated for women must be able to pass a gender test.
- Anyone who refuses to take a drug test or who fails such a test is to be withdrawn of any medals awarded.
- Any sanctions imposed by the IOC do not negate the possibility of additional sanctions from international sport federations. ("Olympic Rules and Regulations" 1974, 14–15)

The new rules were implemented at the Montréal Games, and eight competitors tested positive, seven in the weight lifting competition and one in the track-and-field events. Those who failed the test were from five nations: Bulgaria (2), United States (2), Poland (2), Czechoslovakia (1), and Sweden (1) ("Athletics at the 1976 Montréal Summer Games: Women's Discus Throw" 2016; Chidlovski 2009). Two of the athletes who were disqualified were stripped of their gold medals and one of his silver medal, all in weight lifting.

The "cop and robbers" aspect of drug testing has not abated today. Pharmaceutical chemists continue to search for new anabolic steroids that athletes can include in their training programs without violating existing doping rules. And athletic associations continue to keep an eye out for such substances and to include them in their latest list of prohibited performance-enhancing substances. The most recent such list, published by the World Anti-Doping Association (WADA) in 2012, provides a glimpse of that scope of the "cops and robbers" skirmish. That list of substances that are prohibited "at all times" contains 28 endogenous and 46 exogenous anabolic steroids ranging from 1-androstenediol and 1-androstenedione to 19-norandrosterone and 19-noretiocholanolone. The list is actually much longer because it also includes, without naming them, "other substances with a similar chemical structure or similar biological effect(s)" as part of the list of exogenous steroids and all the metabolites and isomers of five basic endogenous steroids. In addition to this list, WADA provides two other lists of prohibited substances, those that are banned during a competition and those that are banned for specific sports ("Prohibited List 2016" 2016, 2–3).

In addition to the lists of banned substances, WADA provides a list of certain procedures that are not allowed. These procedures fall into three major categories: those that increase the concentration of oxygen available to a competitor, various forms of physical and chemical manipulation of body systems, and so-called gene doping, which involves altering a person's DNA, RNA, or genetic composition ("Prohibited List 2016" 2016, 5).

Testing Methodology

A critical feature to be noted from the preceding discussion is the absolute necessity of adequate testing procedures for detecting the presence of a prohibited substance in a person's body. This statement is especially true for anabolic steroids among all banned substances because of the complexity of steroid chemistry. As one can see from the structural formulas for testosterone and other anabolic steroids discussed earlier in this text, these substances have very complex molecular structures that make them difficult to detect, identify, and distinguish from other substances present in a sample. This would be the appropriate point in this text, therefore, for a review of the process by which anti-doping tests are conducted.

The testing procedures for endogenous and exogenous anabolic steroids are different. In the latter case, a laboratory can simply look for anabolic steroids that do not occur normally in the human body (exogenous anabolic steroids). If they are present in a person's urine, blood, or other bodily fluid, that person is probably guilty of having ingested the substance. The former case is more of a challenge. Suppose that a test shows that a male athlete has testosterone or its metabolites in his blood or urine. Well, of course, they will be. All males have testosterone in their bodies, so it or its metabolites will occur naturally in their blood or urine. Some other technique is needed to decide if a person has ingested an endogenous anabolic hormone, such as having taken a "testosterone pill," for example, in order to boost his body's natural level of the hormone. (Note that women also have testosterone in their bodies, but the following discussion will focus on testosterone testing for males only.)

One basis for such a test might be to determine, first of all, the "normal" level of some anabolic steroid, such as testosterone, in the male body. That research has already been done and a normal testosterone range can be given for most males. However, as with almost any human characteristic, that normal range varies from man to man and can vary significantly even for any one person. One solution to this problem is to measure a man's testosterone level over long periods of time so that a normal range for that person can be determined. But such a procedure is too expensive to be used in practice.

And, as part of the cops and robber game between drug testers and athletes, the former are always trying to develop new and better methods for testing for the presence of banned substances. One of the more recent of these technologies has been the carbon-isotope ratio test. That test is based on the fact that the carbon atoms that occur everywhere in nature exist in two similar, but somewhat different, forms called *isotopes*. Isotopes are forms of an atom that have the same number of protons in their nuclei but different numbers of neutrons. For example, by far the most common form of carbon in nature is carbon-12 (also written as 12C), whose nucleus has six protons and six neutrons. A much less common form of carbon, however, is carbon-13 (13C), which has six protons and seven neutrons. It is relatively easy to distinguish between 12C and 13C in the laboratory.

The important point about the carbon isotopes for testing is that exogenous anabolic steroids contain a smaller fraction of 13C than do endogenous anabolic steroids. So the ratio of 13C to 12C will be lower in the blood of someone who has been taking exogenous testosterone than in someone who has not. Again, the problem is to figure out what constitutes a normal 13C-to-12C ratio for any particular person. But that problem can usually be solved (de la Torre, et al. 2001).

Testing for exogenous anabolic steroids presents a somewhat different kind of challenge. The challenge here is to look for substances in blood, urine, sweat, and other bodily fluids for substances that are banned from use in athletic competitions. The fundamental steps involved in such tests were outlined in the 1970s and remain essentially the same today (see Beckett 1976). The technology involved in testing has, of course, evolved, but the chain of events involved in a test are essentially the same today as it was in 1976. The first step in that chain of events is the selection of the individual(s) to be tested. Various sporting groups and events have differing rules as to who will be tested and under what circumstances. In some cases, all athletes involved in a competition may be tested, while in other instances, only a random sample of athletes may be selected for testing. Testing may occur before, during, or after a competition on one occasion or more. One of the more recent elements of a testing program is the so-called *whereabouts provision*, in which an athlete must notify the testing agency where he or she can be found during one specific part of every day during the testing period. The agency may then appear unannounced during the whereabouts period and administer a drug test ("Drug Testing in Sport" 2014; for an example in one sport, see Wallace 2016).

An athlete to be tested will be asked to provide a sample of a bodily fluid. In theory, that fluid could be saliva, blood, urine, or some other fluid, although primarily for reasons of expense urine testing is by far the most common type of procedure. An athlete is typically asked to provide about 100 milliliters of urine, which is then divided into two parts, known as Sample A and Sample B.

Although technically feasible, sample testing typically does not occur at the same place that a sample is collected. Instead, it is sealed and transmitted to a certified testing laboratory. Precautions in the sealing and transmittal of a specimen are critical, because chemical changes may occur within the sample that can invalidate the test results. One of the most common objections raised by athletes to adverse testing results is that individuals in charge of the sample have not cared properly for the sample and the results reported for the specimen are not, therefore, accurate. Keeping a careful record of the location of a sample, the conditions under which it was held, the individuals responsible for the sample, and other relevant factors is known as the *chain of custody* for that sample. (Current instructions for chain of custody procedures and the form used for such procedures can be found at "Chain of Custody Form" 2016; "Doping Control Officer (DCO) Instructions: Chain of Custody Form" 2015.)

Once the samples have reached a testing laboratory, the first sample (Sample A) is subjected to chemical analysis, which may consist of two steps: the screen and the confirmatory test. In anti-doping terminology, the term *screen* refers to the first test performed on a sample. That test is performed to decide whether the sample is a candidate for further testing. For example, the test might find the presence of no substance on the list of banned substances, and, therefore, the athlete who supplied the specimen can be regarded as "clean." On the other hand, the screen might find the presence of one or more chemicals that suggest that a banned substance may be present. In such a case, a second screen test is usually performed on the sample to determine whether the first result was reliable or not. (The term *reliability* refers to the extent to which two or more tests produce similar or the same results.)

If, after both screening tests, there is reason to believe that a banned substance may be present in the sample, a second test is performed. That test is called a *confirmatory test* because it is accurate enough to determine at a high level of reliability that the sample does or does not contain the banned substance. If the banned substance is present, the person who supplied the sample is assumed to have ingested a prohibited substance and is subject to penalties laid down in the sporting organization's guidelines ("World Anti-Doping Code International Standard: Laboratories" 2016).

The most common screening test used for anti-doping analyses today is called an immunoassay or radioimmunoassay test. The term *immunoassay* provides a hint as to how such tests are carried out. The test works, in general, the way the human body does when exposed to some foreign substance, such as pollen. When pollen, called an *antigen*, enters the body, it is captured and inactivated by chemicals in the body called *antibodies*. This system protects the body from harmful attacks by foreign substances.

In preparing for an immunoassay test, an anti-doping laboratory prepares a "test" solution by producing one or more substances (call them "A," "B," and "C") against which can be made a second set of substances (call them "anti-A," "anti-B," and "anti-C") that combine with the first set of substances, that is, "A" with "anti-A," "B" with "anti-B," and "C" with "anti-C." The testing solution consists of anti-A, anti-B, anti-C, and as many other "antibodies" as one might choose. When this solution is added to the urine sample taken from an athlete, any A present in the urine will bind to anti-A in the testing solution, any B will bind with the anti-B in the testing solution, and so on. Making the anti-A, anti-B, and anti-C in the testing solution radioactive simply makes the products formed during this reaction (anti-A/A, anti-B/B, and so on) easier to see because they give off radiation that can easily be detected. One of the most popular types of immunoassay is called an enzyme-linked immunosorbent assay (ELISA). For more technical information about an ELISA test, see "Enzyme-Linked Immunosorbent Assay (ELISA)" 2017.

An immunoassay screen is quite good at detecting the presence of prohibited substances in a sample, but not good enough. A sample thought to contain a banned substance is then tested a second time. The usual procedure used in the confirmatory test is *gas chromatography-mass spectrometry*. This procedure actually consists of two discrete operations. The first operation, gas chromatography, depends on the fact that different substances move through a medium at different rates of speed. Imagine, for example, that a piece of blotting paper is just barely placed into contact with a container that holds three different colors of ink. Under the proper circumstances, those three different colors migrate upward through the blotting paper at different speeds.

That process is known as *liquid chromatography* because the material moving through the blotter is a liquid (ink). The only way in which gas chromatography is different is that the three colors of ink are carried upward through the blotter in a column of gas, rather than a liquid solution, which is technically a bit more difficult, but not much. (A good demonstration of the operation of a gas chromatograph can be found at "Gas Chromatography" 2008.)

In some chemical procedures, the liquid or gas chromatography procedure can be refined sufficiently so that different substances can be separated from each other quite well. But GC-MS adds a second procedure, *mass spectrometry* (MS). In mass spectrometry, charged particles are caused to spin around the inside of a metal container, like the horses on a carousel. As these particles spin, they are flung outward toward the inner sides of the container. Where they end up on the container depends on how heavy they are, how fast they are moving, and other properties. What makes the MS test work is that scientists know where a testosterone molecule will end up in an MS machine when it is spun at a certain speed: where a methandrostenolone molecule will end up, and where any other anabolic steroid molecule will end up under experimental conditions. (A technical description and diagram of the GC-MS procedure can be found at Brailsford, et al. 2012. Also see Saugy, et al. 2000.)

The GC-MS test, then, combines these two procedures. An athlete's urine is first subjected to a GC test, in which "suspect" molecules can be seen separating from other substances in the mixture. These suspect molecules can then be removed from the GC apparatus and injected into a mass spectrometer. When the MS test is performed, the test supervisor can determine whether the suspect molecules ended up in places where testosterone would have been expected, where methandrostenolone would have been expected, and so on. In other words, she or he would be able to say which substances were present in the sample being tested.

Problems Associated with Testing

The basic principles of drug testing, as outlined here, are relatively simple. But there are a number of circumstances under which important complications may arise. Two of the most important of those circumstances are so-called *false positive* and *false negative* results. False positive tests are also known in statistics as Type 1 errors and false negatives as Type 2 errors. A false positive is a case in which a test appears to show that a sample contains a banned substance when, in fact, it does not. In such a case, an individual would probably be accused of having violated a regulation. That individual would be banned from competition, and if she or he had won any awards those awards would be stripped from her or him. A false negative is a case in which an individual has taken an illegal substance but the testing procedure fails to detect that substance. In such a case, the person "got away with it" by violating a drug test ban without getting caught.

False positives and false negatives can be caused by any number of factors, including human error, machine error, or a break in the chain of custody. The bottom line is that neither machines nor humans are perfect, so that some error is always a part of any testing procedure. Testing laboratories make every possible effort to reduce such errors to zero, but achieving that goal is probably not completely possible.

The important point to note about false results is how much more serious a false positive result is than a false negative. A false negative means that someone may have recorded an achievement he or she did not deserve (a gold medal after using a banned substance), but a false positive means that someone will be accused of using illegal substances when he or she has not actually done so. That individual may eventually be cleared of the accusation, but achieving exoneration may be time consuming and expensive, and members of the general public and that person's colleagues may never fully accept the "true" decision. It is for this reason that one observer has written that "[s]port authorities must ensure that the possibility of a false positive is virtually nonexistent" (Connolly 2006, 49).

According to one fairly sophisticated mathematical analysis of this problem, the rate of false positives in sports anti-doping programs can be expected to range from 0.0 percent to 0.53 percent. While that number does seem very low, one needs to remember the number of athletes tested each year: 146,539 in this particular study. In such a case, one might expect to find 777 false positives, a fairly large number ("WADA Statistics 2005" 2006).

Another problem associated with the issue of false positives is the intentional or unintentional ingestion of products that may contain prohibited substances. In some cases, for example, athletes may have to take certain prescribed medications for the treatment of chronic or acute medical problems. (Chronic problems are those that continue for an extended period of time, such as cancer, while acute problems are those that last a relatively short period of time, such as common cold.) All organizations responsible for the testing of athletes are aware of and sensitive to such problems and provide special conditions for the testing of such athletes. The WADA, for example, makes available certificates that athletes can fill out and return explaining why they need to take certain medications that might cause positive results in drug tests ("Frequently Asked Questions (FAQ). Therapeutic Use Exemptions (TUEs)" 2016).

Some examples of medications that are eligible for consideration under the therapeutic use exception policy of the USADA are the analgesics/anti-inflammatories acetaminophen, aspirin, and codeine; the antacids Maalox, Myalanta, and Tums; the antianxiety/antidepressant agents Celera, Elavil, Valium, and Zoloft; the anti-diarrheals atropine, Donnagel, Immodium, and Loperamide; the antifungals Cruex, Micatin, and Sporonox; the antinausea/antivertigos Antivert, Kytril, and Motionaid; the antihistamines Allegra, Benadryl, and Claritin; the antiseizure medications Lyrcia, phenobarbital, and Topamax; and the cold medications Advil cold and sinus, Pepto Bismol, and Sudafed ("Therapeutic Use Exemptions" 2017).

"Beating the Game"

Dealing with the use of prohibited substances in athletic competitions would be much less of a problem (probably not a problem at all) if some athletes were not committed to finding a way to "get around" rules and regulations and actually use one or another of the drugs that have been banned. There are a number of ways of achieving this objective. One of the most obvious approaches, of course, is to find new anabolic steroids that may recently have been discovered or developed by a reputable (or not-so-reputable) drug company. In such a case, an athlete might legally be able to use that substance unless and until anti-doping agencies found out about the drug and decided to place it on their list of prohibited substances. For example, news began to leak out in the early 2010s about a newly developed compound with properties similar to those of anabolic steroids but with a somewhat different chemical structure. The substance had been developed by the pharmaceutical firm of Merck/Schering-Plough Pharma and its subsidiary Gtx and was given the temporary designation of MK-0773. Clinical trials on its effectiveness for the treatment of sarcopenia (loss of muscle mass) in women began in late 2007.

MK-0773 belongs to a category of compounds known as selective androgen receptor modulators (SARMs). Some SARMs have molecular structures similar to those of anabolic steroids, but some have very different molecular structures. The characteristic that all SARMs share is that they attach to androgen receptors, just as anabolic steroids do. In some cases, they produce responses that are many times greater than those produced by anabolic steroids themselves. MK-0773, for example, is said to initiate a response four times that of testosterone itself. One can assume that, once MK-0773 becomes available, either legally or illegally, some athletes will want to experiment with its use as a muscle-building supplement (see, for example, "Merck's New Anabolic Steroid: MK-0773" 2010; "MK 0773" 2015).

In some ways, the game of catching athletes who try to cheat on their drug tests is stacked against regulatory agencies in favor of those athletes. There are far more anabolic steroids and other performance-enhancing drugs available to athletes than there are tests for those drugs. One of the most knowledgeable experts on the use of anabolic steroids in sports, William Llewellyn, has been quoted as saying that "there are more than 500 steroids in here [referring to a book in which he has collected all known anabolic steroids, legal and illegal, tested and untested]. All the drug tests in the world can maybe find 50" (Assael and Hirshberg 2012). An even more authoritative assessment of the problem comes from Don Catlin, formerly professor of molecular and medical pharmacology at the University of California at Los Angeles Medical School and director of the UCLA Olympic Analytical Laboratory. In testimony before the U.S. Senate Committee on Commerce, Science, and Transportation in May 2005, Catlin observed that "[a]thletes determined to cheat have little trouble beating the test . . . and there are legions of doctors telling them how to do it" (United States Senate, One Hundred Ninth Congress 2005, 18. Also see Berkowitz and Meko 2016).

Individuals concerned about not being able to pass a drug test have developed a number of imaginative techniques for avoiding a positive test. One technique involves the substitution of one's own urine (assumed to contain evidence of illegal drug use) with a "clear" product. A number of suggestions have been made as to how this objective can be achieved, such as collecting and substituting urine from a friend or using "synthetic" urine. A well-known example of the latter option is a kit called the Whizzinator, which consists of an artificial penis, dried urine, a syringe, and a heater pack to warm reconstituted urine to body temperature. As of early 2017, the product was still available and being advertised on the Internet as "an awesome discreet synthetic urine device." A comparable product for women is sold under the name "Go Number One." ("Number #1 Urine Substitution Kit" 2017; "The Whizzanator Touch!" 2017)

Another common approach to avoiding a positive drug test is the use of some type of masking agent or masking procedure. The term *masking* refers to any substance or procedure used to prevent an anti-doping agency from detecting the presence of a prohibited substance in a person's body. Some substances act as masking agents because they react chemically with the substance for which one is being tested. The chemical reaction converts the substance into a form that cannot be recognized by the testing process. Perhaps the most common form of masking is urine dilution. In this process, a person attempts to increase one's rate of urination as much as possible with the intent of "washing out" traces of any prohibited substance or its metabolites. One way to achieve this objective is with diuretics, substances that increase the loss of water and electrolytes through an increased rate of urination. A number of commonly available substances, including coffee and tea, are diuretics (Cadwallader, et al. 2010).

Anti-doping agencies now include diuretics and other types of masking agents among the substances for which they test in a typical drug screen. Among the banned diuretics and masking agents on the current WADA list of prohibited substances are acetazolamide, amiloride, bumetanide, canrenone, chlortalidone, etacrynic acid, furosemide, indapamide, metolazone, and spironolactone ("Prohibited List 2016" 2016, 5).

The efforts to avoid drug detection described here are only the most common of all such procedures that have been tried by athletes in the past. A summary of other methods for avoiding detection is provided on the web page Sports and Drugs, part of the ProCon.org website. ("What Are the 19 Known Methods of Cheating to Pass Performance Enhancing Drug Tests?" 2009; as an example of the types of commercial products available for such purposes, also see PassYourDrugTest.com 2017.)

So, in the end, how effective are current anti-doping programs at identifying athletes who have used performance-enhancing drugs? A great deal of dispute remains on this issue. On the one hand, many experts, including administrators of high-level anti-doping programs, argue that these efforts have been very successful in the past and are likely to become even more successful in the future. In response to a series of questions about drug testing in sports, for example, Gary I. Walder, chair of the WADA Prohibited List and Methods Subcommittee, noted that

> The detection methods are accurate and reliable. They undergo rigorous validation prior to being introduced . . . [WADA] has funded a number of studies in anticipation of the seeming inevitability of gene doping in the years ahead . . . The I.O.C. [International Olympic Committee] retains ownership of the athlete's samples

(blood and urine) for eight years following the Olympic Games . . . if a technique is developed that would enable the detection of a prohibited substance . . . the stored specimen could be tested for that specific substance and the athlete would be held accountable. ("Dr. Gary Wadler of the World Anti-Doping Agency Gives His Answers to Your Questions (Part I)" 2008)

More recently, a number of individuals, groups, and organizations have begun to speak more openly about the lack of success of testing programs, especially in light of the 2016 revelations about massive and widespread cheating in testing programs by the Soviet Union and Russia over a number of years. For example, at its board meeting of May 18, 2012, WADA decided to appoint a committee to look into the reasons that anti-doping testing programs have been less successful in identifying "cheats" and "dopers" than had been expected. In summarizing its report, that committee noted that "[t]o date, testing has not proven to be particularly effective in detecting dopers/cheats" (Report to WADA Executive Committee on Lack of Effectiveness of Testing Programs 2013, 3). The committee report contained a total of 90 recommendations for ways in which WADA, international sports organizations, national anti-doping agencies, governments, testing laboratories, athletes, and event organizers could improve the effectiveness of drug testing. These recommendations were, in turn, based on more than a hundred "weaknesses" that the committee found among these groups. In addition to reports from testing agencies themselves, independent researchers have studied the history of a variety of testing programs to determine their effectiveness in detecting drug use. One such study concluded that

anti doping does not offer any protection of athletes right to participate in doping free sport; that it does not offer significant health protection; and that it does not protect fairness and equality for athletes worldwide, [leading to the conclusion that] anti-doping under the auspices of WADA has been unsuccessful and counter-productive. (Møller 2016, 111)

The 1970s: Doping Gone Wild

The 1970s can be remembered as a decade of great progress in the development of regulations against the use of anabolic steroids in athletic events and the implementation of sophisticated testing programs for banned substances. But it was also a period that witnessed some of the most egregious uses of anabolic steroids to gain unfair advantages in some of the most prestigious athletic competitions in the world. By most accounts, the worst offender in this regard was the German Democratic Republic (GDR; Deutsche Demokratische Republik), more commonly known as East Germany. One piece of data often cited to reinforce this accusation is the improvement in the performance of East German Olympic competitors between 1968 and 1980. As Table 2.2 shows, the East Germans won a total of 25 medals in the 1968 Games, the first year in which East Germany competed as an entity distinct from West Germany. Over the next three Games, the East Germans quintupled the number of medals they received, vastly outdistancing their colleagues from West Germany. How did such a dramatic improvement take place in East German athletic skill?

Throughout the 1970s, athletes from almost any nation who competed against their East German colleagues often noted certain physical characteristics that made them wonder about the nature of the training program in which these individuals were engaged. They observed that women athletes, for example, often had physical traits more commonly associated with males than females, such as large muscle mass, deeper voices, and facial hair. One of the most outspoken of these observers was Brigitte Berendonk, who competed in the discus throw in the 1968 and 1972 Olympic Games. Berendonk had been

Table 2.2   Olympic Medals Won by West Germany and East Germany, 1968–1988

Year	West Germany				East Germany			
	Gold	Silver	Bronze	Total	Gold	Silver	Bronze	Medal
1968 (S)	5	11	10	26	9	9	7	25
1968 (W)	2	2	3	7	1	2	2	5
1972 (S)	13	11	16	40	20	23	23	66
1976 (S)	10	12	17	39	40	25	25	90
1976 (W)	2	5	3	10	7	5	7	19
1980 (S)	DNC	DNC	DNC	DNC	47	37	42	126
1980 (W)	0	2	3	5	9	7	7	23
1984 (S)	17	19	23	59	DNC	DNC	DNC	DNC
1984 (W)	2	1	1	4	9	9	6	24
1988 (S)	11	14	15	40	37	35	30	102
1988 (W)	2	4	2	8	9	10	6	25

DNC, Did not compete; S, Summer Games; W, Winter Games.

Source: Databaseolympics.com. 2011. http://www.databaseolympics.com/. Accessed on February 25, 2017.

born in Dankmarshausen, then part of the GDR. At the age of 16, she defected from East Germany with her family and settled in West Germany, where she eventually joined the West German Olympic track-and-field team. On a number of occasions, she mentioned her doubts about East German athletes to her superiors and the press, who largely ignored or ridiculed her concerns (Ungerleider 2001, 10).

In fact, it was not until the fall of the Berlin Wall in 1989 that information about the East German doping program began to leak to the Western world. Over a period of years, documents about the program were slowly uncovered by a number of committed researchers until a final picture of the program eventually emerged (see especially Franke and Berendonk 1997). The East German doping program appears to have originated on a somewhat informal basis in the late 1960s as the GDR government attempted to improve its international image as a modern and powerful national state. One element in that effort was the development of a national athletic program that would achieve international recognition at events such as the Summer and Winter Olympic Games. Boys and girls who showed promise in one or another athletic field were diverted into special training programs aimed at developing their maximum potential. An important component of these training programs was the use of anabolic steroids to improve muscle mass, strength, endurance, and other physical characteristics. The primary substance used for this purpose, as noted earlier in this chapter, was the chlorinated derivative of methandrostenolone sold commercially as Oral Turinabol. That substance had not yet been prohibited in the late 1960s when the East German program got under way, although it was later listed as a banned substance by the IOC.

The East German program was expanded in the 1970s and formalized in 1974 with adoption of the so-called Research Program 08 (later called State Plan Research Theme 14.25). The top secret legislation creating this program (see Franke and Berendonk 1997, 1267–1268) included a number of elements with regard to the use of anabolic steroids:

- They would be an integral part of all training programs for international competitions.
- They would be under central control and subject to regular evaluation by sports physicians.
- They would be under direct control of the Sports Medical Service (Sportmedizinischer Dienst).
- An ongoing research program would develop and test the efficacy of new anabolic steroids and new and improved methods of administration of the drugs.
- Information about their use would be taught in formal programs to coaches and sports physicians.
- The program for the use of anabolic steroids would be highly classified and regarded as an official state secret.

Overall responsibility for the security of the program was under the control of the notorious East German agency the Ministry for State Security (Ministerium für Staatssicherheit, most commonly known as the Stasi). The director of the program was Manfred Ewald, minister of sport for the GDR from 1961 to 1988 and president of the GDR national Olympic committee from 1973 to 1990. His chief assistant was Dr. Manfred Höppner who, in 1977, issued a report to his Stasi superiors describing the success of State Plan 14.25. He wrote that

> At present anabolic steroids are applied in all Olympic sporting events, with the exception of sailing and gymnastics (female) . . . and by all national teams. . . . The positive value of anabolic steroids for the development of a top performance is undoubted. [He then provides a few examples from track and field for both men and women to support his statement.] Remarkable rates of increase in performances were also noted in the swimming events of women. . . . From our experiences made so far it can be concluded that women have the greatest advantage from treatments with anabolic hormones with respect to their performance in sports. . . . Especially high is the performance-supporting effect following the first administration of anabolic hormones, especially with junior athletes. (quoted in Franke and Berendonk 1997, 1264)

The scope of the East German program was truly amazing. According to one source, more than 10,000 athletes received anabolic steroids during the 1970s and 1980s, with as many as 1,500 full-time scientists and doctors and 8,000 trainers involved in the program at its height. During its final year of operation, in 1989, the East German government budgeted 400 million marks (about US$200 million, at the official exchange rate) for the program (Gilbert, et al. 2009).

As international sports organizations, such as the IOC, established stricter rules against the use of anabolic steroids and as their tests became better able to detect prohibited substances, East German officials learned to become more adept at avoiding detection of their doping efforts. For example, they purchased the latest in drug-testing hardware to use on the testing of their own athletes. Their objective was to make sure that East German athletes would not receive positive tests once they reached an international competition. Athletes who did score positive on the East German test would be withdrawn from competition with the explanation that they were "ill" or "injured" (Rosen 2008, 53).

East German athletes also became experts at the art of detection avoidance. Most of the techniques used today by dishonest athletes and described earlier, such as using synthetic urine, were part of the East German arsenal against detection. At the same time, East German researchers were strongly urged to develop new anabolic steroids that could not yet be detected by existing technology (Franke and Berendonk 1997, 1272; Rosen 2008, 54).

The East German doping scandal has actually had two somewhat discrete parts, the first of which involved the two-decade history of the State Plan 14.25 program described here. The second part of that scandal involves the long-term effects of that program on the hundreds or thousands of athletes who were, to a large extent, innocent victims of an experiment of which they were unaware. (The steroids they were given were handed out in the form of small blue or pink pills described as vitamins or nutritional supplements.) The anabolic steroids they were given over a period of many years, often during the formative years of their lives, have had long-term effects that their superiors neither anticipated nor probably much cared about.

As a consequence, many veterans of the GDR training programs have, since details of those programs have slowly come out, taken court action as a way of gaining partial restitution for their misuse by the East German government. One part of that action has involved criminal complaints against leaders of the GDR program. Beginning in 1998, a number of trials were held in Germany that resulted in the conviction of trainers, doctors, and research scientists for their role in the State Plan 14.25 activities (Andrews 1998). The last of these trials, in 2000, resulted in the conviction of Ewald and Höppner for providing steroids to more than 140 young female athletes, some as young as 11 years of age. Ewald was sentenced to 22 months of probation and Höppner to 18 months of probation (Kettmann 2000).

While by far the most extensive and best-known example of steroid abuse, the East German State Plan 14.25 program was by no means the only situation in which elite athletes used anabolic steroids during the 1970s. In cycling, for example, these substances gradually became more popular throughout the decade. As testing programs for amphetamines, previously the drug of choice among cyclists, became more efficient and widespread, competitors began turning to anabolic steroids for the "extra push" they needed in their rides. Finally, in the 1978 Tour de France, the first rider tested positive for an illegal steroid. Belgian cyclist Michel Pollentier won the 13th stage of the tour and earned himself the yellow jersey as tour leader at that point. However, during the drug test that followed the day's race, Pollentier was found to be using a Whizzinator-like device filled with "clean" urine from a friend. He was disqualified from the race and banned from racing for a two-month period (Rosen 2008, 49–50).

The Great Breakthrough: The 1980s

By the early 1980s, the value of anabolic steroids as performance-enhancing drugs was becoming widely known among both amateur and elite athletes. Among weight lifters and bodybuilders, this knowledge was hardly news, but the availability of a greater range of products soon made them an essential part of almost every participant's training schedule. Especially on the West Coast of the United States, a new business for the production, advertising, and sale of anabolic steroids was developing, beginning in 1982 with the publication of the first handbook on anabolic steroids, *Underground Steroid Handbook for Men and Women*, written by Dan Duchaine. Duchaine was a transplant from Maine to the Venice Beach, California, area, a center of weight lifting and bodybuilding in the United States. Duchaine's booklet provided a complete review of the 29 performance-enhancing drugs of which Duchaine knew, with detailed commentaries on each. The slim volume sold for $6 and was first advertised in *Muscle Builder & Power* magazine in early 1982. Duchaine was overwhelmed with orders and had sold 80,000 copies of the book with a profit of a half million dollars by the spring of 1982. (Copies of that publication are virtually impossible to find today.) The popularity of the work prompted Duchaine to produce a revised edition of the handbook two years later and then a larger and more complete version in 1988, *Underground Steroid Handbook II*, a publication that is still in print and available through many booksellers. It is also available online, at http://www.anasci.org/ebooks/USH%20II.pdf (accessed on February 24, 2017).

After the first edition of the handbook came out, Duchaine rapidly became the "go to" man for information about steroids. Before long, he had earned the title of the Steroid Guru. He also realized that his new fame and notoriety held the potential for a lucrative career in dealing with steroids. In February 1986, he and his two friends, David Jenkins and William Dillon, made a deal with a Mexican entrepreneur, Juan Macklis, to manufacture and package steroids for exportation to the United States. Jenkins was a former silver medal winner in the 1972 Olympics and Dillon was a former Mr. Collegiate Illinois bodybuilding champion. Macklis owned a drug manufacturing plant, Laboratorios Milanos, near Tijuana and was regarded as one of the most powerful men in Mexico at the time (Assael 2007, 16).

The Duchaine-Jenkins-Dillon operation quickly became a huge financial success, at one point bringing in so much money that "it was a struggle to spend it all" (Assael 2007, 17). The group's success did not long escape the notice of U.S. officials, however, and in early 1987, an investigator for the U.S. Food and Drug Administration pounced on the operation. The three principals were all arrested and later found guilty of a variety of charges, including conspiracy, mislabeling of drugs, and distribution of illegal drugs. Duchaine was sentenced to a maximum of 3 years in prison and 5 years of probation; Jenkins was sentenced to 7 years in prison, but served only 9 months before being released; and Dillon was sentenced to 16 years in prison for his part in the affair (Cram 2008; Eisendrath 1988; Harrah [2011]). After completing their prison terms, Duchaine and Jenkins joined efforts to create a legitimate nutritional supplement company under the name of Next Nutrition. Jenkins became president of the company when Duchaine died in 2000 at the age of 47.

While the use of anabolic steroids continued to spread throughout the athletic community in the 1980s, attention was also increasingly being paid to other types of performance-enhancing substances, especially the process known as blood doping and the use of a new (to athletics) type of hormone, human growth hormone (hGh). The term *blood doping* refers to any technique or substance that increases the ability of the blood to transport oxygen to cells. Any such procedure increases an athlete's endurance and stamina. Three methods of blood doping are best known: blood transfusions, oxygen transport enhancement, and the use of erythropoietin (EPO). A blood transfusion is simply a way of increasing the total blood volume in a person's body, thus increasing the amount of oxygen the blood can carry. Oxygen-enhancement systems make use of synthetic materials that bind to oxygen in much the way hemoglobin does in normal blood, again increasing the amount of oxygen available to cells during exercise. EPO is a naturally occurring hormone that regulates the production of red blood cells in the body. If the hormone is supplied to the body artificially, the rate of red blood cell production increases, as does the amount of oxygen available to cells. EPO was apparently used as a performance-enhancing substance as early as the 1970s, and deaths among cyclists have been attributed to the use of the substance. The addition of exogenous EPO to the bloodstream can increase the density of blood, causing the heart to work harder, and increasing the risk of cardiac failure. Since EPO was not specifically banned until the early 1990s, insufficient information is available on its use prior to that time. That information is also difficult to find because a test for EPO was not developed and put into use until the early 2000s (Jenkins 2005; Robinson, et al. 2006).

hGh also occurs naturally in the human body. It is produced in the anterior pituitary gland, from where it travels to other parts of the body. In the liver and other organs, hGh stimulates the production of insulin-like growth factor (IGF-1). The primary function of IGF-1 is the stimulation of cells that produce new cartilage, thus contributing to the growth of new bone, muscles, and organs. Research indicates that the use of exogenous hGh can improve a person's athletic performance both directly and by acting synergistically with anabolic steroids. The IOC banned the use of hGh in 1989, but that action was of little value since no test for the substance was then available. In fact, no athlete was disqualified for using hGh until after 2004, when the first blood test for the hormone was developed ("The Researcher's Perspective" 2007).

One of the factors that long limited the use of both EPO and hGh was the cost and difficulty of collecting these hormones. That problem was solved to a considerable extent when researchers developed methods for synthesizing both hormones by recombinant DNA technology in 1981 for hGh and in the late 1990s for EPO (Winearls 1998; "Human Growth Hormone History" 2014).

According to many observers, the signal event in the history of drug use in the 1980s was the rescinding of the gold medal in the 100-meter dash at the 1988 Olympic Games in Seoul, Korea. The winner of that race, Canadian sprinter Benjamin

Sinclair ("Ben") Johnson, had had a memorable decade in track and field, having won gold medals in the 100-meter dash at the 1985 World Cup in Canberra, the 1985 World Indoor Championship in Paris, the 1986 Goodwill Games in Moscow, the 1986 Commonwealth Games in Edinburgh, and the 1984 bronze medal in the Los Angeles Summer Olympics. His contest in the 100-meter dash with American sprinter Carl Lewis and a star-filled cast in the 1988 Games was expected to be the high point of the Seoul Games.

In that race, Johnson defeated Lewis in the 100-meter dash by 0.13 seconds. Johnson's time, 9.79 seconds, constituted a world record in that event. Three days later, however, the IOC announced that Johnson had tested positive for the anabolic steroid stanozolol, and he was disqualified from the event. The gold medal was given, instead, to Lewis, whose 9.92 seconds was also recognized by the IOC as a new world record in that event.

Johnson's initial reaction to his disqualification was that he had never used illegal substances and that the IOC had made an improper decision. Over time, however, both he and his coach gradually changed their comments about the event. Johnson's coach, Charlie Francis, put forth the argument—first to Johnson and later to the general public—that using illegal substances was not cheating if everyone else was doing the same thing. In such a case, taking steroids was simply a matter of "keeping up with crowd," maintaining a level playing field for all competitors in an event. Johnson later said that he resisted Francis's idea at first but gradually saw the logic in it. Finally, he said to Francis, "Charlie, I'm OK with it. Let's go" (McRae 2014).

Still, at Seoul, Johnson had argued that the case was not so clear. He had tested positive for stanozolol, but he had not taken that drug for some time because of the adverse effects it had produced in his body. Instead, he was taking a drug called furazabol. He hypothesized that some unknown "mystery man" had intentionally spiked one of his drinks with stanozolol and finally identified the person as a "family friend" named Andre

Jackson. Jackson had, Johnson later said, actually confessed to him that he had given Johnson the illegal steroid in a drink (Hurst 2009).

The complex and unpleasant story of Johnson's disqualification finally reached a measure of conclusion in 2010 when Johnson self-published his autobiography, *Seoul to Soul*, in which he presents his final explanation of the event. He still claims never to have taken the illegal substance for which he was banned but does admit that he had used other illegal substances at other times in his career, all under the influence and recommendation of his coach. In any case, his once-promising track-and-field career came to an end in 1988 (Johnson 2010).

Johnson did try to make a comeback in 1991, but it was short lived. At a meet held in Montreál in January 1993, he tested positive for an illegal substance once again, this time testosterone. His measured T/E ratio was 10.3:1 at a time when the highest permissible ratio was 6:1. Two other tests produced comparable results, and the IAAF decided to ban Johnson from competition for life (Cohen 1993).

The 1990s: Steroid Use Ne Plus Ultra

In his excellent history of the use of performance-enhancing drugs in sports since the 19th century, Daniel M. Rosen devotes much of his chapter on the 1990s to a number of specific events in which elite athletes were found to have used illegal anabolic steroids. These events include the following (all page citations from Rosen 2008):

- A number of performers in the World Wrestling Federation testified that they had regularly used illegal anabolic steroids obtained from physician George T. Zaharian III and promoter Vincent McMahon. (81–82)
- Professional football player Lyle Alzado died at the age of 43, possibly from the effects of long-term use of anabolic steroids. (82–84)

- Rumors of an East German–like program for the development of Chinese athletes percolated just below the surface
through much of the decade. Among the confirmed results
of anti-doping tests was the discovery that a number of
participants in the 1994 Asian Games had been using the
banned steroid dihydrotestosterone. (85–89)
- Just prior to the 1998 Tour de France, a car driven by Willy
Voet was stopped at the French-Belgian border and found to
contain very large quantities of a number of performance-
enhancing drugs. Voet was an assistant for the Festina cycling team, based at the time in France. As a result of later
investigations, seven members of the team admitted to taking EPO and were banned from the race. The team doctor,
Eric Rijkaert, was also arrested. (100–102)

The BALCO Scandal

The other event to which Rosen refers in his chapter on the
1990s is the appearance of the Bay Area Laboratory Cooperative (BALCO), an event that actually dates to the early 1980s.
In 1983, Victor Conte, Jr., purchased rights to the use of a
machine used for testing human blood for vitamin deficiencies. Conte had already had a distinguished career as a musician
with a number of major musical groups, including most nota-
bly Tower of Power. By the early 1980s, however, he decided
to look for more mainstream employment and decided that he
could use the blood-testing machine as a basis for advising men
and women about the health of their blood, followed by selling
them nutritional supplements that would improve their overall
health. That scheme rapidly evolved into a somewhat different
type of endeavor.

In 1984, Conte purchased a natural foods shop in Millbrae,
California, and renamed it the Bay Area Laboratory Collective. For more than a decade, Conte struggled to make a living
with BALCO, eventually focusing on a nutritional supplement that featured the minerals zinc and magnesium, which
he marketed as ZMA. Throughout the late 1980s and early

1990s, Conte began making a number of important connections among elite athletes, developing friendships, providing free tests, and then supplying complimentary samples of ZMA to his new friends.

Conte's work took a turn in the late 1990s, however, as he was introduced to a much broader range of "health products" that promised to provide profound performance enhancement. These products included EPO, hGh, an analeptic drug called modafinil, and a number of anabolic steroids, including testosterone, tetrahydrogestrinone (also known as THG or "The Clear"), and norbolethone (Williams and Fainaru-Wada 2004). Before long, he was supplying this collection of illegal substances to a distinguished group of professional athletes that included track and field stars Kelli White, Christie Gaines, Dwayne Chambers, Tim Montgomery, and Marion Jones; National Football League stars Bill Romanowski, Chris Cooper, Barrett Robbins, and Dana Stubblefield; boxer Shane Mosley; cyclist Tammy Thomas; and baseball players Jason Giambi, Barry Bonds, and Gary Sheffield (a list that is almost certainly not complete) ("Victor Conte: BALCO—The Straight Dope on Steroids" 2009).

As it turns out, the issue of illegal steroid use in Major League Baseball had not yet been totally resolved as late as mid-2017. On February 15, 2017, the commissioner's office announced that five minor league players had been suspended for periods ranging from 50 to 72 days for testing positive for a variety of performance-enhancing drugs ("Five Minor League Players Suspended" 2017).

By the turn of the 21st century, major sporting organizations could no longer ignore the increasingly widespread understanding that illegal drug use was rampant in most sports. On October 1, 2000, the USADA was created to assume the testing responsibilities formerly carried out by individual sports organizations for Olympic, Pan American, and Paralympic events. Three years later, on September 3, 2003, a combined task force from the Internal Revenue Service and local law enforcement agencies raided the BALCO offices, collecting a mass of evidence to support a charge of distributing illegal substances. (For a detailed description of the BALCO scandal, see Assael 2007, Chapters 14–18.)

Over the next decade, the BALCO scandal and a number of other revelations revealed the width and depth of illegal anabolic steroid use among amateur and professional athletes in the United States and the rest of the world. One after another, famous names from track and field, cycling, football, weight lifting, bodybuilding, wrestling, baseball, and other sports have come forward to admit their use of steroids, often with explanations of mitigating circumstances. ("I didn't know what I was taking"; "They were legal then anyway"; "Everyone else was using them, so why shouldn't I?"; "In today's world, taking drugs is the only way of remaining competitive"; and so on.) Perhaps hardest hit during this decade was Major League Baseball. A report prepared by former U.S. Senate majority leader George Mitchell in 2007 listed 86 current and previous baseball players who had admitted to or were reasonably suspected of having used steroids during their career. Some of the best known of these names remained in the public eye for years either because they spoke and wrote openly about their drug use (e.g., Jose Canseco) or because they were widely suspected of the practice (e.g., Barry Bonds) (["Players Listed in Mitchell Report"] [2007]).

2012: The Dam Bursts

By 2012, experts on doping and drug testing in world sports found themselves forced to take one of two positions: (1) the number of athletes who used illegal drugs was vanishingly small or (2) existing anti-doping programs were essentially useless. The first position could be supported by the results of anti-doping tests at the 2012 Summer Olympics in London, where only 24 of 5,051 athletes tested for illegal drugs produced a positive result, a rate of 0.48 percent. Those results suggest that only 1 out of every 200 athletes used an illegal drug during the competition ("Factsheet: The Fight against Doping and Promotion of Athletes' Health Update—September 2016" 2016). The other position was reflected by reports such as those by a special committee of the IOC itself (discussed earlier on page 65), which argued that existing testing programs were woefully inadequate at detecting illegal drug use.

On June 12, 2012, the USADA released the results of an investigation bearing on this issue. It concerned possible doping activities by American cyclist Lance Armstrong, winner of seven Tour de France titles and numerous other national and international races, often considered the greatest cyclist of all time. After first denying the USADA charges, Armstrong eventually admitted to their accuracy. He was banned from professional sports for life, and his medals in a number of competitions, including those from the Tour de France, were withdrawn. The Armstrong investigation confirmed that, at least in the field of cycling, the illegal use of drugs was not a rare event that testing programs readily uncovered but a widespread practice that had escaped detection by official agencies for decades ("Lance Armstrong Receives Lifetime Ban and Disqualification of Competitive Results for Doping Violations Stemming from His Involvement in the United States Postal Service Pro-Cycling Team Doping Conspiracy" 2012; Shipley 2012).

One of the most significant events in the history of anti-doping efforts in international sports occurred on December 3, 2014, when the German broadcasting consortium ARD released a documentary called *Secret Doping: How Russia Makes Its Winners*. The documentary provided evidence that officials at the highest level of national sporting organizations had long been operating a doping program for elite Russian athletes, along with a sophisticated program for covering up positive testing results. As one of the primary witnesses interviewed in the documentary said,

That is an internal schema that has established itself over the years. . . . The athlete has no choice. Either you prepare yourself in national team with banned substances, in order to win medals which are also accredited to the Federation—the head coach, the Ministry of Sport, the Federation President, the entire Russian Athletics Federation. And, if you are unable to agree with this scheme, which they offer you, then things can move very quickly and you're out. (Das Erste [2014])

Another interviewee said that she thought 99 percent of athletes in Russia were taking part in national doping programs. (The documentary itself can be viewed at Seppelt 2014.)

Russian authorities responded to the documentary almost immediately, claiming that it was just one more example of the Western press "picking on" Russia by inventing fantastic stories about the country. As Vasily Shestakov, a member of the Russian parliament's Physical Culture, Sports, and Youth Committee said,

Right now it's fashionable to blame Russia for no matter what, and it's a shame they're trying to carry this tendency over into sports, in which our country is undoubtedly one of the world leaders. . . . It seems there are no other ways left to poke us. (Peleschuk 2014)

Other critics admitted that some of the information in the documentary might be correct, but, after all, all other nations were doing the same thing. As former Russian coach Valentin Maslakov observed, performance-enhancing drugs were being used by every country of the world. "Everyone is the same, everyone is equal," he said. "Russia is not the leader in this area" (Luhn 2015).

In spite of these complaints, WADA decided to launch a complete investigation into the charges raised in the ARD documentary. On December 16, 2014, less than two weeks

after the documentary was shown, WADA appointed an independent commission headed by Richard Pound, former world
champion swimmer and current attorney from Canada to
study the problem and make any necessary recommendations.
The report of the Pound Committee, issued on November 9,
2015, provided a devastating confirmation of the charges made
in the ARD program. The IAAF itself quickly acted on the
Committee's recommendations suspending the Russian doping
laboratory a day later and the entire Russian track-and-field organization three days after that ("IAAF Provisionally Suspends
Russian Member Federation ARAF" 2015). The Commission's
complete report can be found at https://www.wada-ama.org/
sites/default/files/resources/files/wada_independent_commis
sion_report_1_en.pdf (accessed on February 25, 2017).

As it transpired, the ARD documentary and the Pound
report were not the end of the Russian sports community's
problems; they were only the beginning. A second bombshell
fell on May 12, 2016, when *The New York Times* printed an
interview with Grigory Rodchenkov, director of the Russian
Anti-Doping Centre in Moscow since 2006, about doping in
that country. In that interview, Rodchenkov described a massive ongoing program designed for use among Russian athletes
in which he, Rodchenkov, not only supplied illegal drugs to
Russian sports authorities for use by their athletes but also
developed a sophisticated system for replacing tainted urine
samples from athletes tested during competitions with clean
samples that allowed them to pass those tests. In particular,
he discussed in considerable detail his efforts to protect drug-
using Russian athletes at the 2014 Winter Olympics in Sochi,
Russia. Rodchenkov described his program as "one of the most
elaborate—and most successful—doping ploys in sports history" that involved "thousands of Olympians" in addition to
untold numbers of athletes from a wide variety of sports (Ruiz
and Schwirtz 2016).

A week later, WADA acted on these charges, appointing
Richard H. McLaren, law professor at Western University in

London, Ontario, and member of the earlier Pound Committee, to study Rodchenkov's claims and issue a report on doping at the Sochi Olympics. McLaren released his preliminary report on July 16, 2016, only two weeks prior to the opening of the 2016 Summer Games in Rio de Janeiro, Brazil. The report essentially confirmed Rodchenkov's claims, but made no recommendations as to any actions that WADA, the IOC, or other organizations should take about the participation of Russian athletes at the Games ("Richard H. McLaren, Independent Person. WADA Investigation of Sochi Allegations" 2016a).

IOC leaders met on July 17 to discuss McLaren's report and decided to uphold the IAAF ban on all Russian track-and-field athletes. But somewhat flummoxed by the challenge of opening a once-in-four-years Games in less than two weeks, it left the decision as to which Russian athletes, if any, could compete in the 2016 Games to individual sports organizations. In the end, 118 Russian athletes were banned from participation, including the entire weight-lifting team and all members, save one, of the track-and-field team. That left 271 athletes who had been cleared by their respective organizations to take part in the Rio events ("Rio Olympics 2016: Which Russian Athletes Have Been Cleared to Compete?" 2016).

Once again, the completion of the Rio Olympic Games did not mean an end to the controversy over doping in world sporting events, either for the Russians or for other countries. On December 9, 2016, McLaren issued the second part of his report, a document that covered doping and anti-doping events in Russia above and beyond those related to the 2014 Sochi Winter Games. McLaren's findings were devastating, indicating that more than a thousand Russian athletes benefitted from

An institutional conspiracy [that] existed across summer and winter sports athletes who participated with Russian officials within the Ministry of Sport and its infrastructure, such as the RUSADA, CSP and the Moscow Laboratory, along with the FSB for the purposes of manipulating doping controls. ("Richard H. McLaren, Independent Person. WADA Investigation of Sochi Allegations" 2016b, 1)

Doping in Horse Racing

Reference to the "doping" of an athlete to improve his or her strength, speed, endurance, or some other quality nowadays most often refers to men and women at every level of athletic competition. Yet, the word *doping* itself is generally thought to have arisen within a non-human context, specifically with regard to the use of performance-enhancing substances in race horses. One etymologist suggests that the first use of the term *doping* to refer to the use of drugs for improving a horse's performance occurred in 1873, when a number of West Coast newspapers began using the term to refer to situations in which race horses were administered any one of a number of substances ranging from whiskey to cocaine to make them run faster (Zimmer 2013). (Interestingly enough, that term later gained a broader context that illustrated the extensive use of drugs with horses, with the use of *doping* also to mean a projection of the outcome of a race, as in "getting the inside dope" on the results of a race ["Dope" 2017].)

Historical vignettes suggest that doping of racing horses was not unknown throughout history. The use of fermented honey to increase the speed of horses during ancient Roman times, giving herbal and animal supplements to war horses in countries ranging from China to the Andes to improve their endurance, and providing race horses with a wide range of supplements that included poisons such as strychnine and arsenic have been well documented by experts in the field (Higgins 2006). But the real beginning of horse doping in competitive races can usually be traced to the last two or three decades of the 19th century. At that point, the practice had become so common that a number of individuals and organizations were commenting on the drugging of horses (see, for example, *The New York Times* article of October 19, 1903, "'Dope' Evil of the Turf," as given in Goldberg, Finley, and Marquardt 2013, 2), and the earliest rules limiting the use of performance-enhancing substances were introduced in the late 1890s and early 1900s (Gleaves 2012).

Over the next half century, a familiar pattern involving the drugging of horses and new regulations to ban such practices continued to play out: the story of doping of racing horses was much the same as it was for the drugging of human athletes. The availability of new performance-enhancing substances produced by chemical research created new options for trainers and veterinarians, while anti-doping laws and agencies continuously adopted new rules and regulations in an effort to gain control over doping activities. Possibly the best single resource dealing with this long story is a series of six articles by Goldberg, Finley, and Marquardt (2013) in *TDN Magazine*.

Monitoring the use of illegal drugs in thoroughbred racing is a substantially different problem than is the case for drug testing in professional or amateur human athletics. In the latter instance, each sport is governed by some specific national and/ or international organization that can establish rules and regulations to which all participants in that sport must conform. And if someone violates those standards, they are punished in a variety of ways, such as having medals revoked or their opportunity to continue participating in the sport withdrawn. The IOC and IAAF are perhaps the two best known of such organizations, although there are dozens of others controlling individual sports.

That is not the case with thoroughbred racing, where the rules and regulations for participation are set by individual state groups that vary considerably as to their title, mandate, concerns over doping, use of testing, forms of punishment, and other issues surrounding drug use. There are currently 37 state racing commissions in the United States and 6 in Canada, including groups such as the California Horse Racing Commission, Florida Division of Pari-Mutuel Wagering, and New York State Racing and Wagering Board. Other major sources of rules and regulations are the individual venues where racing occurs. The Thoroughbred Racing Association now consists of 44 member associations at 40 tracks in the United States and Canada (TRA Member Tracks 2016). It is these decentralized groups that determine which substances may or may not be administered to a horse; what dosage, if any, is permitted; when (how long before a race) the drug may be administered; penalties that may be assessed for ignoring these rules; and other issues relating to the use of performance-enhancing drugs with horses on the track (Allin [2011]; Regulation of US Thoroughbred Racing 2017). For a review of recommended regulations by one major U.S. racing authority, the Jockey Club, see "Reformed Racing Medication Rules" 2012.

As is the case with human sporting events, considerable disagreement remains as to the extent of performance-enhancing drug use by competitors and the efficacy of testing efforts aimed at detecting such events in thoroughbred racing. Some individuals and organizations intimately involved with the sport of thoroughbred racing both in the United States and elsewhere in the world argue that the sport is much more "clean" (much less drug use) than any other form of sporting competition. According to a report issued in 2011 by the Association of Racing Commissioners International, for example, just under 1,600 thoroughbred horses in the United States out of a sample of 324,215 horses tested came back positive, a failure rate of 0.493 percent. Of that number, just under 100 (6 percent) were illegal drugs, while the remaining 94 percent of failures were for excessive amounts of legal drugs ("Drugs in U.S. Racing—2010. The Facts" 2011).

Other observers disagree with the conclusion reached by the authors of this report. They are more likely to agree with the findings of a months-long investigation by a team of *New York Times* reporters in 2012. Those reporters pointed out that an estimated 24 race horses die each week in the United States as a result of doping activities. They concluded from their research that horse racing in the United States is "an industry still mired in a culture of drugs and lax regulation and a fatal breakdown rate that remains far worse than in most of the world" (Bogda-nich, et al. 2012). A similar view was expressed by Senator Tom Udall (D-NM) at a 2012 hearing of the U.S. Senate Commit-tee on Commerce, Science, and Transportation. Unlike other sports, Udall said,

> horseracing lacks a commission or a league office that can issue uniform rules. State racing commissions routinely impose small fines and short suspensions. There is mini-mal deterrence, and chronic doping continues unabated. ("Medication and Performance-Enhancing Drugs in Horse Racing" 2012, 1)

Should Steroid Use Be Legal?

One can hardly read the first two chapters of this book without gaining the distinct impression that most organizations and individuals responsible for the administration of amateur and professional sports programs in all fields and at all levels tend to oppose—usually quite strongly—the use of anabolic ste-roids in athletics. (A similar statement is true for other types of performance-enhancing drugs, such as EPO and hGh.) A key component of this argument is the adverse side effects that ste-roids have on the human body, including shrinking of the tes-ticles, development of breasts in males, decreased sperm count with possible impotence, masculinization in females, develop-ment of acne, jaundice, loss of body hair, cardiac disorders, increased risk of liver disease, tendency of tendon ruptures and tears, increase in cholesterol levels, and a range of emotional and psychological problems that include increased tendencies toward rage, aggression, violence, and mood swings. Reflecting this viewpoint, nearly every amateur and professional sports organization now has a ban on virtually all anabolic steroids that are currently known to science.

Another important component of this argument is fair-ness in athletics. Taking drugs is seen by most authorities as "cheating," a way by which an individual has an unfair advantage over her or his opponents. As Dr. Timothy Noakes, Discovery Health Professor of Exercise and Sports Science at the University of Cape Town, South Africa, has written,

> Sport is meant to be about honesty—what you see is all there is. Doping is part of an evil influence extending to match fixing and gambling that has always been a (hidden) part of professional sport, but which will likely ultimately destroy it. If we do not attempt to control this evil triad, professional sport finally distances itself from the mystical endeavour it is meant to be. Without the illusion that professional athletes are somewhat like ourselves, just better, their profession has no appeal. Rather, sport becomes no different from any other commercially driven activity. (Noakes 2006, 312)

Another argument for drug prohibition in sports and athletics is even more direct: Such drugs are usually illegal in the general society. If such substances are illegal for the ordinary man or woman on the street to take, how can anyone argue that they should be permitted to athletes? In a commentary on the ProCon.org website, Joe Lindsey, a writer for *Bicycling* magazine, pointedly asked the question, "Should people have the right to use a substance that is not legal for human use under ANY circumstances?" The answer to that question, he said, "cannot be anything other than 'no' " ("Should Performance Enhancing Drugs (Such as Steroids) Be Accepted in Sports?" 2016).

This argument for the banning of steroid use in athletics does not, however, have unanimous support from experts in the field. A number of writers have pointed out reasons why sports organizations should reconsider their long-held bans on certain types of performance-enhancing substances such as anabolic steroids. One of the most outspoken of these critics is Norman Fost, professor emeritus of pediatrics and bioethics and former director of the Program in Medical Ethics at the

University of Wisconsin at Madison. Fost offers a number of reasons for, at the very least, raising questions about banning certain substances, such as anabolic steroids, in athletic competitions. (He does agree that such bans are appropriate for children and adolescents whose bodies are still growing and who may, therefore, experience adverse events that would not be observed in older adults. See Collins 2005.)

One of Fost's primary arguments is that peer-reviewed scientific studies on the deleterious effects of steroids on human health are lacking. Supporters of bans on the use of steroids in athletics frequently offer a long list of problems that may develop from their use. But, he says, scientific evidence for these claims is never presented. As he says in one article, "Quick: name an athlete who died, or was diagnosed, with steroid-related cancer, heart disease, or stroke." He then refers to the case of Lyle Alzado, a professional football player who died in 1992 from circumstances that many observers attributed to his long use of anabolic steroids. "What is missing," Fost goes on, "is a single article, or evidence, or even a quote from any authority on the topic to support any connection between steroids and Alzado's tumor" (Fost 2005).

Perhaps even more to the point, according to Fost, is that people who engage in athletic events do so usually knowing fully well what the possible physical consequences of their actions are likely to be. In an interview with sports attorney Rick Collins, Fost pointed out that for men who play professional football, it is "something that competent adults decide to do in exchange for the money, glory and pleasure that they get out of it. We don't think, in America, that people's liberty to take risks like that should be interfered with, just so long as they are not harming anyone else" (Collins 2005). Surveys of people who engage in dangerous sports appear to confirm this position. On a website devoted to choosing the world's 10 most dangerous sports, for example, a reader is struck by the number of respondents who describe the terrible risks they took in horseback riding, gymnastics, football, hockey, and other sports, often pointing out, however, that they would do it all over again if they could and that they had taken part in a sport because they loved it so much ("Most Dangerous Sports" 2017).

Fost is also one of many observers who point out that it is difficult to complain about steroids giving one athlete a "special advantage" over another athlete, when sports competitions are filled with "special advantages." What do observers think of special swimsuits, specially designed golf clubs and tennis rackets, specially fitted and built running shoes, high-altitude training, availability of the best coaches and trainers, and other "perks" used by athletes to reach their maximum potential are? Do spectators at professional football games complain about "drugging" when players are given pain killers that allow them to go back onto the field after an injury? Even more fundamentally, Fost argues, who ever said that "enhancing performance" is unfair? If that were the case, he says, "we should ban coaching and training" (Fost 2005).

Some critics also dispute the notion that anabolic steroids give athletes an extra "boost" of which they are otherwise not capable. For example, Lincoln Allison, founding director of the Study of Sport in Society at England's Warwick University, has written that "[a] sportsman or woman who seeks an advantage from drugs just moves up to the level appropriate to his or her underlying ability." He goes on to point out that

> There are no drugs to enhance the human characteristics of judgment and leadership. If there were, would we not want the prime minister to take them? And if there were drugs for hand-eye coordination, would we not pay more to see a performer who had taken them than one who had not? (Allison 2004)

Proponents and opponents of steroid prohibition also argue over the importance of records in sports: most home runs in a season, most completed passes for touchdowns, fastest 100-meter dash, and so on. When Mark McGwire was found to have used illegal substances in setting new home run records in professional baseball, a number of critics suggested adding an asterisk to the new record in the official books of statistics. As one observer has written, "[s]ports that revere records and historical comparisons (think of baseball and home runs) would become unmoored by drug-aided athletes obliterating old standards" (Murray 2008). A writer with a different view, Scott Long, has responded to that argument, however: "[p]ersonally, I don't have a big problem with some of baseball's greatest records being broken by athletes who are under suspicion as cheaters." Think of all the changes that have taken place in professional baseball over the past century or more: baseballs that are more or less "lively," changes in bat manufacturing, closer or more distance outfield fences, better overall nutrition and conditioning, more or less aggressive play on the bases, changes in the size of the strike zone, more or fewer and better or less-qualified umpires, and a host of other factors. Why should steroid use not be considered as just one more factor that might affect the numbers that eventually make their way into the record books? Long concludes by asking, "[a]re you telling me that the Ty Cobb Tigers or the Gas House Gang Cardinals wouldn't have taken anything they thought that gave them a chance to perform better?" (Long 2006; also see Bagnolo 2010; Vincent 2013).

So perhaps the argument over doping in sports is not entirely settled. For the better part of two centuries, organized sports has battled to keep itself "clean" from performance-enhancing substances it has claimed would introduce dangerous and unsafe practices into athletics. Now that organizations have succeeded to some extent in achieving that goal, the question has arisen whether all that battle was really worth the effort.

References

Allin, Jane. [2011]. "Part 10: Who Rules?" In The Chemical Horse. The Horse Fund. http://horsefund.org/the-chemical-horse-part-10.php. Accessed on February 12, 2017.

Allison, Lincoln. 2004. "Faster, Stronger, Higher." *The Guardian*. http://www.guardian.co.uk/sport/2004/aug/09/athensolympics2004.olympicgames. Accessed on February 26, 2017.

Almond, Elliott, Julie Cart, and Randy Harvey. 1984, January 29. "Testing Has Not Stopped Use of Steroids in Athletics; Soviets Led the Way, but West Has Caught Up." *Los Angeles Times*.

Andrews, Edmund L. 1998. "Swimming: 3 Guilty of Giving Drugs to East German Athletes." *The New York Times*. http://www.nytimes.com/1998/08/21/sports/swimming-3-guilty-of-giving-drugs-to-east-german-athletes.html. Accessed on February 25, 2017.

Assael, Shaun. 2007. *Steroid Nation*. New York: ESPN Books.

Assael, Shaun, and Charles Hirshberg. 2012. "In the Game Behind the Game, the Guys with the Juice Still Have the Edge." ESPN. http://www.espn.com/espn/magazine/archives/news/story?page=magazine-20030707-article16. Accessed on February 24, 2017.

"Athletics at the 1976 Montréal Summer Games: Women's Discus Throw." 2016. SR/Olympic Sports. http://www.sports-reference.com/olympics/summer/1976/ATH/womens-discus-throw.html. Accessed on February 22, 2017.

Bagnolo, P. 2010. "Technology Not Drugs Make Home Run Records." *Science Buzz*. http://www.sciencebuzz.org/blog/technology-not-drugs-made-home-run-records. Accessed on February 27, 2017.

Baker, Millard. 2011. "The Amazing History of Anabolic Steroids in Sports." MESO-Rx. http://thinksteroids.com/articles/history-anabolic-steroids-sports/. Accessed on February 20, 2017.

Beckett, Arnold H. 1976. "Problems of Anabolic Steroids in Sports." *Olympic Review.* 109–110: 591–598. http://library.la84.org/OlympicInformationCenter/OlympicReview/1976/ore109/ore109l.pdf. Accessed on February 22, 2017.

Berkowitz, Bonnie, and Tim Meko. 2016. "Stronger. Faster. Longer. And Higher." *The Washington Post.* https://www.washingtonpost.com/graphics/sports/olympics/doping/. Accessed on February 24, 2017.

Bogdanich, Walt, et al. 2012. "Mangled Horses, Maimed Jockeys." *The New York Times.* http://www.nytimes.com/2012/03/25/us/death-and-disarray-at-americas-racetracks.html?ref=waltbogdanich&_r=0. Accessed on February 12, 2017.

Brailsford, Alan D., et al. 2012. "Two-Dimensional Gas Chromatography with Heart-Cutting for Isotope Ratio Mass Spectrometry Analysis of Steroids in Doping Control." *Drug Testing and Analysis.* 4(12): 962–969. https://www.researchgate.net/publication/228115890_Two-dimensional_gas_chromatography_with_heart-cutting_for_isotope_ratio_mass_spectrometry_analysis_of_steroids_in_doping_control. Accessed on February 23, 2017.

Brooks, R. V., R. G. Firth, and N. A. Sumner. 1975. "Detection of Anabolic Steroids by Radioimmunoassay." *British Journal of Sports Medicine.* 9(2): 89–92.

Cadwallader, Amy B., et al. 2010. "The Abuse of Diuretics as Performance-Enhancing Drugs and Masking Agents in Sport Doping: Pharmacology, Toxicology and Analysis." *British Journal of Pharmacology.* 161(1): 1–16.

"Chain of Custody Form." 2016. World Anti-Doping Agency. https://www.wada-ama.org/sites/default/files/resources/files/wada_chain_of_custody_form_v4.pdf. Accessed on February 23, 2017.

Chidlovski, Arthur. 2009. "The Eraser: History of Disqualifications at the Men's Olympic Weightlifting Tournaments." Lift Up. http://www.chidlovski.net/liftup/l_disqualifications_olympics.asp#eraser. Accessed on February 22, 2017.

Cohen, Roger. 1993. "Johnson Is Banned for Life after Testing Positive for Drugs a 2d Time." *The New York Times*. www.nytimes.com/1993/03/06/sports/track-field-johnson-banned-for-life-after-testing-positive-for-drugs-2d-time.html. Accessed on February 24, 2017.

Collins, Rick. 2005. "Steroids and Sports: A Provocative Interview with Norm Fost, M.D." *Steroid Law*. http://www.steroidlaw.com/steroid-law-45.html. Accessed on February 26, 2017.

Connolly, Ryan. 2006. "Balancing the Justices in Anti-Doping Law: The Need to Ensure Fair Athletic Competition through Effective Anti-Doping Programs vs. the Protection of Rights of Accused Athletes." *Virginia Sports and Entertainment Law Journal*. 5(2): 41–80.

Cram, Steve. 2008. "Jenkins Shows Jones That Cheats Can Prosper." *The Guardian*. The Sport Blog. http://www.guardian.co.uk/sport/2008/jan/15/athletics.sport2. Accessed on February 24, 2017.

"Das Erste." [2014]. WDR. https://presse.wdr.de/plounge/tv/das_erste/2014/12/_pdf/English-Skript.pdf. Accessed on February 25, 2017.

de la Torre, Xavier, et al. 2001. "13C/12C Isotope Ratio MS Analysis of Testosterone, in Chemicals and Pharmaceutical Preparations." *Journal of Pharmaceutical and Biomedical Analysis*. 24(4): 645–650.

"Dope." 2017. *Online Etymology Dictionary*. http://www.etymonline.com/index.php?term=dope. Accessed on February 12, 2017.

"Doping Control Officer (DCO) Instructions: Chain of Custody Form." 2015. World Anti-Doping Agency.

https://www.wada-ama.org/sites/default/files/resources/
files/instructions_wada_chain_of_custody_form_v4_
en.pdf. Accessed on February 23, 2017.

"Dr. Gary Wadler of the World Anti-Doping Agency Gives His
Answers to Your Questions (Part I)." 2008. *The New York
Times*. http://beijing2008.blogs.nytimes.com/2008/06/26/
dr-gary-wadler-of-the-world-anti-doping-agency-gives-his-
answers-to-your-questions-part-i/?_r=0. Accessed on
February 25, 2017.

"Drug Testing in Sport." 2014. The Athlete.org. http://www
.theathlete.org/Drug-Testing-In-Sports.htm. Accessed on
February 22, 2017.

"Drugs in U.S. Racing—2010. The Facts." 2011. Association
of Racing Commissioners International. http://www
.caltrainers.org/ctt_news/drugs-in-u-s—racing-2010-the-
facts.pdf. Accessed on February 12, 2017.

Dvorchak, Robert. 2005, October 2. "Never Enough/
Steroids in Sports: Experiment Turns Epidemic 46 Years
after Steroids Were Injected into Sports, There Is a Frenzy
to Get Rid of Them." *Pittsburgh Post-Gazette*. http://www
.ergogenics.org/123.html. Accessed on February 19,
2017.

Eisendrath, John. 1988. "Confessions of a Steroid Smuggler:
When the Quest for Big Muscles Turns into a Passion for
Big Money." *Los Angeles Times*. http://articles.latimes.com/
1988-04-24/magazine/tm-2306_1_william-dillon.
Accessed on February 24, 2017.

"Enzyme-Linked Immunosorbent Assay (ELISA)." 2017.
Rockland Antibodies and Assays. http://www.rockland-inc
.com/elisa.aspx. Accessed on February 23, 2017.

Eyquem, Marie-Thérèse. 1961. "Women Sports and the
Olympic Games." *Bulletin du Comité International
Olympique*. 73: 48–50. http://library.la84.org/Olympic
InformationCenter/OlympicReview/1961/BDCE73/
BDCE73k.pdf. Accessed on February 20, 2017.

"Factsheet: The Fight against Doping and Promotion of Athletes' Health Update—September 2016." 2016. International Olympic Committee. https://stillmed .olympic.org/media/Document%20Library/OlympicOrg/ Factsheets-Reference-Documents/Medical/Fight-against-Doping/Factsheet-The-Fight-against-Doping-and-Promotion-of-Athletes-Health.pdf#_ga=1.255298568.18 68910684.1481307880. Accessed on February 20, 2017.

Fair, John D. 1993. "Isometrics or Steroids? Exploring New Frontiers of Strength in the Early 1960s." *Journal of Sport History*. 20(1): 1–24.

"Five Minor League Players Suspended." 2017. MLB.com. http://m.mlb.com/news/article/216112410/five-minor-league-players-suspended/. Accessed on February 16, 2017.

"40 Years of Fighting against Doping." 2001. International Cycling Union. http://oldsite.uci.ch/english/health_sante/ docs/40_ans.pdf. Accessed on February 20, 2017.

Fost, Norman. 2005. "Steroid Hysteria: Unpacking the Claims." *AMA Journal of Ethics*. 7(11). http://virtualmentor.ama-assn .org/2005/11/oped2-0511.html. Accessed on February 26, 2017.

Franke, Werner W., and Brigitte Berendonk. 1997. "Hormonal Doping and Androgenization of Athletes: A Secret Program of the German Democratic Republic Government." *Clinical Chemistry*. 43(7): 1262–1279.

"Frequently Asked Questions (FAQ). Therapeutic Use Exemptions (TUEs)." 2016. World Anti-Doping Agency. https://www.wada-ama.org/sites/default/files/resources/ files/2016-11-17-qa_tues_en.pdf. Accessed on February 24, 2017.

"Gas Chromatography." 2008. Royal Society of Chemistry. https://www.youtube.com/watch?v=08YWhLTjlfo. Accessed on February 23, 2017.

Gilbert, Bil. 1969. "Problems in a Turned-On World." *Sports Illustrated*. June 23, 1969. http://www.si.com/vault/issue/43044/72/2. Accessed on February 21, 2017.

Gilbert, Cathrin, et al. 2009. "The Doping Legacy." *Der Spiegel*. http://www.presseurop.eu/en/content/article/80561-doping-legacy. Accessed on February 24, 2017.

Gleaves, John. 2012. "Enhancing the Odds: Horse Racing, Gambling and the First Anti-Doping Movement in Sport, 1889–1911." *Sport in History*. 32(1): 26–52.

Goldberg, Ryan, Bill Finley, and Lucas Marquardt. 2013. "A Painful Truth." *TDN Magazine*. In six parts: May 2, May 9, May 16, May 29, June 15, June 22. http://www.teamvalor.com/news/june2013/tdnseries.pdf. Accessed on February 12, 2017.

Goldman, Denie, and Robert Goldman. 1980. "Father of Dianabol." *Muscle Training Illustrated*. 75: 5.

Harrah, Scott. [2011]. "Dan Duchaine Unchained: The 'Guru' Breaks the Silence on Steroids." Elite Fitness. http://www.elitefitness.com/articledata/dan-duchaine-interview.html. Accessed on February 24, 2017.

Higgins, Andrew James. 2006. "PL04 from Ancient Greece to Modern Athens: 3000 Years of Doping in Competition Horses." *Journal of Veterinary Pharmacology and Therapeutics*. 29(1): 4–8.

"Human Growth Hormone History." 2014. Somatropin. http://somatropin.co/hgh-history.htm. Accessed on February 24, 2017.

Hunt, Thomas Mitchell. 2007. "Drug Games: The International Politics of Doping and the Olympic Movement, 1960–2007." Doctoral thesis. University of Texas at Austin, https://repositories.lib.utexas.edu/bitstream/handle/2152/3255/huntt51425.pdf?sequence%20%EF%80%BD%202. Accessed on February 20, 2017.

Hunt, Thomas Mitchell. 2011. *Drug Games: The International Olympic Committee and the Politics of Doping, 1960–2008.* Austin: University of Texas Press.

Hurst, Mike. 2009. "Johnson Finds His Drink Spiker." *The Telegraph.* http://www.dailytelegraph.com.au/sport/more-sports/johnson-finds-his-drink-spiker/story-e6frey6i-1225813 659234. Accessed on February 24, 2017.

"IAAF Provisionally Suspends Russian Member Federation ARAF." 2015. IAAF. https://www.iaaf.org/news/press-release/iaaf-araf-suspended. Accessed on February 25, 2017.

Jenkins, Mark. 2005. "Erythropoietin." http://www.rice.edu/~jenky/sports/epo.html. Accessed on February 24, 2017.

Johnson, Ben. 2010. *Seoul to Soul.* Ontario, Canada: Ben Johnson Enterprises.

Kettmann, Steve. 2000. "E. German Olympic Dopers Guilty." *Wired.* http://www.wired.com/politics/law/news/2000/07/37631. Accessed on February 25, 2017.

Kicman, Andrew T., and D. B. Gower. 2003. "Anabolic Steroids in Sport: Biochemical, Clinical and Analytical Perspectives." *Annals of Clinical Biochemistry.* 40(Pt. 4): 321–356.

"Lance Armstrong Receives Lifetime Ban and Disqualification of Competitive Results for Doping Violations Stemming from His Involvement in the United States Postal Service Pro-Cycling Team Doping Conspiracy." 2012. U.S. Anti-Doping Agency. http://www.usada.org/lance-armstrong-receives-lifetime-ban-and-disqualification-of-competi tive-results-for-doping-violations-stemming-from-his-involvement-in-the-united-states-postal-service-pro-cycling-team-doping-conspi/. Accessed on February 25, 2017.

Long, Scott. 2006. "The Happy Hypocrite Takes on Jason Grimsely." The Juice Blog. http://thejuice.baseballtoaster.com/archives/398606.html. Accessed on February 26, 2017.

Luhn, Alec. 2015. "Russia Has Been Singled Out over Doping, Claims Former Athletics Coach." *The Guardian*. https://www .theguardian.com/sport/2015/aug/02/valentin-maslakov-russia-singled-out-doping-drugs. Accessed on February 25, 2017.

Mantell, Gregory. 2011. "Doping and the Global Fight against Doping in Sport: Nandrolone." http://minebuilding.org.ua/. Accessed on February 20, 2017.

McRae, Donald. 2014. "Ben Johnson: 'My Revelations Will Shock the Sporting World.'" *The Guardian*. http://www .guardian.co.uk/sport/2010/oct/05/ben-johnson-drugs-olympics. Accessed on February 24, 2017.

"Medication and Performance-Enhancing Drugs in Horse Racing." 2012. U.S. Senate Committee on Commerce, Science, and Transportation. https://www.gpo.gov/fdsys/pkg/CHRG-112shrg76248/pdf/CHRG-112shrg76248 .pdf. Accessed on February 12, 2017.

"Merck's New Anabolic Steroid: MK-0773." 2010. ergo-log .com. http://www.ergo-log.com/newsteroidmk0773.html. Accessed on February 24, 2017.

"MK 0773." 2015. Adis Insight. http://adisinsight.springer .com/drugs/800024550. Accessed on February 24, 2017.

Møller, Verner. 2016. "The Road to Hell Is Paved with Good Intentions—A Critical Evaluation of WADA's Anti-Doping Campaign." *Performance Enhancement & Health*. 4(3–4): 111–115.

"Most Dangerous Sports." 2017. The Top Tens. http://www .the-top-tens.com/lists/most-dangerous-sports.asp. Accessed on February 26, 2017.

Mullegg, Gaston, and Henry Montandon. 1951. "The Danish Oarsman Who Took Part in the European Championships at Milan in 1950; Were They Drugged?" *Bulletin du Comité International Olympique*. 28: 25–26. http://library.la84.

org/OlympicInformationCenter/OlympicReview/1951/
BDCE28/BDCE28l.pdf. Accessed on February 19, 2017.

Murray, Thomas H. 2008. "Sports Enhancement." The Hastings
Center. http://www.thehastingscenter.org/briefingbook/
sports-enhancement/. Accessed on February 26, 2017.

"1952 Helsinki Medal Tally." 2017. Topend Sports. http://
www.topendsports.com/events/summer/medal-tally/1952
.htm. Accessed on February 19, 2017.

"1936 Berlin Medal Tally." 2017. Topend Sports. http://www
.topendsports.com/events/summer/medal-tally/1936.htm.
Accessed on February 19, 2017.

"1932 Los Angeles Medal Tally." 2017. Topend Sports. http://
www.topendsports.com/events/summer/medal-tally/1932
.htm. Accessed on February 19, 2017.

Noakes, Timothy. 2006. "Should We Allow Performance-
Enhancing Drugs in Sport? A Rebuttal to the Article by
Savulescu and Colleagues." *International Journal of Sports
Science and Coaching*. 1(4): 289–316. http://journals
.sagepub.com/doi/pdf/10.1260/174795406779367710.
Accessed on February 26, 2017.

"Number #1 Urine Substitution Kit." 2017. Urine King.
http://syntheticurine.co/index.php/product/number-
1-urine-substitution-kit/. Accessed on February 24, 2017.

"Olympic Rules and Regulations." 1974. Lausanne: Comite
International Olympique. https://stillmed.olympic.org/
Documents/Olympic%20Charter/Olympic_Charter_
through_time/1974-Olympic_Charter-Olympic_Rules_
and_Regulations.pdf. Accessed on February 22, 2017.

PassYourDrugTest.com. 2017. PassYour Drug Test.com.
http://www.passyourdrugtest.com/text.htm. Accessed on
February 24, 2017.

Peleschuk, Dan. 2014. "Here's Something Else You Can Pin
on Russia." PRI. http://www.pri.org/stories/2014-12-09/

here-s-something-else-you-can-pin-russia. Accessed on February 25, 2017.

"A Piece of Anti-Doping History: IAAF Handbook 1927–1928." 2006. IAAF. https://www.iaaf.org/news/news/ a-piece-of-anti-doping-history-iaaf-handbook. Accessed on February 20, 2017.

Pilgrim, Jill, and Kim Betz. 2008. "A Journey through Olympic Drug Testing Rules: A Practitioner's Guide to Understanding Drug Testing within the Olympic Movement." *The Sport Journal.* http://thesportjournal.org/article/a-journey-throu gh-olympic-drug-testing-rules-a-practitioners-guide-to-un derstanding-drug-testing-within-the-olympic-movement/. Accessed on February 20, 2017.

["Players Listed in Mitchell Report"]. [2007]. [Major League Baseball]. http://mlb.mlb.com/mlb/news/mitchell/players .jsp. Accessed on February 25, 2017.

"Prohibited List 2016." 2016. World Anti-Doping Agency. https://www.wada-ama.org/sites/default/files/resources/files/ wada-2016-prohibited-list-en.pdf. Accessed on February 22, 2017.

Quinn, T. J. 2009. "Pumped-Up Pioneers: The '63 Chargers." ESPN. http://www.espn.com/espn/otl/news/ story?id=3866837. Accessed on February 20, 2017.

"Reformed Racing Medication Rules." 2012. The Jockey Club. http://www.jockeyclub.com/pdfs/reformed_rules.pdf. Accessed on February 12, 2017.

"Regulation of US Thoroughbred Racing." 2017. Gamblingsites .com. https://www.gamblingsites.com/horse-racing/us/ regulation-control/. Accessed on February 12, 2017.

"Regulations: Doping Control for FIFA Competitions and Out of Competition." [2004]. Fédération Internationale de Football Association. http://www.fifa.com/mm/document/ afdeveloping/medical/6.17.%20fifa%20doping%20 control%20regulations_1533.pdf. Accessed on February 20, 2017.

Reinold, Marcel, and John Hoberman. 2014. "The Myth of the Nazi Steroid." *The International Journal of the History of Sport*. 31(8): 871–883.

"Report to WADA Executive Committee on Lack of Effectiveness of Testing Programs." 2013. Working Group Established Following Foundation Board Meeting of 18 May 2012. https://www.wada-ama.org/sites/default/files/resources/files/2013-05-12-Lack-of-effectiveness-of-testing-WG-Report-Final.pdf. Accessed on February 25, 2017.

"The Researcher's Perspective." 2007. *Play True*. 2: 15–18. https://www.wada-ama.org/sites/default/files/resources/files/PlayTrue_2007_2_Science_Honing_In_On_Doping_EN.pdf. Accessed on February 24, 2017.

"Richard H. McLaren, Independent Person. WADA Investigation of Sochi Allegations." 2016a. World Anti-Doping Agency. https://www.wada-ama.org/sites/default/files/resources/files/20160718_ip_report_newfinal.pdf. Accessed on February 25, 2017.

"Richard H. McLaren, Independent Person. WADA Investigation of Sochi Allegations." 2016b. World Anti-Doping Agency. https://www.wada-ama.org/sites/default/files/resources/files/mclaren_report_part_ii_2.pdf. Accessed on February 25, 2017.

"Rio Olympics 2016: Which Russian Athletes Have Been Cleared to Compete?" 2016. BBC. http://www.bbc.com/sport/olympics/36881326. Accessed on February 25, 2017.

Riordan, Jim. 1993. "The Rise and Fall of Soviet Olympic Champions." http://library.la84.org/SportsLibrary/Olympika/Olympika_1993/olympika0201c.pdf. Accessed on February19, 2017.

Robinson, N., et al. 2006. "Erythropoietin and Blood Doping." *British Journal of Sports Medicine.* 40(Suppl 1): 30–34.

Rosen, Daniel M. 2008. *Dope: A History of Performance Enhancement in Sports from the Nineteenth Century to Today.* Westport, CT: Praeger.

Ruiz, Rebecca R., and Michael Schwirtz. 2016. "Russian Insider Says State-Run Doping Fueled Olympic Gold." *The New York Times.* http://www.nytimes.com/2016/05/13/sports/russia-doping-sochi-olympics-2014.html?_r=0. Accessed on February 25, 2017.

Saugy, Martial, et al. 2000. "Test Methods: Anabolics." *Baillière's Best Practice & Research. Clinical Endocrinology and Metabolism.* 14(1): 111–133.

Schudel, Matt. 2010. "Harold Connolly, Olympic Gold Medalist in Hammer Throw, Dies at 79." *The Washington Post.* http://www.washingtonpost.com/wp-dyn/content/article/2010/08/21/AR2010082102538.html. Accessed on February 19, 2017.

Schulze, Jenny Jakobsson, et al. 2008. "Doping Test Results Dependent on Genotype of Uridine Diphospho–Glucuronosyl Transferase 2B17, the Major Enzyme for Testosterone Glucuronidation." *The Journal of Clinical Endocrinology and Metabolism.* 93(7): 2500–2506.

Scott, Jack. 1971, October 17. "It's Not How You Play the Game, But What Pill You Take." *The New York Times.* 40–41. http://www.nytimes.com/1971/10/17/archives/its-not-how-you-play-the-game-but-what-pill-you-take-its-not-how.html?_r=0. Accessed on February 19, 2017.

Seppelt, Hans. 2014. *The Secret of Doping—How Russia Makes Its Winners.* YouTube. https://www.youtube.com/watch?v=iu9B-ty9JCY. Accessed on February 25, 2017.

Shipley, Amy. 2012. "Lance Armstrong Faces Fresh Doping Charges from USADA." *The Washington Post.* https://www

.washingtonpost.com/sports/lance-armstrong-faces-fresh-doping-charges-from-usada/2012/06/13/gJQAefnPaV_story.html?utm_term=.e10d2570e136. Accessed on February 25, 2017.

"Should Performance Enhancing Drugs (Such as Steroids) Be Accepted in Sports?" 2016. ProCon.org. http://sportsand drugs.procon.org/view.answers.php?questionID001200. Accessed on February 26, 2017.

Sumner, N.A. 1974. "Measurement of Anabolic Steroids by Radioimmunoassay." *Journal of Steroid Biochemistry*. 5(4): 307.

"Therapeutic Use Exemptions." 2017. World Anti-Doping Agency. https://www.wada-ama.org/en/what-we-do/science-medical/therapeutic-use-exemptions. Accessed on February 24, 2017.

Todd, Jan, and Terry Todd. 2001. "Significant Events in the History of Drug Testing and the Olympic Movement." In Wayne Wilson and Ed Derse, eds. *Doping in Elite Sport: The Politics of Drugs in the Olympic Movement*. Champaign, IL: Human Kinetics. 65–104.

Todd, Terry. 1965. "The Jovial Genius of Dr. John Zeigler." *Strength & Health*. 33: 44–45.

"TRA Member Tracks." 2016. Thoroughbred Racing Associations. http://www.tra-online.com/members.html. Accessed on February 12, 2017.

"Transgender and Intersex Olympians." 2011. *The Hitchhiker's Guide to the Galaxy: Earth Edition*. http://www.h2g2.com/entry/A87724588. Accessed on February 20, 2017.

Ungerleider, Steven. 2001. *Faust's Gold: Inside the East German Doping Machine*. New York: Thomas Dunne Books; St. Martin's Press.

United States Senate, One Hundred Ninth Congress. 2005, May 24. First Session, Hearing before the Committee on Commerce, Science, and Transportation. https://babel

.hathitrust.org/cgi/pt?id=pst.000058148266;view=1up; seq=24. Accessed on February 24, 2017.

Van Eenoo, P., and F. T. Delbeke. 2006. "Metabolism and Excretion of Anabolic Steroids in Doping Control—New Steroids and New Insights." *Steroid Biochemistry and Molecular Biology*. 101(4–5): 161–178.

"Victor Conte: BALCO—The Straight Dope on Steroids." 2009. *Diet, Health & Fitness News*. www.diethealthandfit nessnews.com/balco-book-victor-conte.html. Accessed on February 25, 2017.

Vincent, David. 2013. "Top 10 Reasons Why You Can't Credit Steroids for the Increase." 500 Home Run Club. http://www .500hrc.com/500-hrc-articles/top-10-reasons-why-you-cant-credit-steroids-for-the-increase.html. Accessed on February 26, 2017.

"WADA Statistics 2005." 2006. Now THAT's Amateur. http://now-thats-amateur.blogspot.com/2006/04/wada-statistics-2005.html. Accessed on February 24, 2017. A continuation of this article dealing with technical issues can be found at http://now-thats-amateur.blogspot.com/ 2006/07/wada-statistics-2005-part-2.html and http://now-thats-amateur.blogspot.com/2006/07/ wada-statistics-2005-part-3.html.

Wallace, Wade. 2016. "A Look Inside the Whereabouts Program." Cycling Tips. https://cyclingtips.com/2016/06/ living-with-the-whereabouts/. Accessed on February 22, 2017.

Ward, R. J., C. H. Shackleton, and A. M. Lawson. 1975. "Gas Chromatographic-Mass Spectrometric Methods for the Detection and Identification of Anabolic Steroid Drugs." *British Journal of Sports Medicine*. 9: 93–97.

Werner, T. C., and Caroline K. Hatton. 2011. "Performance-Enhancing Drugs in Sports: How Chemists Catch Users." *Journal of Chemical Education*. 88(1): 34–40.

"What Are the 19 Known Methods of Cheating to Pass Performance Enhancing Drug Tests?" 2009. ProCon.org. http://sportsanddrugs.procon.org/view.resource.php? resourceID 002706. Accessed on February 24, 2017.

"The Whizzanator Touch!" 2017. ALS. http://www.thewhizzi nator.com/whizzinator.html. Accessed on February 24, 2017.

Williams, Lance, and Mark Fainaru-Wada. 2004. "An Unlikely Cast of Characters at Center of Doping Scandal." SFGate. http://www.sfgate.com/sports/article/An-unlikely-cast-of-characters-at-center-of-2796932.php#page-1. Accessed on February 25, 2017.

Winearls, Christopher G. 1998. "Recombinant Human Erythropoietin: 10 Years of Clinical Experience." *Nephrology, Dialysis, Transplantation*. 13 (Suppl 2): 3–8.

"World Anti-Doping Code International Standard: Laboratories." 2016. World Anti-Doping Agency. https://www.wada-ama.org/sites/default/files/resources/files/isl_june_2016.pdf. Accessed on February 23, 2017.

Yesalis, Charles E., et al. 1990. "Incidence of the Nonmedical Use of Anabolic-Androgenic Steroids." *National Institute on Drug Abuse Research Monographs*. 102: 97–112. http://archives.drugabuse.gov/pdf/monographs/102.pdf. Accessed on February 19, 2017.

Zimmer, Ben. 2013. "The Straight Dope on 'Doping.'" Visual Thesaurus. https://www.visualthesaurus.com/cm/wordroutes/the-straight-dope-on-doping/. Accessed on December 27, 2017.

Introduction

Discussions of steroids and doping in sports depend very much on understanding the background, history, and factual issues involved in such topics. However, they are also laden with a variety of opinions and emotional views. The essays in this chapter provide both types of perspectives about a variety of topics in the field of steroids and doping in sports.

Steroid Abuse and Body Image
Mark L. Fuerst

Blame the Rock, *People* magazine's current "Sexiest Man Alive." Add in the beefed-up versions of movie superheroes Superman and Batman and Chris Helmsworth as Thor. They represent the new version of what the ideal man is supposed to look like.

But these media images of increasingly muscular men, along with muscle-enhancing techniques now available to today's

---

Jamaica's sprinter Steve Mullings hits the tape to win the 100 meters race during the Prefontaine Classic track and field meet in Eugene, Oregon, June 4, 2011. The Jamaica Anti-Doping Commission announced on November 21, 2011, that Mullings had been banned for life after being found guilty of doping by a three-member disciplinary panel. It was Mulling's second doping offense as he was banned in 2004 for two years after failing a drug test during qualifications to compete in the 2004 Olympics. (AP Photo/Don Ryan)

youth, are a cause for concern. Teens across the country are taking drugs, including potentially dangerous anabolic steroids, under the misconception they will enhance strength, speed, and their looks.

Hundreds of thousands of teens have used steroids. A recent survey of nearly 2,800 diverse adolescents, average age 14, from 20 urban middle and high schools assessed the use of five muscle-enhancing behaviors: changing eating habits, exercising, consuming protein powders, using steroids, and taking other muscle-enhancing substances (Eisenberg, Wall, and Neumark-Sztainer 2012). Muscle-enhancing behaviors were found common, for both boys and girls. More than one-third said they used protein powders or shakes and 5.9 percent reported steroid use. These behaviors were significantly more common among boys, but overweight and obese girls were significantly more likely to use protein powders or shakes than girls of average weight.

The majority of teenage steroid abusers are male athletes who want to perform better in sports, to be more competitive in gaining an athletic scholarship, or simply to look better. The most common reason for teenage girls to use steroids is for aesthetic purposes. Shockingly, both males and females report they have tried steroids as early as age 11.

Kids' interest in steroids may begin with the use of vitamins, supplements, and protein powders from the health-food store. If athletes happen to perform well while taking supplements, they may look for something stronger to become even better.

A recent analysis estimates that as many as four million Americans, nearly all of them men, have used anabolic steroids at one time in their lives (Pope, Khalsa, and Bhasin 2017). These drugs are widely available through an underground black market, mostly through weight-lifting gyms. But even in suburban health clubs, the guys in the weight room often know where to find steroids. Whether they are called "juice" or "roids," taken in pill form or by injection, steroids have become a major problem.

With constant exposure to muscular male images on magazine covers, in advertisements, on television, and in movies, many young men have become overly concerned with their musculature. This is reflected in an increasing prevalence of "muscle dysmorphia," a form of body image disorder characterized by an obsessive preoccupation with a muscular appearance. Men with muscle dysmorphia say they are dissatisfied with their body size and shape. They are preoccupied with the idea that they do not have enough muscles.

Teens are particularly sensitive about how they look, and they feel the effects of not meeting society's standards. A recent study examined 1,666 male and female secondary students, aged 12–18 years, who completed a survey that included measures of dissatisfaction and preoccupation with their weight and shape, psychological distress, and eating disorder behaviors (Mitchison, et al. 2017). Preoccupation with weight and shape was particularly significant in girls. The boys who were dissatisfied with their body shape were more likely than girls to criticize their own looks and feel distress. Unrealistic media images may have contributed to the low satisfaction with body image among these teens.

To get more buff, most men with muscle dysmorphia engage in weight lifting, and more than 40 percent of them report they have used anabolic steroids at some time in their lives. Many of them use dietary supplements to enhance performance and appearance, but they may not realize that unregulated, over-the-counter supplements may contain anabolic steroids or other similar compounds, including chemicals called selective androgen receptor modulators.

Emerging evidence implicates steroid use with an increasing number of health problems. These include an increased risk of premature death, heart disorders, psychiatric effects (think "roid rage"), suppression of testosterone levels, and possible neurotoxic effects. Among young people who are known steroid users, the long-term effects of steroid use have been linked to heart attack and stroke, serious damage to the heart muscle, and acceleration of atherosclerosis. The end result is that the body is ravaged by steroids.

It's imperative that teens understand all of the dangers of steroid use. Luckily, if the steroid use is not too prolonged, some of the side effects are reversible when the teen stops taking the drugs. However, many of them are not reversible, such as heart problems. At the moment, no one can predict for any one person whether the side effects of steroid abuse will be reversible.

References

Eisenberg M. E., M. Wall, and D. Neumark-Sztainer. 2012. "Muscle-Enhancing Behaviors among Adolescent Girls and Boys." *Pediatrics*. 130(6): 1019–1026.

Mitchison D., et al. 2017. "Disentangling Body Image: the Relative Associations of Overvaluation, Dissatisfaction, and Preoccupation with Psychological Distress and Eating Disorder Behaviors in Male and Female Adolescents." *International Journal of Eating Disorders*. 50(2): 118–126.

Pope, H. G., J. H. Khalsa, and S. Bhasin. 2017. "Body Image Disorders and Abuse of Anabolic-Androgenic Steroids among Men." *JAMA*. 317(1): 23–24.

Mark L. Fuerst is a freelance health and medical writer based in Brooklyn (www.marklfuerst.com). He holds a graduate degree in journalism from the University of Missouri. He has written hundreds of articles for major women's and health magazines and is the coauthor of 11 books for consumers, including the Sports Injury Handbook *and* Tennis Injury Handbook. *His most recent book is* The Harvard Medical School Guide to Tai Chi.

Competing Motives in Sports Doping
Dean A. Haycock

In the first edition of *Steroids and Doping in Sports*, I argued against legalizing performance-enhancing drugs (PEDs) for athletes. I concluded "as quixotic as it might sound, it might be noble to draw the line at steroids and accept the fact that sports police will be doomed forever to chasing down cheaters and the new ways they find to cheat" (Haycock 2014, 141–142).

It's now clear that not only many ambitious athletes are motivated to cheat, but unions and employers have reasons not to push too hard for rigorous testing. As Roni Selig and Gupta Sanjay of CNN point out, "Major League Baseball, the NFL and others craft their testing policies as part of the collective bargaining process between the players' union and the league" (Selig and Gupta 2017). In other words, the terms under which these players are tested are negotiated.

The results of these negotiations hinder the ability of drug testers to detect drugs. NFL players, for instance, can be tested only six times a year, and they can never have a blood test on the day they compete. Once tested six times, they could use any PED they like; no one can detect what they can't test.

Furthermore, there is a delay lasting 3 to 24 hours between the time players are notified of a test and the time they provide a sample for testing. And when they provide a urine sample, they do so in private. This delay and privacy raise the possibility that some players could submit fake samples.

This may not matter if, as the NFL claims, only a small minority of players use PEDs. But the truth is nobody knows how many players are cheating with anabolic steroids, human growth hormone, stimulants, and other PEDs. Even the director of external affairs for the NFL Players Association, George Atallah, admitted he doesn't know how many players use PEDs. "Only the players in the locker room know," he told CNN (Selig and Gupta 2017).

A former Notre Dame and NFL quarterback thinks he knows why more than half a dozen NFL players were injured—some seriously—two months into the 2015 season. Brady Quinn suspects that between 40 and 50 percent of them were taking PEDs, which enable players to push their bodies beyond their normal limits and so increase their risk of injury (Knowlton 2015).

Admirably, mixed martial arts fighters under contract with the Ultimate Fighting Championship deal with tougher testing standards than football or baseball players. They would have much more trouble finding ways to deceive drug testers because they are tested by the United States Anti-Doping Agency (USADA). The USADA has stricter testing procedures than other testing services.

"An important part of USADA's testing program," its website explains, "is the ability to test athletes without any advance notice in an out-of-competition setting. Athletes are subject to testing 365 days a year and do not have 'off-seasons' or cutoff periods in which testing does not occur. Whereabouts information (dates, times, locations, etc.) is information submitted to USADA by an athlete that allows the athlete to be located for out-of-competition testing" (U.S. Anti-Doping Agency 2014).

As soon as a fighter is notified by USADA about a test, he or she is accompanied by a chaperone. If the fighter is not at his listed location, the tester will wait one hour. The chaperone ensures that the fighter provides a reliable sample for testing, going so far as to observe the fighter providing the sample.

USADA also tests members of the U.S. Olympic team. Unfortunately, not all Olympians who competed in the 2014 Olympics underwent such scrutiny. In fact, the director of Russia's anti-doping laboratory, Grigory Rodchenkov, said he created a cocktail consisting of three banned substances and gave them to dozens of Russian competitors (Ruiz and Schwirtz 2016).

Later, Russian intelligence agents and anti-doping personnel substituted clean urine samples for around 100 PED-containing samples during the international competition. The Russians earned more medals than their closest competitor, the United States, during those Olympic Games. No Russians tested positive at the time.

After the discovery of extensive state-sponsored cheating, anti-doping officials retested samples saved from the 2008 and 2012 Olympics Games. This time they were able to use more sensitive tests. This resulted in more than 75 doping violations missed earlier. Most of the newly discovered cheaters represented Russian or eastern European countries. These "enhanced" athletes were stripped of the medals they won (Ruiz 2016).

Olympic Committee member Gian-Franco Kasper reacted to the results of retesting by noting that "the numbers are just impossible, incredible. We lose credibility. Credibility is a major concern" (Ruiz 2016).

This essay started with a reference to a quixotic goal and it ends with one, but one tinged with a touch of cynicism, or realism. To avoid losing more credibility, all sporting competitions should require participants to be tested using the most rigorous standards, such as those used by the USADA and its international counterpart, the World Anti-Doping Agency. Athletes should be banned from competition for life if three independent, certified drug-testing labs confirm the presence of steroids and other PEDs.

Of course, cheating athletes will not be banned. Football and baseball teams and their owners have millions of dollars at stake. Losing players would cost money. And nations desperate for recognition will go further; they will actively encourage cheating.

Thus, we remain stuck with simultaneous games; athletic competition on the field, for profit; and competition between cheaters and drug testers off the field, for our culture. Right now, the profit motive is edging out the culture motive.

References

Haycock, Dean A. 2014. *Steroids and Doping in Sports*. Santa Barbara, CA: ABC-CLIO, 139–142.

Knowlton, Emmett. 2015. "Former NFL Player Thinks Performance-Enhancing Drugs Are on the Rise in the NFL." *Business Insider*. http://www.businessinsider.com/brady-quinn-peds-nfl-injuries-2015-11. Accessed on February 4, 2017.

Ruiz, Rebecca R. 2016. "Olympics History Rewritten: New Doping Tests Topple the Podium." *The New York Times.* https://www.nytimes.com/2016/11/21/sports/olympics/olympics-doping-medals-stripped.html?emc=edit_na_20161121&nlid=15430158&ref=cta&_r=2. Accessed on February 12, 2017.

Ruiz, Rebecca R., and Michael Schwirtz. 2016. "Russian Insider Says State-Run Doping Fueled Olympic Gold." *The New York Times.* https://www.nytimes.com/2016/05/13/sports/russia-doping-sochi-olympics-2014.html?_r=0. Accessed on February 1, 2017.

Selig, Roni, and Sanjay Gupta. 2017. "Is the NFL Doing Enough to Test for PEDs?" CNN. http://www.cnn.com/2017/02/05/health/performance-enhancing-drugs-nfl-investigative-explainer/index.html. Accessed on February 1, 2017.

U.S. Anti-Doping Agency. 2014. "Testing." http://www.usada.org/testing/ Accessed on February 10, 2017.

Dean A. Haycock, PhD, is a science and medical writer. He is the author of Murderous Minds, Exploring the Criminal Psychopathic Brain *and* Characters on the Couch, Exploring Psychology through Literature and Film.

Therapeutic Use Exemptions in Sport
Jon Heshka

Sport tied itself up in knots in 2016 over the conundrum of doping with the leak by the reputed Russian hackers, Fancy Bears, of legalized doping by dozens of Olympians. What separates these athletes' use of banned performance-enhancing substances is that they are medically authorized and have been issued a therapeutic use exemption (TUE).

Canadians (full disclosure—I'm Canadian) have a particular expertise in the doping department, having survived the cathartic experience of celebrating Ben Johnson's spectacular win in the 100-meter dash at the 1988 Seoul Olympics only to survive the disappointment of his positive doping test for stanazolol three days later. This led to an inquiry into doping led by Ontario Appeal Court Chief Justice Charles Dubin, which involved hundreds of hours of testimony resulting in a 638-page report on the Commission of Inquiry into the Use of Drugs and Banned Practices Intended to Increase Athletic Performance released in 1990.

Let's first be clear about doping. Doping is the use of prohibited substances intended to enhance sporting performance. Anti-doping proponents hide behind the shibboleth that doping is either extremely dangerous to the user or destructive to sport by conferring an unfair competitive advantage on the user. In other words, doping is bad because it tilts the playing field in favor of the athletes who benefit from the pharmacological effects of the banned substances.

Lost in the miasma of the discussion is that the playing field is already tilted. A court of law once naively held that a fair race should involve only an athlete's own skills, strength, and spirit but not his or her own pharmacologist. If only it were true. The reality is that an elite athlete's skill and strength are optimized through a legion of support personnel, which often includes coaches, trainers, physiotherapists, psychologists, and sometimes even sports scientists and biomechanical engineers.

This cold war of sport pitting what's fair versus what's not fair isn't always clear. It is posited that doping is bad because it benefits only those who dope. Eliminate doping and the playing field is level, goes the argument.

However, as already noted, the field of competition is skewed depending on the extent to which the athlete is supported by private elite track-and-field clubs like ALTIS or publicly by countries that have built systems and artifices employing arsenals of personnel designed with the sole purpose to win.

For example, the Australian Institute of Sport has its 100-million-dollar Winning Edge project grounded by a commitment to cutting-edge sports science/sports medicine services.

Canada's Own the Podium program has its own Top Secret Wing and 200,000-dollar treadmill. Other examples are the English Institute of Sport and the U.S. Olympic Committee's Sport Performance Division, whose mandates are to improve sporting performance through science, medicine, technology, and engineering.

Do programs like these tilt the playing field? You bet they do. How else can it be explained, for example, that athletes from ALTIS finished just outside the top 10 in the medals table at the 2015 IAAF (the governing body for track and field) World Championships or that athletes from developing countries have won less than 4 percent of all men's Olympic swimming medals whereas three countries that comprise 7 percent of the world's population (the United States, Australia, and Japan) account for more than half of all medals ever awarded?

Not every athlete or country has access to such resources, so let's not delude ourselves into thinking that this is just about fairness and leveling the playing field of competition.

One of the rationales that underpin doping is dizzyingly bewildering in its attempt to justify why taking a substance that enhances sporting performance is bad. One of the three criteria used by the World Anti-Doping Agency to ban a substance is if it has the potential to enhance or if it enhances sport performance. But isn't that the whole point?

High-performance sport is about trying to gain advantages over the competition. It's argued performance-enhancing drugs are unfair because of the advantage conferred on the user and that it would only be fair if all athletes could benefit from the same competitive advantages. The point here is that performance-enhancing drugs are only one way athletes gain an edge over the competition; there are many other ways in which some athletes are advantaged while others are not.

The doping horse has already left the barn, so let's move on and go back to Fancy Bears and the leaking of those confidential medical records. The leaks revealed such world-class athletes as American gymnastics star Simone Biles, who won four gold medals and a bronze at the 2016 Rio Olympics, American tennis icon Serena Williams, Tour de France winner and Olympic gold-medal-winning cyclist Bradley Wiggins of Great Britain, and many others who got exemptions for performance-enhancing drugs.

The hack has thrown TUEs into the spotlight, as well as those identified athletes under the bus beneath a cloud of suspicion that they were cheats. It succeeded, temporarily at least, at shifting the spotlight away from the issue of state-sponsored doping and smearing the reputations of athletes who played within the rules.

Relying upon the rationale that doping is bad because it enhances performance has been stretched to the breaking point with the leaking of so many athletes benefiting from their use, albeit via a TUE. It's disingenuous for an athlete to be permitted to take a banned substance to treat an illness (with the pharmacological rationale that its effect is to merely create a level playing field) but to be prohibited to take the same substance with the same pharmacological benefit if there is no medical condition.

This leads to the almost inevitable possibility some athletes will exploit TUE rules. Three-time Tour de France winner Chris Froome has said the exemption system is open to abuse and is something that urgently needs to be addressed. Richard Ings, the former president of the Australian Anti-Doping Agency, has said there is no doubt exemptions can be abused. Even Wiggins's former team doctor expressed skepticism about the coincidental timing of injections of intramuscular steroids ostensibly to treat his asthma at the precise time before his most important races of the season.

How prevalent are TUEs? The World Anti-Doping Agency approved 1,330 TUEs in 2015, a 109 percent increase from the 636 in 2013. Three countries—the United States, Australia, and France—accounted for 63 percent of the TUEs granted in 2015 (Brown 2016).

Fancy Bears succeeded in shifting the spotlight away from institutionalized doping and onto TUEs, the extent to which they are used, and by whom and under what circumstances.

The confidence in the sporting establishment is shaken. The IOC's stickhandling of the Russian state-sponsored doping program has left the venerable institution vulnerable and open to criticism. Rather than thoughtfully discussing how to square this circle of permitting performance-enhancing substances that would otherwise be banned and allowing their use as TUEs, like a bickering married couple on the verge of divorce, the world of sport is playing the blame game with the IOC thinking about a divorce from the World Anti-Doping Agency that is forced to defend it's every move.

Reference

Brown, Andy. 2016. Sports Integrity Initiative. http://www .sportsintegrityinitiative.com/us-australia-appear-to-lead- world-in-approved-tues/. Accessed on February 16, 2017.

Jon Heshka is the associate dean of law at Thompson Rivers University in Kamloops, British Columbia, Canada. He also teaches a course in sports law. Jon has coauthored a university textbook, written two book chapters plus 59 articles, and presented at more than 30 conferences nationally and internationally. He has played semi–pro volleyball in Brazil; competed in many marathons and Ironman triathlons; and climbed in Alaska, the Andes, and the Himalayas, but now mostly spends his recreational time trying to catch up to his two teenage kids.

Cheating with Drugs in Thoroughbred Racing
Barry Irwin

Drug usage in thoroughbred horse racing involves two basic types: legal (mostly of the therapeutic variety) and illegal (banned substances and designer drugs). Most of the news reports about positive drug tests are likely the result of human error by trainers, stable staff, or veterinarians in the use of legal drugs. These positives usually occur because the drugs were administered too close to race time.

Only one drug, the so-called anti-bleeder medication furosemide (Lasix, Salix), is allowed by racing regulators on race day. The other legal drugs must not have traces above a designated level.

The least-reported instances of positives are for illegal or designer drugs. A designer drug is a synthetic substance that closely mirrors a known banned drug except for a slight molecular change that allows it to retain its potency while evading detection. The BALCO scandal involved designer drugs for human athletes (Fainaru-Wada and Williams 2014).

Human connections (veterinarians, trainers, owners) who want to enhance performance focus on altering the state of horses by using illegal drugs as follows.

Pain management. Masking pain can make a horse more willing to perform. Opioids alter the state of a racehorse and mask pain. New York racing authorities discovered in two post-race samples a synthetic opioid named AH-7921 ("Two Horses Test Positive for Opioid" 2015). This designer drug closely mirrors morphine.

Demorphin is another opioid sourced from a South American tree frog. This naturally occurring substance has much in common with its relative morphine, in that it not only numbs pain but puts a horse in a euphoric state (Dockterman 2012).

Oxygen delivery. Red blood cells carry oxygen to the lungs. The more oxygen in its lungs, the better a horse can perform. Eryhtropoietin (Epogen) is a naturally occurring hormone secreted by the kidneys to increase red cell production. A test for this illegal drug was first developed for racehorses in the early 2000s by Dr. George Maylin in New York. Experts say that detection of the drug is difficult because traces are difficult or impossible to find unless a test is done within hours of a horse being dosed. Standard-breds (harness horses) have tested positive in New Jersey (Little 2006).

Cobalt, a metallic element, is yet another substance recently in vogue among cheaters because of its ability to stimulate red blood cell synthesis by indirectly activating the EPO gene. Its effectiveness is less scientific and more apocryphal at this time (Brewer, et al. 2016).

Increased muscle mass. This process allows horses to perform better because muscles enable the skeletal structure to move faster and with more power. Horses treated with anabolic steroids such as stanozolol (Winstrol) also are thought to recover quicker from racing and training. Increased red blood cell production is another benefit (Angst 2015).

Buffering lactic acid. Commonly known as "milk-shaking," this practice consists of mixing baking soda and sugar in a pail and delivering it from a nasogastric tube directly into the stomach in order to neutralize the build-up of lactic acid that slows down a horse in the later stages of a race. It also comes in paste form (Fidanza 2006).

Stimulation. Opiates and amphetamines have been illegally used for years to "light up" horses and are given close to a race for best results. These drugs are tricky, because a stimulated horse can become unmanageable and unable to perform up to expectations (Tobin 2005).

Depressant. Tranquilizers, such as Acepromazine, have been used to make a horse run both below or above its ability level. Not all cheating is done to win with a particular horse. Some cheating is done to eliminate a horse from competition. Interestingly, Ace was cited by a famous racetrack vet as his drug of choice, stating that most horses are too highly strung and the use of Ace would take off the edge and allow their speed to come out ("Horse Owned By CHRB Commissioner Tests Positive for Tranquilizer" 2015).

A form of misconduct by vets and trainers also takes place with the legal drug clenbuterol (Ventipulmin), which was used illegally for at least a decade in America before the Food and Drug Administration made it legal in 1998. California made it legal for use as a therapeutic drug in 2002. When used for its intended purpose and for the prescribed time period, it is an effective drug to treat certain types of respiratory issues because of its ability to increase the speed with which minute hairs clear mucous from the trachea. But when overused or used for more than 14 days in a row, the side effects outweigh the advantages of any respiratory help and actually worsen air passages.

But trainers have seen the steroidal impact the drug has on the physique of their stock, so they use clenbuterol as much for its perceived muscle-building qualities as its respiratory help, even though the evidence from trials shows the questionable benefits of the product's steroidal impact on the respiratory system.

References

Angst, Frank. 2015. "Anabolic Steroids Still an Issue in U.S. Racing." BloodHorse. http://www.bloodhorse.com/horse-racing/articles/109169/anabolic-steroids-still-issue-in-u-s-racing. Accessed on February 13, 2017.

Brewer, K., et al. 2016 "Cobalt Use and Regulation in Horseracing: A Review." *Comparative Exercise Physiology.* 12(1): 1–10. DOI: http://dx.doi.org/10.3920/CEP140008.

Dockterman, Eliana. 2012. "Frog Juice: Horse Racing's New Doping Scandal." *Time.* http://www.newsfeed.time.com. Accessed on February 13, 2017.

Fainaru-Wada, Mark, and Lance Williams. 2014. *Game of Shadows: Barry Bonds, BALCO, and the Steroids Scandal That Rocked Professional Sports.* New York: Gotham Books.

Fidanza, Bob. 2006. "Milkshaking." The Horse. http://www.thehorse.com. Accessed on February 13, 2017.

"Horse Owned By CHRB Commissioner Tests Positive for Tranquilizer." 2015. Paulick Report. http://www.paulickreport.com. Accessed on February 13, 2017.

Little, Dave. 2006. "Horse Positive, Trainer Is Barred."
    Daily News. http://www.nydailynews.com. Accessed on
    February 17, 2017.

Tobin, Thomas, et. al. 2005. "Equine Drugs, Medications,
    and Performance Altering Substances: Their Performance
    Effects, Detection, and Regulation." http://www
    .thomastobin.com. Accessed on February 13, 2017.

"Two Horses Test Positive for Opioid." 2015. BloodHorse.
    http://www.bloodhorse.com/horse-racing/articles/200
    239/two-horses-test-positive-for-opioid. Accessed on
    February 13, 2017.

Barry Irwin began in thoroughbred racing as a journalist for The
Blood-Horse *in 1969 and later wrote a column for* Daily Racing
Form. *He is a frequent op-ed contributor to industry publications
around the world. He is president of Team Valor International
racing stable and the author of* Derby Innovator: The Making of
Animal Kingdom.

The Problematic Character of the Case for Regulation of Steroids
Lewis Kurlantzick

The seemingly simple question of the proper treatment of steroid use in professional athletics is, in fact, highly complicated.
That complexity reflects a mix of controverted justifications,
enforcement mechanisms that implicate privacy interests and
feature an inverse relationship between expense and reliability, and historically untrustworthy national and international
enforcement authorities. (Recent years have provided ample
evidence of the undependable character of these bodies [Powell
2016, B7].)

At the core of the debate, though, is the matter of rationale. What are the justifications proffered for a ban on steroid
use? Probably most common is the "unnatural" performance-
enhancing quality of these substances. This rationale, apparently

simple, is, in fact, hardly free of difficulty. The problem is that over time the ingestion by athletes of a large range of supplements and "restorative" substances, the use of novel training methods and diets, and, of course, advances in equipment have all "enhanced" performance (Fost 1986, 5–6; Murray 1987, 11, 13). A difficulty lies in articulating a convincing distinction between these enhancers and steroids. If the claimed difference is rooted in a notion of naturalness, we presently have no convincing explanation of why some substances, including synthetic vitamins, are considered "natural" and others, including naturally occurring hormones, are considered "unnatural." This task of differentiation may be not only difficult but impossible, as the debates on this topic among philosophers of sport suggest that composition of a satisfying distinction between permissible and impermissible substances may be beyond our powers of conception and articulation (Carr 2008, 193, 194; Simon 2004, 72, 89). There appears to be no moral distinction between various natural and unnatural assists to performance. And the absence of such a distinction underlines the ambiguity of a moral evaluation of drug use (and of the meaning of our cultural notion about the "right" way to obtain success— through hard work).

A second justification rests on a concern for the athlete's health. Yet, assuming that accurate information is available and therefore ignorance of any physical risk of steroid use is not present, this rationale is problematic, at least for competent adults. Athletes are in a position to make a decision about what behavior is in their best interests, to weigh the risks and benefits according to their own values. And a paternalistic rule that attempts to prevent them from harming themselves runs counter to the important values of independence and personal choice. Moreover, it is likely that the feared harm is neither life threatening nor irreversible. Indeed, one might wonder about the disingenuousness of this justification in a universe where the risks of competing in the sport itself often far exceed the risks of the drugs causing concern. (Presumably, under this health rationale, if performance is enhanced by substances that cause neither short-term nor long-term harm to the athlete, these substances should not be banned.)

A third justification, though more intricate and less often voiced, is more promising. This justification is rooted in a concern for a form of "coercion" in the athlete's decision making and his or her inability to coordinate a response without outside intervention. If one person is perceived to have an advantage in using a drug, others may feel compelled to use it in an effort to try to stay even. That decision is not necessarily troubling, any more than the initial decision to engage in a risky sport. After all, the athlete can choose to forego the opportunity and any attendant risks. However, if a large percentage of participants in a particular sport would choose not to use steroids if left to their own independent decisions but feel pressured to use them in order to remain competitive with users, a case can be made for intervention in the form of a rule banning (or limiting) use. In light of the large number of potential users, the costs of contractually establishing an advance arrangement that would serve the collective interest of assurance of nonuse would be prohibitive. Thus, a rule here could be seen as a response to a problem of coordination that the interested parties cannot resolve themselves. Under this justification, the athletes' situation, then, can be seen as analogous to that of the fishermen who will "overfish" and excessively deplete the stock in the absence of a legal rule limiting the permitted catch. The coordination function, though, need not be effected by public intervention. Indeed, in the case of all major professional sports leagues, a private mechanism, the players' union, exists to effectuate the players' interests, and the union and management can adopt a rule by contract. But, of course, even if this justification is theoretically persuasive, there remains the empirical question of whether the assumption about participant attitudes is accurate.

A decision by owners and players to ban or limit the use of steroids might proceed from a quite different perspective, that of entertainment. That is, the parties are engaged in the joint sale of an entertainment product and consequently the views of their consumers are of critical concern to them. Hence, if present and potential fans are likely to change their preferences with respect to consumption of the sport in that absence of league action against steroid use, it would make sense simply as a matter of sound commercial judgment to take action to avoid this customer alienation. League action would be rooted in a practical concern about the financial implications of athletes with bad images. The rationale for this response, though, has nothing to do with concern for athletes' health, preservation of an "even" playing field, or a distinction between natural and unnatural substances. Rather, the decision to condition employment on abstention from use of steroids derives from a judgment about the marketing of the product.

There is reason to question the prevailing view in the sports community that performance-enhancing drugs are bad and that their use should be banned. Cogent criticisms of the arguments for prohibiting steroid use exist. Recognition of the incoherence of many of these claims and, more generally, that the moral foundations of drug testing in sports are suspect should inform decisions and beget caution about both establishment of testing schemes and the design and implementation of such schemes. Robert Simon has suggested that, assuming the lines of argument for or against the view that steroid use is immoral are inconclusive, sports authorities have reasonable grounds to impose a ban, and their decisions, if reached pursuant to a proper process, have normative force (Simon 2004, 86–88, 90). While this perspective has some merit, its persuasiveness is weakened in the not-uncommon situations where—unlike professional sports leagues—the athletes have no representation in the policy-making process that formulates (and executes) governing rules. The NCAA and the IOC are examples of this kind of structure.

Just as the normative justifications offered for a ban on the use of steroids are problematic, the empirical assumptions underlying the case for a ban are questionable. The legitimacy of these assumptions is simply taken for granted, when, in fact, their validity is dubious.

Take, for example, the efficacy of steroid use. The assumption is that such use generally produces significant, if not dramatic, effects on athletic performance, particularly in baseball. But that assumption is far from certain. In a *New York Times* op-ed piece, two respected professors reported the results of their statistical research on the question of whether performance-enhancing drugs improve performance in professional baseball (Cole and Stigler 2007, A25). Their examination of the data on the players featured in the Mitchell Report—pitchers and hitters—suggests that in most cases drugs had either little or a negative effect. While they were unable to test the possibility that one effect of drugs is to help players compensate for decline as they age, there was no evidence in the data for performance enhancement above previous levels. Noteworthy is the fact that these results, which run contrary to the prevailing wisdom, have not penetrated the universe of sports talk radio. In fact, skepticism about the impact of steroids is warranted. And the popular perception that slugging across baseball has increased during the "steroid era" is likely wrong.

Another assumption concerns the health effects of steroid use. Here, the premise is that drug consumption will necessarily produce adverse side effects resulting in serious, permanent—perhaps life-threatening—damage. Again, the health picture is more complicated. Despite oft-cited anecdotal reports, such as the self-diagnosis of ex–football player Lyle Alzado linking cancer and steroid use, the long-term, high-dose effects of steroid use are in fact largely unknown. Moreover, many health hazards of short-term effects are reversible. Also, most data on the long-term effects of anabolic steroids on humans come from case reports rather than formal epidemiological studies. And from these reports, the incidence of life-threatening effects appears to be low. Similarly, there is little evidence of a direct link between steroids and negative psychological effects. Despite popular reference to "roid rage," aggression, while a potentially serious effect of steroid use, appears to be relatively rare. My point is not that steroids have no harmful physical and psychological effects or that they have no performance-enhancing effects for some individuals, especially in individual sports. But rather the evidence for these effects and the contentions derived from them are far from clear. The need is to identify and evaluate the underlying assumptions.

References

Carr, Craig L. 2008. "Fairness and Performance Enhancement in Sport." *Journal of the Philosophy of Sport*. 35(2): 193–207.

Cole, Jonathan R., and Stephen M. Stigler. 2007, December 22. "More Juice, Less Punch." *The New York Times*. A25.

Fost, Norman. 1986. "Banning Drugs in Sports: A Skeptical View." *Hastings Center Report*. 16(4): 5–10.

Murray, Thomas H. 1987. "The Ethics of Drugs in Sport." In Richard H. Strauss, ed. *Drugs & Performance in Sports*. Philadelphia: W. B. Saunders.

Powell, Michael. 2016, December 9. "After Russia's Spree of Doping, A Time to Reform." *The New York Times*. B7.

Simon, Robert. 2004. *Fair Play: The Ethics of Sport*, 2nd ed. Boulder, CO: Westview Press.

Lewis Kurlantzick is the Zephaniah Swift professor of law emeritus at the University of Connecticut School of Law. A 1965 graduate of Wesleyan University, Professor Kurlantzick received his law degree in 1968 from Harvard, where he was a member of the Board of Editors of The Harvard Law Review. *He regularly teaches a seminar on sports and the law and writes on copyright and sports law issues for both popular and legal newspapers and journals.*

An Overview of Hormone Replacement Therapy for Transsexual Patients
Jessica Sideways

Few people in our modern society truly understand the process of transsexual transition, including the social, legal, and medical aspects. The purpose of this essay is to discuss one of the medical aspects of transition, known as hormone replacement therapy (or HRT). There are several benefits of HRT, allowing the patient to settle more easily into his or her target gender role. This process is achieved through simple medication that is already in use either for the hormone replacement therapy of cissexual patients (people who identify with the gender that they were assumed to be by way of their birth sex) or for other purposes. There are three ways that most transsexual people begin HRT. Two of these involve a primary care physician and one does not; that last one is obviously not recommended due to the high risk to the patient.

The question why people change their sex is often asked, but the answer is not clear cut. There is insufficient medical research as of yet to show that transsexualism is a neurological abnormality that occurs in utero thanks to a hormonal flush that influences the brain's development. However, what we do know is that people choose to change their sex when they feel that they cannot live comfortably or genuinely as a member of their birth sex. They do this because they feel frustrated that they are not being seen as who they see themselves as and understand that in order to live a more genuine life, they must transition. While many people over the last few decades have transitioned later in life, we are now seeing more people transition at younger ages and parents supporting their child's wishes to transition. HRT is one of the first steps to start on the path of medical transition and can be done at a younger age, unlike more serious medical interventions such as facial feminization surgery or sex reassignment surgery (SRS).

The benefits of HRT are a calmer state of mind and the development of secondary sex characteristics. While it may limit the development of secondary sex characteristics that are associated with the patient's birth sex, it cannot reverse the development of secondary sex characteristics. The secondary sex characteristics that are often developed include facial hair, breast development, and elongation of vocal chords (thus creating a deeper voice). Some other characteristics can be changed, such as emotions, body hair, fertility, sexual function, and physical strength/endurance. However, HRT can also cause a number of side effects, such as sensitivity to sun burns, dehydration, osteoporosis, stroke, blood clots, and cancer (breast and colon). This is the reason that persons interested in HRT should consult a physician, so that such side effects can be prevented or minimized.

HRT often involves hormones that are associated with the target gender. This would be estrogen (and possibly progesterone) for transsexual women and testosterone for transsexual men. Additionally, preoperative (or pre-op, meaning prior to SRS) patients will receive a chemical way to block their natural hormones until they can have sufficient SRS to block the natural hormone production (vaginoplasty or orchiectomy for transsexual women, hysterectomy for transsexual men) or, in the case of teenage patients, puberty blockers.

The first way someone can begin HRT is with a physician's prescription following an extreme form of psychotherapy. This extreme form is codified in the World Professional Association for Transsexual Health's Standards of Care (SOC). The SOC can be interpreted in a number of ways by a variety of psychotherapists and psychiatrists and allows the therapists to retract their recommendation for whatever reason. In my years of advising people on how to get HRT, I have heard horror stories of therapists abusing this privilege to coerce people to continue to see them. It is for this reason that I do not recommend this path because it exercises a great deal of control over people who do not need it. However, I definitely do recommend this path for those who may not be mentally stable enough to realize the gravity of such a decision.

The second way is a physician's prescription following light psychotherapy or counseling. There are modalities by which one can get hormone therapy with little to no psychotherapy. However, formal consent and education about the potential problems and effects of the treatments are undertaken so that physician liability is limited while making hormone therapy to be more accessible to the public. This is what I recommend for most people because it allows people who may not have an urgent need for psychotherapy to put the appropriate focus on their medical care. This path is often found in free or low-income medical clinics, and there are treatment modalities developed for this purpose, such as the Tom Waddell Health Clinic Protocols for Hormonal Reassignment of Gender, used by the staff at the Tom Waddell clinic in San Francisco, along with other clinics across the country. Additionally, this path is almost exclusively used even by physicians who would require the SOC in other cases if the patient has had SRS.

The third way is often called "self-medicating." This is achieved either by purchasing or stealing substances needed for proper hormone replacement therapy or other off-label methods of hormone replacement therapy. Off-label vehicles for hormone replacement therapy are either natural phytoes-trogens (which are estrogens that naturally occur in plants, including breast enhancement tablets, which have little to no lasting effects) or birth control. Self-medicating can also be achieved by ordering hormone therapy through online retailers abroad. In recent years, however, U.S. Customs and Border Protection have been putting the squeeze on anyone who has ordered from overseas pharmacies by intercepting packages from these pharmacies.

The reasons why self-medicating must be discouraged are varied. The first is that operating outside the care of a primary care physician means that the patient may not be getting a dose that is right for the patient. Furthermore, the patient is not being properly monitored with blood tests in order to catch and treat the side effects in a timely manner. The second is the illegality of it, as ordering from overseas pharmacies is illegal, even more so for female-to-male transsexual persons, whose hormone therapy often involves drugs that are considered a controlled substance. (Many forms of testosterone are listed as a Schedule III controlled substance, per the U.S. Drug Enforcement Administration.) The third is that using off-label or "natural" means for HRT may not be effective. There are many physicians and low-income or free clinics that, in an effort to help people avoid the risks of self-medication, allow people who are self-medicating to get under the care of a physician and have their hormone replacement therapy monitored and moderated by a physician.

So, hormone replacement therapy for transsexual patients is a very complex situation, and it is my hope that this essay has helped you to gain some understanding of the reasons why people transition from one gender to another, the effects of hormone replacement therapy, and the ways by which one can receive hormone replacement therapy.

Jessica Sideways is a 28-year-old postoperative transsexual woman with an associate's degree in web design and interactive media from the Art Institute of Colorado. She writes extensively on topics related to gender transformation.

The Politicization of Doping in Sports
Rick Sterling

Background

There is a long history of politics interfering with international sports. In 1979, the United States and Saudi Arabia supported radical "mujahadin" travelling to Afghanistan to overthrow the socialist government. Ultimately, this led to the Soviet Union's sending troops into Afghanistan in support of the Afghan government. To protest the Soviet intervention, the United States led a campaign to boycott the 1980 Moscow Summer Olympics. Four years later, the Soviet Union retaliated by leading a campaign to boycott the Los Angeles Olympics.

Current Geopolitical Situation

There is rising geopolitical conflict today. Since 2011, Saudi Arabia and the United States have supported an armed opposition seeking to overthrow the Syrian government. Russia has supported Syria diplomatically and more recently with air support. Adding to the international tension, the Ukrainian government was overthrown in February 2014 with U.S. involvement. That was followed by the secession of Crimea from Ukraine and "reunification" with Russia. In eastern Ukraine, the largely Russian-speaking population declared their opposition to the new Kiev government, leading to a bloody conflict. These events have led to increasing geopolitical tension between Russia (and allies China and Iran) and the West (including Turkey and the Gulf monarchies).

Accusations of Russian "State-Sponsored" Doping

As the coup took place in Ukraine, the 2014 Winter Olympics were happening in Sochi, Russia. At the time, there was no discussion of excess Russian doping or its being "state sponsored." Since then, the situation has changed dramatically.

- In December 2014, German TV showed a documentary *The Secrets of Doping: How Russia Makes Its Winners*. The documentary features interviews with Vitaliy and Yuliya Stepanov alleging that "all athletes" in Russia take performance-enhancing drugs (PEDs).
- In January 2015, the World Anti-Doping Agency (WADA) established an Independent Commission to look into the documentary's allegations.
- In November 2015, the WADA's Independent Commission released a 300-plus-page report claiming widespread use of

PEDs in Russian athletics. The report recommended the prohibition of numerous athletes, coaches, and trainers plus decertification of Moscow Laboratory.

- In December 2015, Russian authorities suspended or fired numerous officials, including Grigory Rodchenkov.
- On May 8, 2016, the American TV program *Sixty Minutes* broadcast a story about Russian doping based on testimony from Vitaliy and Yuliya Stepanov, now living in the United States. The following week, *The New York Times* published articles about Russian doping test manipulations based on the revelations of Rodchenkov, also living in the United States.
- Days later, WADA appointed Richard McLaren to investigate the media allegations.
- On July 16, three weeks before the start of the Rio Olympics, WADA published the McLaren report #1. McLaren acknowledged that the report was incomplete and "left much of the possible evidence unreviewed." The report was based on the testimony of the fired former Moscow laboratory director Grigory Rodchenkov. McLaren's report asserted there was a "state-dictated failsafe system" and that the "Ministry of Sport directed, controlled and oversaw the manipulation of athlete's analytical results or sample swapping."
- Before his report was published, McLaren spoke confidentially with leaders of the International Association of Athletics Federation (IAAF). On that basis, the IAAF banned Russian track-and-field athletes from the Rio Olympics. The International Olympic Committee decided to not ban all Russian athletes and instead advised each sport federation to decide on its own.
- On December 9, 2016, WADA published McLaren's final report along with an Evidence Disclosure Package. The conclusions were that over 1,000 Russian athletes were complicit or benefiting from an "institutional conspiracy" to violate and evade doping restrictions.

Big Accusations, Flimsy Evidence

The following problems underscore the need for a critical assessment of McLaren's conclusions.

1. McLaren's report says, "Over 1000 Russian athletes . . . can be identified as being involved in or benefiting from manipulations to conceal positive doping tests." The examination is ongoing but early results indicate the evidence is weak. For example, the International Biathlon Union recently evaluated McLaren's information and cleared 22 of 29 Russians who had been implicated. Investigation of the other seven continues. Even if all seven are ultimately found guilty, that means that 76 percent were not and suggests that McLaren's accusation of 1,000 complicit Russian athletes was hugely exaggerated.

2. This lack of evidence has now been acknowledged by WADA itself. On February 23, 2017, the International Olympic Committee reported "it was admitted by WADA that in many cases the evidence provided may not be sufficient to bring successful cases."

3. McLaren says there was an "institutional conspiracy" of athletes and officials within the Ministry of Sport and the FSB (Federal Security Service). However, he does not present supporting evidence. When this author contacted Richard McLaren asking where the evidence of the involvement of the Russian Ministry of Sports, FSB and RUSADA (the Russian Anti-Doping Agency) in the conspiracy is, he replied "The EDP [Evidence Disclosure Package] is divided into categories so you can locate the documents you are looking for" (Sterling 2017).

   The Evidence Disclosure Package contains 1,031 evidence documents. A chart assigns each document to 1 of 12 general categories. McLaren's major accusations do not reference a specific document. In effect, the Independent Person tells readers to find it for themselves. This is a very curious way to persuade or convince anyone. It raises the question whether the evidence is weak or non-existent. McLaren admits that there is "no direct evidence of ROC (Russian Olympic Committee) involvement in the conspiracy."

3. McLaren's bias is shown in his contradictory statements to the IAAF representative on June 14, 2016, as he encouraged their banning of all Russians from the Rio Olympics (EDP1163). In one paragraph, McLaren states: "I am satisfied that we have a level of evidence to establish that there was a state run manipulation of laboratory analytical results." In the next paragraph, he states, "I have to [emphasize] that this is a preliminary finding and we have limited cross verification."

4. One can fairly ask whether WADA's goal was to "protect clean athletes" or to punish and isolate Russia. Russian athletes preparing for the Rio Olympics were having their urine and blood samples analyzed at the WADA certified laboratory in London, England. The actions of the IAAF and IPC banning all Russians harmed clean Russian athletes and reduced attendance and was a major distraction for the Rio Olympics.

5. Western media have generally failed to examine the evidence or lack of it in McLaren's reports. On December 13, 2016, *The New York Times* editorial board wrote: "With Russia standing accused of meddling in American politics and in Syria and Ukraine, new revelations about Russian doping in sports might seem anti-climactic. Yet the mountain of new evidence laid out by Richard McLaren . . . is astounding." The doping manipulations by Director Rodchenkov have been known for two years and are not under dispute. The *Times* writers apparently did not bother to check if there is evidence of Russian government involvement for which there appears to be little or no evidence.

6. McLaren falsely claims his first report was not challenged. In fact, it was strongly criticized in the web publication

Sports Integrity Initiative and other publications. McLaren's unwillingness to seek or consider a response from the Russian side before publishing his first report was criticized for failing a basic standard of fairness.

7. Much of the "forensic evidence" in McLaren's final report is regarding the findings of the "scratches and marks expert" who could determine whether a urine sample bottle had been tampered with. Here again, the evidence is not very persuasive. Why did McLaren not obtain a cross-check from the Swiss company that manufactures the "tamper evident" bottles? Why is the expert anonymous? Was there any effort to authenticate his determinations? Otherwise, this evidence also requires a large leap of faith.

Where Is This Controversy Headed?

A key upcoming issue is how to remove politics, bias, and cheating from drug testing in sports. The International Olympic Committee is proposing to establish an independent organization that will be responsible for testing internationally instead of relying on each country to test their own athletes. Other forces are seeking to empower WADA to have more authority. The U.S. Congress is discussing the issue and considering to dramatically increase their funding of WADA. This would very likely increase the politicization of anti-doping control and management.

Some forces seek to further punish Russia by preventing them from hosting international sporting events and barring their athletes from upcoming events, including the 2018 Winter Olympics. Other forces are pushing against this, preferring to restore Russian participation.

Russian president Putin has recently offered an olive branch to WADA. While mentioning the shortcomings of the McLaren Report and saying there never was a "state sponsored" doping system, he acknowledges that there were violations and failures. He says these should be admitted and corrected in coordination with WADA guidelines.

The goal of the Olympic movement is to promote international friendship and peace. The politicization of doping in sports runs counter to this goal.

Reference

Sterling, Rick. 2017. "The Politicization of Doping in Sports." Global Research. https://www.globalresearch.ca/the-politicization-of-doping-in-sports/5582163. Accessed on October 6, 2017.

Rick Sterling is an investigative journalist. He can be reached at rsterling1@gmail.com.

Drug Testing High School Athletes and Fitness Trainers
Katinka van de Ven and Kyle Mulrooney

The recreational use of steroids and other image enhancing drugs (SIEDs) to enhance image and/or performance has been firmly recognized as a public health concern (McVeigh, et al. 2016). In a meta-analysis of 187 studies exploring the recreational use of SIEDs, an overall global lifetime prevalence of 3.3 percent, and a lifetime prevalence of 2.3 percent for high school students who use SIEDs, was found (Sagoe, et al. 2014). In addition, looking at fitness training–related groups, such as bodybuilders, we see much higher numbers, with prevalence rates in gyms as high as almost half of all members. While most countries focus on prevention and education to deal with this growing issue, a handful have taken the drastic step of introducing dope-testing programs in gyms (only EU countries) and high schools (mainly the United States).

In 2003, Belgium (in particular in Flanders) became the first country to introduce doping controls in gyms. In Belgium, recreational trainers, like elite athletes, are not allowed to use substances banned by the World Anti-Doping Agency's code and are also subject to the same sanctions. If a person tests positive and if it is a first offence, the national anti-doping agency may ban that person for two years from every gym and any form of organized sport. The person may also receive a fine of, on average, 1,000–2,000 euros ($1,060–2,120), although fines can be as high as 25,000 euros ($26,600). In addition, the police are able to conduct a home search based on a positive test, and a trainer may therefore face both a doping and a drug investigation for the same offence. Other EU countries that have adopted dope-testing programs in gyms include Denmark, Norway, and Sweden.

With regard to testing in high schools, in 2006, New Jersey became the first state in the United States to require steroid testing for high school athletes. While three states (Florida, Illinois, and Texas) have followed suit, the only other state that currently also has a statewide steroid-testing program is Illinois. As a result of the program, any person who tests positive or who refuses to provide a testing sample in these two states will be banned from participating in competitions for a one-year period and any individual honor earned while in violation will be forfeited. In addition, the student must undergo counseling, or successfully complete an educational program, and must produce a negative test result before being allowed to compete again. However, this is not just a U.S. phenomenon; since 2014, high school students in South Africa are likewise tested for performance-enhancing drugs and face similar sanctions for positive tests.

There are several reasons why these steroid-testing schemes have been implemented in gyms and high schools: firstly, because the use of SIEDs can potentially lead to adverse health effects, in particular in young people; secondly, in the case of high school athletes, SIED use can give users an unfair advantage over their competition and is therefore considered "cheating." This argument in principle does not apply for fitness trainers as most train for recreational and not competitive purposes. Therefore, to mitigate health risks and clamp down on "cheating," it is argued that testing for steroids helps deter use among high school students and fitness trainers. Other scholars have critically discussed anti-doping in the name of health and a "level playing field" (e.g., Mauron, et al. 2007). Here, we briefly consider how effective these controls are in deterring SIED use.

Aside from privacy and human rights issues, such as undressing in front of a doping officer and the disproportionate targeting of certain groups (so-called muscle profiling), research shows that doping tests in gyms may be ineffective at preventing or reducing doping substance use (Van de Ven 2016). Rather, there are possible unintended outcomes that may increase health risks. For instance, users may opt to train in basements, stop training altogether, displace to other countries with no controls, or undertake more dangerous doping practices to avoid a positive test. Indeed, drug testing in high schools appears to have a limited effect in preventing students from trying doping substances (Bahrke 2015). For example, one study found that a high school drug-testing program known as SATURN not only had a limited effect on prevention and reduction but also increased risk factors for future substance abuse (Backhouse, et al. 2014).

While doping tests appear to have little deterrent effect, they are also very expensive. For these reasons—both the ineffectiveness and the costs—Texas and Florida dropped their steroid-testing programs. For example, without even accounting for procedural costs such as transportation and labor, it is estimated that one test in the United States costs at least $100. Furthermore, the per-positive-result cost of the testing program is estimated to be $250,000. In the case of Texas, during the eight years the program was implemented, the state's initial six-million-dollar investment paid for 19,000 tests, which resulted in only nine positive results (less than 0.05 percent). The legitimacy of drug-testing programs in high schools and gyms and its supposed deterrent effects are therefore highly questionable.

Nevertheless, it has become clear that (young) people are increasingly using SIEDs outside of elite sports—an issue that needs to be addressed. As such, attention should be paid to methods that have proved to be successful in addressing the use of SIEDs within the general population, such as education and harm reduction. In relation to high school athletes, research has shown that anti-doping education programs, such as the Athletes Training and Learning to Avoid Steroids program, are effective in preventing doping substance use, particularly when combined with practical strength training (Backhouse, et al. 2014). However, additional measures need to be put in place for recreational users who currently are unwilling or unable to halt their SIED consumption in an effort to minimize harms. For example, in several countries, individuals who inject steroids are a growing population in needle and syringe programs and in some clinics even represent the biggest client group.

Dope-testing of high school athletes and fitness trainers is invasive and expensive and has limited effects and therefore seems to be a fruitless investment. Efforts to curb SIED use need to be led by the evidence surrounding "what works," which currently suggests promising outcomes for prevention programs combined with practical strength training and initiatives that seek to reduce harms associated with SIED use, including empowering users to make informed decisions through education.

References

Backhouse, S. H., et al. 2014. "Study on Doping Prevention: A Map of Legal Regulatory and Prevention Practice Provisions in EU 28." http://ec.europa.eu/assets/eac/sport/news/2014/docs/doping-prevention-report_en.pdf. Accessed on February 12, 2017.

Bahrke, M. S. 2015. "Drug Testing US Student-Athletes for Performance-Enhancing Substance Misuse: A Flawed Process." *Substance Use & Misuse*. 50(8–9): 1144–1147.

Mauron, Alexandre, Bengt Kayser, and Andy Miah. 2007. "Current Anti-doping Policy: A Critical Appraisal." *BMC Medical Ethics*. 8(1): 1–10.

McVeigh, Jim, et al. 2016. "Harm Reduction Interventions Should Encompass People Who Inject Image and Performance Enhancing Drugs." *BMJ*. 353: 1189.

Sagoe, Dominic, et al. 2014. "The Global Epidemiology of Anabolic-androgenic Steroid Use: A Meta-Analysis and Meta-Regression Analysis." *Annals of Epidemiology*. 24(5): 383–389.

Van de Ven, Katinka. 2016. "Blurred Lines: Anti-Doping, Domestic Policies and the Performance and Image Enhancing Drug (PIED) Market in Belgium and the Netherlands." *Performance Enhancement & Health*. 4(3): 94–102.

Dr. Katinka van de Ven is a research fellow at the National Drug and Alcohol Research Centre, University of New South Wales, and Kyle Mulrooney is a doctoral fellow at the University of Kent and Universität Hamburg. Kyle and Katinka are the founders of the Human Enhancement Drug Network.

Introduction

This chapter contains brief sketches of individuals and organizations that are important in understanding the history of performance-enhancing drugs in the United States and around the world. The number of such individuals and organizations is legion, and only some especially significant organizations and individuals, or those typical of other organizations and individuals, are included.

Patrick Arnold (1966–)

Arnold is an organic chemist best known for his synthesis of a number of synthetic anabolic steroids, including tetrahydrogestrinone (THG; also known as "The Clear"), norbolethone, and desoxymethyltestosterone (DMT). He also introduced to the United States and the sports world other testosterone-like steroids with strong anabolic effects: androstenedione, 1-androstenediol, and methylhexanamine. At the time, the chemicals that Arnold synthesized and popularized were not on the list of substances prohibited for use by athletes by any major sports organization. Those substances were, however,

BALCO founder Victor Conte holds up one of the nutritional supplements he sells, at his office in Burlingame, CA, October 21, 2003. Conte served a four-month prison sentence for orchestrating an illegal steroids distribution scheme that reportedly involved Barry Bonds and Jason Giambi. (AP Photo/Paul Sakuma)

later added to such lists. During the 1990s, he collaborated with the drug "guru" Dan Duchaine to promote the use of these drugs among bodybuilders, weight lifters, and amateur and professional athletes from many sports. He was also very much involved in the synthesis, production, and distribution of testosterone analogs through the Bay Area Laboratory Co-operative (BALCO). In 2006, Arnold was convicted of conspiracy to distribute illegal anabolic steroids and sentenced to three months in prison and three months of house arrest. At his sentencing, U.S. district judge Susan Illston told Arnold: "It's a really destructive path you've been on, and a very serious crime you've committed." Arnold responded: "I'm very regretful for what I've done and especially what it has precipitated in sports and society. Now, more than ever, I'm very much against sports doping. I do believe there should be a level playing field, and this whole thing needs to be addressed."

Patrick Arnold was born in 1966 in Guilford, Connecticut, into a middle-class home. His mother was a high school teacher and his father a professor of industrial engineering active in Democratic politics. He became interested in bodybuilding at the age of 11 when his grandfather gave him a set of weights, with which he started working out. He was introduced to anabolic steroids when he received a shot as treatment for his attention deficit disorder condition that had caused him to drop out of the University of New Haven (UNH) after his freshman year. He found that he quickly added substantial muscle to his body, an important benefit in the construction job that he had taken after leaving UNH. Intrigued by the potential benefits of these chemicals, Arnold decided to return to UNH, from which he eventually received his BS degree in chemistry in 1990.

After completing his college degree, Arnold took a number of jobs, none of which seemed to suit his background and expectations. He maintained his interest in steroids, however, taking classes at the University of Connecticut and Montclair State College (now Montclair State University). During this time, he also became a regular contributor to an Internet news group called misc.fitness.weights, through which he came to know Dan Duchaine, then known as the guru of steroids. Duchaine helped connect Arnold with others interested in the development and sale of anabolic androgenic steroids (AASs), including Bill Phillips, at Experimental and Applied Sciences, and Stan Antosh, founder and owner of Osmo Therapeutics, in San Francisco. The connection between Arnold and Phillips went nowhere, but Antosh offered Arnold a job with Osmo with the provision that any discovery Arnold made would be shared with the company for development and distribution. Antosh also convinced Arnold to do his research at a small pharmaceutical company, Bar North America, in Seymour, Illinois. The rural setting provided the privacy and solitude that Arnold needed to do the literature searches and laboratory experiments needed to uncover and develop a variety of new testosterone-like compounds.

Arnold made his first breakthrough in 1996, when he came across a scientific paper on androstenedione, a steroid that had proved to have excellent anabolic properties but had never been developed commercially. (Androstenedione eventually became popular under the common name of Andro.) He obtained samples of the substance from a manufacturer in China and presented his discovery to Antosh. The product soon proved its value when St. Louis Cardinals star Mark McGwire began using the product. Five years later, Arnold came through with another successful product, 1-androstenediol. Both androstenedione and 1-androstenediol are prohormones, compounds that are not hormones themselves but that are converted in the body to testosterone or a testosterone-like hormone.

The focus of Arnold's research changed in 2005 when all of the prohormones that he had introduced and developed were added to the prohibited list under amendments to the Controlled Substances Act of 1970 (CSA). Instead, he began to search for new substances that were not included under the CSA's prohibited list and, most important, could not be detected by existing drug tests. The most important of those new discoveries were the drugs norbolethone and THG, which he provided to BALCO for retail sales. It was largely his involvement with BALCO that eventually led to his arrest and conviction for the distribution of illegal substances in 2006.

After settling in Seymour in 1996, Arnold arranged to establish a new company, LPJ Research, in conjunction with the owner of Bar North America, Ramlakhan Boodram. In 2003, the owners changed the name of the company to Proviant Technologies. The company markets nutritional supplements under the name of ErgoPharm. In 2009, Arnold left Proviant to create his own company, which supplies AAS-type products under the names of E-Pharm and Prototype Nutrition. On the Prototype Nutrition website, Arnold summarizes his career in the development of performance-enhancing drugs and concludes with the observation that "[h]e continues to be perhaps the number one driving force in the advancement of performance enhancing nutritional supplementation."

Joe Biden (1942–)

Joe Biden was coauthor (with Senator Strom Thurmond [R-SC]) of the Crime Control Act of 1990, Title XIX of which was the Anabolic Steroids Control Act of 1990. That Act placed anabolic steroids on Schedule III of the CSA, meaning that they could be prescribed, dispensed, and distributed for therapeutic purposes only. The Act essentially outlawed the use of anabolic steroids for many of the purposes for which they have become so popular among bodybuilders, weight lifters, and other amateur and professional athletes. A decade later, Biden coauthored (with senator Orin Hatch [R-UT]) an extension of the 1990 Act, the Anabolic Steroids Control Act of 2004, which extended the listing of prohormones and other synthetic AASs under Schedule III of the CSA.

Both pieces of legislation were very popular in both houses of Congress and among the general public. They were each proposed at times when news of the use of AAS by amateur and professional athletes had become major stories that resulted in the downfall in the public esteem of stars such as Marion Jones and Ben Johnson in track and field, Lyle Alzado and Bill Romanowski in professional football, Floyd Landis in professional cycling, and Mark McGwire and Barry Bonds in professional baseball. Most observers at the time and since have argued that no politician (or very few politicians) could have taken a strong stand against steroid legislation at the time it was proposed by Biden and his colleagues. Indeed, some observers have suggested that Biden undertook the campaign against steroid use at least in part because of a failed nomination campaign for president of the United States with the Democratic Party in 1988.

Joseph Robinette Biden, Jr., was born in Scranton, Pennsylvania, on November 20, 1942. He was the first of four children born to Joseph R. Biden, Sr., and Catherine Eugenia Finnegan Biden. A 2008 *New York Times* article described Joseph, Sr., as someone who had "had it all" in the 1920s, "sailing yachts off the New England coast, riding to the hounds, driving fast cars, flying airplanes." As a result of "drunken, faithless bosses and a thieving partner," the senior Biden eventually found himself out of work and virtually destitute. When Joseph, Jr., was 10, his family moved to Claymont, Delaware, where his father found work as a used-car salesman. There he attended Archmere Academy, from which he graduated in 1961. He then matriculated at the University of Delaware, in Newark, where he majored in history and political science. He then continued his education at the Syracuse University College of Law, where he received his JD degree in 1968. He is reputed not to have been a particularly remarkable student at either institution, finishing 506th in his class of 688 at Delaware and 76th out of 85 at Syracuse.

After graduating from Syracuse, Biden returned to Delaware, where he worked first as a public defender before organizing his own law firm, Biden and Walsh, in 1969. In a relatively short period of time, Biden found that he was more interested in politics than in the legal profession, and he ran for the New Castle County Council in 1970. He was elected and served for two years on the council, while still retaining his law practice. In 1972, Biden decided to run against sitting U.S. senator J. Caleb Boggs, a long-serving Republican from Delaware. He started his campaign with virtually no name recognition, funding, or staff. At one point in the campaign, the 29-year-old Biden trailed the popular Boggs by more than 30 points. He continued to work for his election, however, and in November 1972 won a startling upset victory with 116,006 votes (50.48 percent of the total) to Boggs's 112,844 votes (49.10 percent).

Less than six weeks after his reelection, Biden's wife and 1-year-old daughter were killed in an automobile accident in Hockessin, Delaware. His two young sons were also critically injured in the accident. This terrible event caused Biden to reconsider his potential career in the U.S. Senate but was eventually dissuaded from resigning his seat by Senate majority leader Mike Mansfield.

Biden was reelected six more times to the U.S. Senate, in 1978, 1984, 1990, 1996, 2002, and 2008. His two primary interests in the Senate have been (1) the Judiciary Committee, of which he was chairman from 1987 until 1995 and ranking minority member from 1981 until 1987 and from 1995 until 1997 and (2) the Foreign Relations Committee, which he chaired from 2001 until 2003 and again from 2007 until 2008. In mid-2008, Biden was chosen by Democratic presidential nominee Barack Obama to serve as his vice presidential candidate. The Obama-Biden slate won the 2008 election and was reelected in 2012.

Barry Bonds (1964–)

Bonds is widely regarded as one of the finest baseball players in the history of the sport. He holds a number of records, including the most home runs in a lifetime (762) and the most home runs in a single year (73 in 2001). He also holds the record for the most walks (2,558) and the most intentional walks (688) in a career. His skills have been recognized by his selection as the Most Valuable Player in Major League Baseball a record seven times and his receiving the Golden Glove award (for being the best defensive player at his position) on eight occasions. He was selected to play in Major League Baseball's All-Star Game on 14 occasions. His lifetime batting average is .298, and he stole 514 bases in his career. His career statistics have been somewhat diminished by his arrest and conviction in 2011 on charges of obstruction of justice in connection with the illegal use of anabolic steroids reputedly provided by the BALCO drug-testing laboratory in San Francisco.

Barry Lamar Bonds was born on July 24, 1964, in Riverside, California, to Bobby Lee Bonds, a renowned professional baseball player in his own right, and Patricia Howard Bonds. He grew up in San Carlos, California, and attended Junipero Serra High School, where he excelled in three sports: football, basketball, and baseball. After graduating from high school, Bonds was drafted by the San Francisco Giants professional baseball team, but he was unable to come to terms with the team and decided to go to college instead. He matriculated at Arizona State University (ASU) in 1983, planning to major in physical education. He continued to star in baseball at ASU, with a three-year batting average of .347 and a number of honors for his play in the PAC-10 conference, the College World Series, and other venues. In 1985, the Pittsburgh Pirates major league baseball team drafted Bonds again. This time he agreed to terms offered by the Pirates, and he joined the team in 1986 for his first season in Major League Baseball. Bonds played for seven seasons with the Pirates, winning his first Most Valuable Player award in 1990, followed by repeats in 1992 and 1993. Bonds became a free agent in 1993 and signed a six-year, $43.75 million contract with the San Francisco Giants, with whom he remained until he retired from professional baseball in 2007. He set most of his Major League Baseball records with the Giants, including a record-setting string of four Most Valuable Player awards in 2001–2004.

Allegations that Bonds might have used anabolic steroids to improve his body muscle mass and strength began to appear in 2003. His trainer since 2000, Greg Anderson, worked out of a gym that was two blocks from the offices of the BALCO in Burlingame, California. When agents of the U.S. Food and Drug Administration (FDA) raided BALCO's offices in September 2003, questions were raised as to the possible involvement of Anderson and Bonds in the use of anabolic steroids. An important basis for those questions was the significant increase in Bonds's physical appearance during the previous decade, when he had increased his weight from 185 pounds in 1991 to 228 pounds in 2001. Bonds claimed that his improvement in body size and strength was the result of conditioning and improved nutrition, but a number of observers suspected that other factors might also have been involved, including drug use.

In a testimony before a grand jury in December 2003, Bonds admitted to using nutritional supplements supplied to him by Anderson but said that they were only natural treatments for his arthritis. The cases against four individuals involved in the BALCO investigation brought by the grand jury were eventually dismissed in early 2005 in an action that included provisions for keeping private the names of any sports figures who may have used drugs supplied by the company. In April 2006, Bonds was in the news again when federal investigators announced that they were going to prosecute him for lying in his grand jury testimony of December 2003. That effort reached its climax in November 2007 when a federal grand jury indicted Bonds for lying in that testimony. Bonds pleaded not guilty to these charges, and, after a number of delays, a trial was held on the matter on March 21, 2011. Three weeks later, a jury found Bonds guilty of obstruction of justice. On December 15, 2011, U.S. district judge Susan Illston sentenced Bonds to 30 days of house arrest, 2 years of probation, and 250 hours of community service. On May 3, 2012, Bonds's attorney filed a brief asking the 9th U.S. Circuit Court of Appeals to vacate Justice Illston's sentence based on the fact that Bonds's original testimony was "rambling and irrelevant," even if "truthful" to the grand jury. Bonds's conviction was eventually overturned on April 22, 2015, by the U.S. Court of Appeals for the Ninth District by a vote of 10 to 1.

In 2012, Bonds announced to the press that he was interested in returning to Major League Baseball again, perhaps in the role of batting coach for the Giants. Observers met that announcement with mixed emotions, acknowledging that Bonds had a great deal of knowledge and experience to share with young players but that he still had a cloud of doubt about drug use lying over his long and very successful career. In any case, Bonds did achieve his goal in 2016, when he served as hitting coach, not for the Giants but for the Miami Marlins. He was not rehired for the 2017 season.

Charles Brown-Séquard (1817–1894)

Brown-Séquard was a physiologist and neurologist who is perhaps best known today for his research on the nervous system and his discovery of the function of the adrenal glands. His name remains a part of the medical literature as a medical condition known as *Brown-Séquard syndrome*, also called *Brown-Séquard's hemiplegia* or *Brown-Séquard's paralysis*. The condition occurs as the result of damage to the spinal cord that results in a loss of sensation and motor function in the extremities.

In the history of anabolic steroids, Brown-Séquard is also known for a series of experiments that he conducted rather late in life to determine whether he could restore some of the normal bodily functions that he had lost as a result of the process of aging. In these experiments, he injected himself with extracts taken from the testicles of guinea pigs and dogs. He discovered that this treatment produced a "radical change" that renewed his body strength and intellectual vigor. Some historians doubt that Brown-Séquard actually conducted the experiments that he described, that the observed effects actually occurred, or that the effects were the result of the injections. In any case, word of Brown-Séquard's experiments rapidly spread through the medical world and was put to practical use on behalf of many aging men around the world who were seeking a "remedy" for the old age that was robbing them of their physical and intellectual powers. Materials like those produced by Brown-Séquard became commonly known as the Elixir of Life. Countless numbers of charlatans, as well as many well-meaning medical men, made small fortunes in selling these materials to their patients and customers.

Charles Édouard Brown-Séquard (also Charles Edward Brown-Séquard) was born in Port Louis, Mauritius, on April 8, 1817. His father, Charles Edward Brown, was an American naval officer from Philadelphia of Irish heritage and his mother was Charlotte Séquard, of French birth and a native of the island of Mauritius. Captain Brown lost his life at sea shortly after his son's birth. He was in command of a ship delivering provisions to Mauritius, which was undergoing famine at the time. Under the circumstances, young Charles grew up under his mother's care under modest circumstances. He obtained his early education at a private school in Port Louis, where he was also in charge of two small circulating libraries. In 1838, he traveled to Paris with hopes of becoming a writer. When he made little progress in that direction, he turned his attention to medicine, a field in which he earned his bachelor of letters diploma in 1838 and his bachelor of science diploma in 1839 from the University of France and his medical degree in 1846 from the medical faculty of the University of France. While studying for his medical degree, he also taught natural history, chemistry, natural philosophy, and physiology.

Brown-Séquard's doctoral thesis was entitled "Vital Properties and Functions of the Spinal Cord," a topic that was to occupy his interest for many years following his graduation. He soon discovered that medical research was of at least as much interest to him as was patient care, and he attached himself to some of the best researchers in the field then working in Paris. In the years following his graduation, he published a series of papers describing the condition now known as Brown-Séquard syndrome, outlining the consequences of severing the spinal cord at various locations on sensory function at various parts of the body.

Brown-Séquard's living and working conditions in Paris were far from satisfactory. He is said to have carried out most of his experiments in his own small and cramped apartment, where he also kept his experimental animals. Finally, in 1852, he decided that he could not make a living in France, and he left for the United States. There, he survived by teaching French, giving lectures, and, according to one biographer, "delivering babies at cut-rate prices." Even an appointment at the Medical College of Virginia (which lasted only four months) was not enough to keep him in the United States, however. With his new wife, Ellen, he returned to Paris, and then traveled on to Port Louis, when conditions in France were no better than they had ever been.

In fact, Brown-Séquard spent most of the rest of his life traveling from place to place, trying to find a site at which he could settle down and focus on his medical research. He always seemed to end up in Paris, where he lived and worked from 1847 to 1850, in 1855, from 1857 to 1859, in 1865, from 1869 to 1873, and, finally, from 1878 to his death in 1894. Sandwiched in between these stays in France, he also taught at the Royal College of Surgeons in London in 1858 and worked as a physician at the National Hospital for the Paralysed and Epileptics, in London, from 1860 to 1863. In 1864, he was offered the chair of physiology and pathology at the Harvard Medical School, an appointment he held until 1867. In 1873, he moved from Paris to New York, where he established a private practice. Finally, in 1878, Brown-Séquard received a job offer with the promise of a permanent position to his liking, the post of professor of experimental medicine at the Collège de France, in Paris. In that post, he replaced one of the world's greatest medical experimentalists of the time, Claude Bernard. Brown-Séquard held that appointment until his death on April 2, 1894, in Sceaux, France.

Brown-Séquard received awards from the French Academy of Science on five separate occasions and twice from the British government. He was elected to the National Academy of Sciences in 1868 and to the Royal College of Physicians of London in 1860. He was the founder and editor of three important journals in medicine: *Journal de la physiologie de l'homme et des animaux*, *Archives de physiologie normale et pathologique*, and *Archives of Scientific and Practical Medicine*.

Adolf Butenandt (1903–1995)

"One can say that he was always a 'first.'" That accolade was suggested by one of Butenandt's good friends and coworkers upon his death in 1995. He was the first person to isolate a number of sex hormones, the first person to discover the action of genes in the production of hormones, the first person to isolate an insect hormone, and the first person to isolate and study a pheromone. He was awarded a share of the 1939 Nobel Prize in Chemistry for the first of these achievements and for his work on sex hormones in general.

Adolf Friedrich Johann Butenandt was born in the town of Lehe, a section of Bremerhaven, Germany, on March 24, 1903. He was the second son of Otto Louis Max Butenandt, a businessman, and his wife, Wilhelmina Thomfohrde Butenandt. He attended the Bremerton Oberrealschule for his secondary education before enrolling at the University of Marburg in 1921, where he majored in biology and chemistry. Before graduating, he transferred to the University of Göttingen, where his most influential teacher was Adolf Windhaus, who had won the 1928 Nobel Prize in Chemistry for his research on sterols. Sterols are a family of organic compounds that consist of a characteristic four-ring structure to which is attached at least one hydroxyl (—OH) group. Butenandt was awarded his

Ph.D. in biochemistry in 1927 for research on a compound found in insecticides.

After earning his degree, Butenandt remained at Göttingen to complete his habilitation. (Habilitation is a characteristic European type of study that involves original research and writing of a thesis beyond the level normally presented for awarding of the doctoral degree.) He then took the post of professor of organic chemistry at the Danzig Institute of Technology, where he remained until 1936. Butenandt left Danzig in 1936 to become director of the Kaiser Wilhelm Institute for Biochemistry (later the Max Planck Institute for Biochemistry) in Berlin. When the institute was moved to Tübingen in 1945 because of air raids on Berlin, he also assumed the post of professor of physiological chemistry at the University of Tübingen; when the institute was moved once again in 1956 to Münich, he also was named professor of physiological chemistry at the University of Münich. He retired from his post at Münich in 1971. For an extended period of time, from 1960 to 1972, Butenandt served as president of the Max Planck Society for the Advancement of Science, the most powerful and famous research institution in Germany.

Butenandt's first scientific breakthrough came in 1929, when he announced the discovery of the female sex hormone estrone (also, oestrone). He followed up that discovery with the announcement of a comparable male sex hormone, androsterone, in 1931, and another female sex hormone, progesterone, in 1934. Butenandt and Leopold Ruzicka, cowinner of the 1939 Nobel Prize in Chemistry, independently isolated the primary male sex hormone testosterone in 1935, after which they were successful in synthesizing both estrogen and testosterone. After the war, Butenandt continued his work on hormones, isolating the first insect hormone, ecdysone, in 1954. Ecdysone is the hormone responsible for the transformation of a caterpillar into a butterfly. In 1959, Butenandt also discovered the first hormone used by insects as a sexual attractant, a substance known as a *pheromone*. He named that substance *bombykol*.

Prior to and during the war, Butenandt was a member of the Nazi party, an affiliation for which he was severely criticized by many colleagues outside of (and some within) Germany. His membership in the party did not allow him to travel to Stockholm to receive his Nobel Prize in 1938, nor to accept an earlier invitation from Harvard University to join its faculty in 1935. He did, however, use his membership to justify and support requests for funding for some wartime research projects that he defended as being critical to the war's success. Butenandt died in Münich on January 18, 1995.

Butenandt received many honors and awards throughout his lifetime. In addition to the Nobel Prize, he was awarded the Gold Cross for Federal Services of West Germany and the gold and silver Adolf von Harnack medals of the Max Planck Association for the Advancement of Science. In addition, he was awarded honorary doctoral degrees by the universities of Graz, Leeds, Madrid, Münich, and Tübingen, as well as Cambridge University. He was also elected as a corresponding or honorary member of the Academy of Sciences at Göttingen, Royal Society of London, New York Academy of Sciences, Japanese Biochemical Society, Deutsche Akademie der Naturforscher Leopoldina at Halle, and Austrian Academy of Sciences. In his honor, the University of Münich named its molecular biology unit the Adolf Butenandt Institut Molekularbiologie. In 1969, Butenandt was also named a commander of the Legion of Honor of France.

Jose Canseco (1964–)

Canseco was a Major League Baseball player from 1985 to 2001, during which time he set a number of records and won many accolades as one of the leading players of his time. He was chosen American League Rookie of the Year in 1986, American League Most Valuable Player in 1988, and American League Comeback Player of the Year in 1994. He was named to the All Star game on six occasions and played for seven different major league teams during his career, the Oakland Athletics, Texas Rangers, Boston Red Sox, Toronto Blue Jays, Tampa Bay Devil Rays, New York Yankees, and Chicago White Sox. In 2005, he published his autobiography, *Juiced: Wild Times, Rampant 'Roids, Smash Hits & How Baseball Got Big*, in which he described his own use of anabolic steroids and suggested that as many as 85 percent of all Major League Baseball players had also used AAS at some time in their career. Among the players he named as steroid users were stars such as Jason Giambi, Juan González, Mark McGwire, Rafael Palmeiro, and Iván Rodríguez. Over time, some of the individuals named by Canseco admitted to steroid use, while others have continued to deny that they were ever involved in drug use.

José Canseco Capas, Jr., and his twin brother, Osvaldo (Ozzie), were born on July 2, 1964, in Havana, Cuba, to José Canseco, an oil company executive, and his wife, Barbara. In 1965, the Cansecos received permission to leave Cuba and moved to Opa-Locka, Florida. There, the Canseco boys attended Coral Park High School, where they both played baseball. After completing high school, both Canseco boys were drafted by Major League Baseball teams, Ozzie by the New York Yankees and José by the Oakland Athletics. José made his major league debut at the end of the 1985 season in a game against the Baltimore Orioles and by the next year had improved to the point of being named the American League Rookie of the Year. His peak year came in 1988, when he batted .307, hit 42 home runs, had 124 runs batted in, and stole 40 bases, the first Major League Baseball player in history to register a "40–40" year.

In 1992, he was traded to the Texas Rangers, where he played for three years, before moving on to a number of other teams, with whom he never stayed for more than two years (Boston). He spent the 2000 season with Tampa Bay and the Yankees, before completing his major league career with Chicago in 2001. Since leaving Major League Baseball, Canseco has pursued a number of athletic careers, including a single mixed martial arts contest (which he lost), a brief prize fighting career, and short stints with six minor league baseball teams. Among the most recent of those contracts was with the Quintana Roo Tigers of the Mexican League in 2012, which ended when Canseco declined to take a drug test for testosterone. In 2007, the first year he was eligible, Canseco received six votes for Baseball's Hall of Fame, disqualifying him from being listed on the Hall of Fame ballot vote by sportscasters for future years. (He could still be elected by the Hall's Committee of Baseball Veterans, although, as of late 2017, that action has not occurred.)

Canseco has always been an outgoing individual, somewhat interested in promoting himself to the general public. He has appeared on a variety of television and radio programs, including *The Simpsons*, *60 Minutes*, *The Late Show with David Letterman*, *The Howard Stern Show*, and *The Celebrity Appearance*. He has been troubled by a number of run-ins with the law, including an arrest for reckless driving in 1989, an arrest for carrying a loaded handgun in his car in 1989, a charge of aggravated battery for a dispute with his then-wife in 1992, an arrest for battery on his second wife in 1997, an arrest for violating his parole agreement for using steroids in 2003, and an arrest for bringing an illegal drug into the United States from Mexico in 2008.

In recent years, Canseco has appeared with (or at least signed a contract with) a variety of professional and amateur baseball teams, including the Worcester Tornadoes (2012), Fort Worth Cats (2013), Valley Rays (2011), and Rio Grande Valley White Wings (2012).

Don Catlin (1938–)

Catlin has sometimes been called the father of drug testing in sports. In 1981, the International Olympic Committee (IOC) asked Catlin to be in charge of drug testing for the 1984 Olympic Games to be held in Los Angeles. At the time, Catlin was a member of the faculty at the University of California at Los Angeles (UCLA) School of Medicine. He had spent most of his professional career on issues related to drug abuse, so he seemed the ideal candidate for the job. At first, he declined the IOC offer, but later changed his mind when he realized that the university would be allowed to keep the drug-testing equipment. He continued his affiliation with the IOC for two decades while retaining his academic position in the UCLA Department of Molecular and Medical Pharmacology. He left UCLA and resigned from his IOC position in 2005 to open his own business, Anti-Doping Research, Inc. (ADRI), in Los Angeles.

Don Hardt Catlin was born on June 4, 1938, in New Haven, Connecticut, to Kenneth Catlin, an insurance executive, and Hilda Catlin, a homemaker. He attended Yale University, from which he received his bachelor's degree in psychology and statistics in 1960. He then continued his studies at the University of Rochester Medical School, from which he received his MD in 1965. After completing his residency and internship, Catlin enlisted in the U.S. Army and was assigned to the Walter Reed Army Medical Center, in Washington, D.C. He very soon became interested in the problem of drug addiction, to a large extent because of the problem posed by military men and women returning from duty in Vietnam who had become addicted to one or another illegal substance. He later said that he had a running battle with superior officers who preferred simply to imprison such individuals rather than offering them medical care, as Catlin preferred and continued to recommend.

In 1972, Catlin resigned his commission in the army and accepted a position as assistant professor at the UCLA School of Medicine in the Department of Pharmacology. He was later promoted associate professor and full professor at UCLA. After his retirement from UCLA, Catlin was named professor emeritus of molecular and medical pharmacology at UCLA.

When Catlin accepted the IOC's offer to conduct drug tests for the 1982 Olympics, the whole course of his professional

career changed. He spent the better part of the next two decades carrying out drug tests, not only for the IOC but also for
groups such as the U.S. Olympic Committee (USOC; since
1985); the National Collegiate Athletic Association (NCAA;
since 1986); National Football League (NFL; since 1990); National Center for Drug Free Sport, which runs the drug-testing
program for the NCAA (since 1999); the U.S. Anti-Doping
Agency (USADA), which runs the USOC anti-doping program (since 2000); and Minor League Baseball (since 2004).
His team's responsibilities include testing for illicit drugs and
providing education to athletes, coaches, sporting organizations, and other groups about the risks of illegal substances.

Over the years, an increasingly important part of Catlin's
work has been the isolation and identification of designer
drugs. Designer drugs are analogs of natural and/or known
synthetic drugs that are synthesized to produce comparable results as those drugs but are difficult or impossible to detect by
conventional analytical techniques. Among the substances that
Catlin has identified are the steroids norbolethone, THG, and
madol, as well as the blood enhancer darbepoetin and the aromatase inhibitor 4-androstene-3,6,17-trione (popularly known
as 6-OXO). He has also developed new technologies for the
identification of prohibited substances, perhaps the most important of which is the carbon isotope ratio test, which allows
for the differentiation between natural testosterone in the body
and exogenous forms of the hormone. One of his team's most
recent accomplishments was the development in 2009 of a test
for the drug methoxy polyethylene glycol-epoetin beta, originally developed for the treatment of anemia, but sometimes
used illegally to improve blood volume (and, thus, racing performance) in race horses.

Catlin founded ADRI, as a nonprofit organization whose
goal it is to conduct research on illegal substances used in
sport, as well as to develop new technology for the detection
of such materials. The company's major project at the current
time is the development of a test for human growth hormone,

a substance believed to be in wide use among athletes at all levels of sport but for which no reliable test yet exists. In addition to his work at ADRI and UCLA, Catlin currently serves as chairman of the Equine Drug Research Institute's Scientific Advisory Committee, member of the Federation Equestre Internationale Commission on Equine Anti-Doping and Medication, and member of the IOC's Medical Commission. He is the author or coauthor of more than 100 peer-reviewed scientific papers on drugs and drug technology.

Victor Conte (1950–)

Conte is perhaps best known as the founder and president of BALCO. Conte founded the business in 1984, officially for the purpose of conducting blood and urine tests and for providing food supplements to the general public. In fact, the primary function of the laboratory was to supply performance-enhancing drugs, primarily to professional athletes. In 1988, he established a close working relationship with a number of U.S. Olympic competitors by offering them free blood and urine tests. His connections to the sports world grew rapidly after that point and eventually became associated with leading performers in Major League Baseball, the NFL, U.S. Track and Field, and other major sports. Because of his role in the spread of anabolic steroids and other drugs among professional athletes, he eventually earned the nickname of "the Darth Vader of sports."

Victor Conte was born in Death Valley, California, on July 10, 1950. His father owned a gas station adjacent to a restaurant owned by his aunt. At the age of 4, Conte's family moved to Lake Tahoe, California, where his father had taken a job in construction. The family later moved back to southern California and settled in Fresno, where Victor attended McLane High School. He participated in track at McLane, but his real passion was music. While still in high school, he formed a band with two cousins, but set his musical ambitions aside briefly to attend Fresno City College. His track skills were good enough to earn him an athletic scholarship to Fresno State College, but he decided to pursue a career in music instead. Over the next 15 years, he played with a number of bands, including the Tower of Power, Pure Food and Drug Act, the Jump Street Band, Common Ground, and Herbie Hancock's Monster Band. Overall, he was involved in the production of more than 15 albums.

By the end of the 1970s, Conte had achieved considerable success in the field of music. Interestingly, as he has pointed out, he was one of the few professional musicians who were not involved in the use of drugs. His interest in that field came about when he was introduced to the field of holistic medicine. In 1980, he decided to open a small business in Millbrae, California, that sold vitamins. He called the business the Millbrae Holistic Health Center. As his interest in medical products grew, he expanded his business to include blood and urine testing and renamed his business the Bay Area Laboratory Cooperative. Between 1984 and 1995, Conte gradually expanded the number of his contacts in amateur and professional sports until some of the most famous names in athletics had become his customers. A federal investigation of BALCO records in 2003 found evidence connecting Conte to a long list of athletes that included Major League Baseball players Barry Bonds, Benito Santiago, Jeremy Giambi, Bobby Estalella, and Armando Rios; hammer thrower John McEwen; shot putters Kevin Toth and C. J. Hunter; sprinters Dwain Chambers, Marion Jones, Tim Montgomery, Raymond J. Smith, Zhanna Block, and Kelli White; middle-distance runner Regina Jacobs; boxer Shane Mosley; and cyclist Tammy Thomas.

Based on evidence collected in 2003, U.S. attorney general John Ashcroft announced a 42-count indictment against Conte and three other men for a variety of offenses, including conspiracy to distribute and possess with intent to distribute anabolic steroids, conspiracy to defraud through misbranded drugs, and money laundering. On July 15, 2005, Conte pleaded guilty to two charges, steroid distribution and money laundering, and was sentenced to four months in prison. He served that sentence at the end of 2005 and the beginning of 2006, and was released on March 30, 2006.

Since his release from prison, Conte has returned to his work with nutritional supplements for athletes, but now in a more carefully focused and controlled manner. He has chosen to work primarily with prize fighters, helping them to develop a nutritional program that will allow them to achieve the maximum potential possible with the bodies they have. He lists as his clients Shane Mosley, Zab Judah, Andre Berto, Karim Mayfield, Brandon Gonzales, and Nonito Donnaire. He says he has turned down some of the best-known names in boxing because he suspects that they use performance-enhancing drugs, and he does not care to become involved in that field again. What he does focus on is his athletes' blood chemistry, nutrition, and training schedules to help them achieve their goals. Many of the people who now work with Conte in the field of prize fighting believe that he has really changed. They also say that his background may offer a huge benefit to the sport, which many argue is among the "dirtiest" (in terms of performance-enhancing drug use) of all forms of competition. As one colleague has said, "he is somebody who understands the problem. If you can't listen to someone like that, you're really doing the athletes a disservice."

Daniel Duchaine (1952–2000)

Duchaine is widely regarded as the person most responsible for making the potential of anabolic steroids in improving body strength and muscle mass known to the world of bodybuilding and weight lifting. He is often referred to as the "guru of steroids" for this contribution to athletics and sports. In 1982, he and his partner of the time, Michael Zumpano, published one of the most memorable books on AAS ever written, an 18-page pamphlet entitled *Underground Steroid Handbook for Men and*

Women (sometimes referred to as *The Original Underground Steroid Handbook*), listing the steroids available and outlining their use for weight lifters and bodybuilders. Copies sold at 6 dollars each and almost immediately became enormously popular worldwide. Within the first year of publication, more than 80,000 copies were sold and produced an income of more than half a million dollars for Duchaine and Zumpano. Copies of Duchaine's original book are extremely rare today. He later produced an updated version, *The Underground Steroid Handbook*, in 1983, and a third version, *Underground Body Opus: Militant Weight Loss & Recomposition* (XIPE Press) in 1996. These two books are both generally available.

Daniel Duchaine was born on a date not generally available in 1952 in Connecticut. His mother, whom he barely knew, was a single mother who was later admitted to a psychiatric hospital for a personality disorder. (The admitting physician wrote that she was "without personality.") Duchaine was taken in by a childless pair of mill workers in Westbrook, Maine, who soon died, the adoptive mother when Duchaine was 10 and his adoptive father two years later. After that time, Duchaine essentially raised himself, living on his own in his adoptive parents' cottage outside of town. Those with a memory of his early days have noted that Duchaine's dress and behavior made him stand out in the quite rural community. Perhaps in keeping with this image, Duchaine attended Boston University, where he majored in theater arts and earned his bachelor of arts degree in 1975. He then returned to Maine, where he worked at a bicycle shop for two years.

By this time, Duchaine had become interested in bodybuilding, perhaps as a way of improving his own self-image. He persuaded his personal physician to prescribe steroids to improve his body mass, strength, and endurance, and rapidly experienced a significant improvement in all of these areas. He became convinced that, used in moderation, steroids could be a powerful and safe way of improving one's performance in weight lifting and bodybuilding.

In 1978, he decided that Maine was not the most appropriate location for him to pursue his interests in steroids and bodybuilding, so he moved to Venice, California, where he quickly became a regular member of the local gym culture. He later said that his own experience with steroids made him the resident expert on performance-enhancing drugs "by default." He appeared to know more about the subject than anyone with whom he came into contact. In a short biographical sketch he wrote toward the end of his life, Duchaine noted the following major accomplishments during this period:

1983—Introduced Ultimate Orange as the first MRP [(meal-replacement product]) using maltodextrins and MCTs [(minimum chain triglycerides]).

1984—Started the first mail-order steroid business, the John Siegler Fan Club, that delivered steroids via UPS C.O.D.

1985—Cofounded Laboratories Milano, the largest black market steroid-manufacturing plant in Tijuana, Mexico.

The U.S. government soon became interested in Duchaine's activities, and the next item on his biographical list was arrest for conspiracy and mislabeling of drugs produced in his Tijuana factory. He pled guilty and was sentenced to three years in jail, although he served only a few months. In 1991, while he was still on probation for his first conviction, Duchaine was picked up by agents of the FDA and arrested again, this time for trading in a restricted substance, gamma-hydroxybutyrate (GHB). This time he was sentenced to the full three-year term. Duchaine's final entry in his short autobiography, dated 1997, notes that he was the first person to introduce the steroid androstenedione to the bodybuilding world.

Dan Duchaine died on January 12, 2000, at the age of 47. The cause of death was polycystic kidney disease, a hereditary condition about which he had learned from a long-lost sister he first met in 1987. Until the end of his life, Duchaine never stopped speaking out about the value of anabolic steroids, when used in moderation. In 1988, *The New York Times* featured a story on Duchaine, briefly outlining his career with steroids. In the article, he described himself as "a guiding light" for the use of AAS in weight lifting, bodybuilding, and other sports. He also appeared on a number of radio and television programs, including *60 Minutes* and *20/20*, promoting his views on steroids.

International Association of Athletics Foundation

The International Association of Athletics Foundation (IAAF) is the international governing organization for the sport of athletics. The term *athletics* refers to a number of sports involving running, walking, jumping, and throwing. Included among these sports are track-and-field events, cross country, road running, and race walking. The IAAF was founded in 1912 when 17 national sporting organizations joined together to form an international association through which the sport of athletics could standardize the approach to equipment, record keeping, and other activities essential to the sport. The organization was originally called the International Amateur Athletics Federation as a way of emphasizing its commitment to athletic competition among individuals who participated not because of the hope of financial or other awards but for the love of the sport. Over time, the demands of commercialization became more pronounced in athletics, and the IAAF changed its name to its present title in 2001. The association has had its headquarters in Stockholm (1912–1946), London (1946–1993), and, most recently, Monaco (1993–present).

As of 2017, the IAAF has 214 national member federations organized into 6 so-called area associations: Asian Athletics Association in Asia; Confédération Africaine d'athlétisme in Africa; Confederación Sudamericana de Atletismo in South America; European Athletic Association in Europe; North American, Central American and Caribbean Athletic Association in North America; and Oceania Athletics Association in

Australia and Oceania (Australasia). One of the primary responsibilities of the IAAF is record keeping. Records in every athletics event for men and women can be found on the association's website at http://www.iaaf.org/statistics/recbycat/index .html. The organization also sponsors and operates a number of world championships in various fields of athletics, including the World Championships in Athletics, World Indoor Championships in Athletics, World Cross Country Championships, World Half Marathon Championships, World Junior Championships in Athletics, World Youth Championships in Athletics, World Race Walking Cup, World Marathon Cup, and the IAAF Continental Cup (involving team, rather than individual, competitions). All of these events are held biennially except for the Continental Cup, which is held every four years.

The IAAF was the first sports organization to adopt a policy prohibiting the use of performance-enhancing substances in athletic competitions. In 1982, it added a section to its *Handbook* that said:

> Doping is the use of any stimulant not normally employed to increase the poser of action in athletic competition above the average. Any person knowingly acting or assisting as explained above shall be excluded from any place where these rules are in force or, if he is a competitor, be suspended for a time or otherwise from further participation in amateur athletics under the jurisdiction of this Federation.

That statement was largely symbolic because tests were not yet available for most of the substances that athletes had been using—or would begin to use in the near future—to improve their athletic performance.

Since its original statement, the IAAF has tended to work closely with the World Anti-Doping Agency (WADA) and the IOC in achieving most of its anti-doping objectives. In 1979, for example, the IAAF Council accepted the rules for accreditation of testing laboratories developed by the IOC and, in 1981, designated the first laboratories approved for this purpose. Since the creation of WADA in 1999, the IAAF has followed that organization's lead in defining substances to be prohibited from athletic competition, policies for testing, and other issues relating to the ban of performance-enhancing drugs in athletic competitions. At its 44th Congress held in Paris in 2003, the IAAF voted to accept the World Anti-Doping Code as its own statement of anti-doping principles. Like other national organizations, however, the IAAF has the right to adjust the WADA's prohibited list to correspond with its own individual objectives and policies. For example, the IAAF does not list alcohol and beta-blockers on its list of prohibited substances although both substances do occur on the WADA list.

IAAF anti-doping policies are set by the IAAF Council, the chief administration group of the organization. Those policies are then implemented by a troika of three divisions: the Medical and Anti-Doping Commission, the Doping Review Board, and the IAAF Anti-Doping Administrator. The Medical and Anti-Doping Commission is responsible for constantly reviewing the IAAF's anti-doping rules and guidelines and making suggestions for changes that may be needed. As its name suggests, the Doping Review Board is responsible for considering the legal and regulatory status of specific cases of suspected doping and deciding by what means such cases are to be resolved. Finally, the anti-doping administrator is responsible for the day-to-day operation of the IAAF's anti-doping program. Specifically, he or she is responsible for reviewing the results of drug tests and determining what sanctions, if any, shall be assessed for positive results of such tests.

Charles Kochakian (1908–1999)

Kochakian has been called the father of anabolic steroids because of his extensive research and important discoveries on the members of this family of biochemical compounds. Probably his most notable work was completed very early in his career, when he was still a graduate student in endocrinology at the University of Rochester. He arrived at Rochester; he wrote in his autobiography, *How It Was: Anabolic Action of Steroids and Remembrances*, knowing almost nothing about the subject of endocrinology. But he registered to take a course in the subject and was soon excelling in his studies. In fact, his instructor told him that he no longer had to take exams in the course, but suggested, instead, that he become involved in some original research being conducted in the department.

The focus of this research was the relationship between certain components of male urine and the basal metabolic rate (BMR), the minimum amount of energy an organism needs to maintain basic bodily functions such as respiration, digestion, and circulation. Early studies had suggested that extracts prepared from male human urine increased the BMR in castrated dogs. The hypothesis Kochakian set out to test, then, was whether in fact there is a positive correlation—and, perhaps, a cause-and-effect relationship—between the extract and BMR in dogs and maybe even humans.

Kochakian's own experiments failed to confirm the earlier results, even after they had been modified and repeated a number of times. What he did discover, however, was that the urine extract significantly affected the nitrogen balance in the castrated dogs. It appeared that injection of the extract increased the amount of nitrogen used up during the dog's metabolism, suggesting that the element was being used to synthesize new body tissue. Indeed, he found that both castrated dogs in the study gained body weight in response to additional injections of the urine extract.

These experiments were going on at just the time that researchers in other laboratories were beginning to identify the essential elements of male urine that produce primary and secondary male sex characteristics. The first sex hormone, estrone, had been discovered in 1929 and the first sex hormone to be synthesized artificially, androsterone, was produced in 1934. The key to the whole process of masculinization, the hormone testosterone, was itself discovered only a year later, in 1935. By the time Kochakian was well into his research, samples of synthetic testosterone, androsterone, and some of their analogs were commercially available. Kochakian began to make use of these commercial products to continue his tests on the castrated dogs. Kochakian devoted the rest of his productive professional career on the synthesis, characterization, and study of dozens of anabolic hormones, the precursors, and metabolites.

Charles Daniel Kochakian was born in Haverhill, Massachusetts, on November 18, 1908. His parents were immigrants from Armenia, his father in 1900 and his mother in 1904. He has written that, like many immigrants, his parents had only a meager elementary school education themselves, but were insistent that their children receive the most extensive and best education possible. His mother hoped, in particular, that her son would pursue a career in dentistry, an ambition that young Charles did not himself share. Upon graduation from high school, he matriculated at Boston University (BU), from which he received his AB in chemistry in 1930. He then continued his studies at BU, earning his AM in organic chemistry a year later.

The early 1930s were a difficult time for a young man to be seeking work, even with a master's degree in organic chemistry. His applications for work produced no results until September 1933, when he was offered a position in the graduate school at the University of Rochester in the field of endocrinology. The offer was accompanied by a modest scholarship that was, he later wrote, adequate only for a "bare living." It was at Rochester that he began his work on anabolic steroids, which was to occupy his professional career for the next half century. He was awarded his Ph.D. in physiological chemistry by Rochester in 1936.

After completing his graduate work, Kochakian remained at Rochester as an instructor (1936–1940), associate professor (1940–1944), and assistant professor (1947–1951) in the Department of Physiology and Vital Economics (a somewhat unusual division in which teaching and research were focused on hygiene and human nutrition). In 1951, Kochakian accepted an appointment as head of biochemistry and endocrinology at the Oklahoma Medical Research Foundation in Oklahoma City, where he also served as associated director, coordinator of research, and professor of research biochemistry until 1957. In 1957, he left Oklahoma to become professor of physiology at the University of Alabama at Birmingham (UAB), where he spent the remainder of his academic career. While there, he held the titles of professor and director of experimental endocrinology (1961–1979), professor of biochemistry (1961–1979), and professor of physiology and biophysics (1964–1975). In 1979, he was named professor emeritus at UAB.

Among his honors, Kochakian was awarded the Claude Bernal Medal of the University of Montreal in 1950 and the Osaka Endocrine Society Medal in 1962. Kochakian was particularly proud of his religious involvement, listing a number of church-related activities in his curriculum vitae. These activities included secretary of the Men's Club at the Centre Congregational Church in Haverhill; chair of the Christian Education Committee at the Brighton Presbyterian Church in Rochester; member of the Building Committee of the Westminster Presbyterian Church in Oklahoma City; and active elder of the Southminister Presbyterian Church in Birmingham. He was listed in a number of "who's who" books, including *Who's Who in American History*, *Who's Who in America*, *Who's Who in American Education*, *Who's Who in the South and Southwest*, *Who's Who in the World*, *International Who's Who in Community Service*, *Notable Americans*, and *American Men of Science*. Kochakian died in Birmingham on February 12, 1999.

Floyd Landis (1975–)

Landis is an American cyclist best known for his remarkable victory in the 2006 Tour de France, the premier cycling event in the world. A two-day period in the race that will forever be a part of cycling history began on July 16 during the 182-kilometer race from Bourg-d'Oisans to La Toussuire. Landis had a miserable day and trailed the stage leader Michael Rasmussen by more than 10 minutes. On the next day, however, Landis made one of the most amazing comebacks in racing history, winning the 201-kilometer run from St. Jean de Maurienne to Morzine by nearly 6 minutes. The stage was notable for an especially difficult 18.3-kilometer climb up the Alps. Only a few days after the race had been completed, anti-doping officials notified Landis's manager that he had failed a drug test conducted just prior to the historic St. Jean de Maurienne to Morzine stage. The test had shown that Landis's testosterone to the hormone epitestosterone ratio, a common doping test, was 11 to 1. The normal ratio for someone who is not taking steroid supplements is 4 to 1.

These test results set into motion the normal series of events leading to a consideration of voiding Landis's eventual triumph in the Tour de France. Less than a month after Landis had been declared winner on the 2006 Tour de France, the USADA confirmed Landis's test results, and he was disqualified from the race. Spanish cyclist Óscar Pereiro was declared winner of the event. Landis appealed the USADA decision, but an appeals board confirmed that decision on September 20, 2007, and Landis was banned from professional cycling for two years. Landis appealed again, this time to the Court of Arbitration for Sport (CAS), an international tribunal to hear disputes having to do with athletic competitions. On June 30, 2008, the CAS announced its decision, an affirmation of earlier decisions and the ban on Landis's participation in cycling for two years. In May 2010, Landis finally admitted to the use of illegal steroids in the Tour de France, largely negating the long campaign he had fought to overturn his conviction for those actions.

Floyd Landis was born on October 14, 1975, in Farmersville, Pennsylvania, to Paul and Arlene Landis. The Landis family was part of a devout Mennonite community in Lancaster

County, in which many otherwise typical activities are often (but not always) forbidden, such as the wearing of "modern" clothes, using motorized transportation, and listening to radio and watching television. Floyd's own father was so concerned about his son's "frivolous" bicycle riding that he assigned the boy extra chores to keep him busy during the day. In response, Floyd changed his riding to the evening hours, often enjoying his hobby in the wee hours of the morning.

Nonetheless, Landis seemed to have been born for riding. At his first cycling competition, he reputedly showed up wearing "a garish jersey, a visored helmet, and a pair of brilliantly colored Argyle socks, pulled high," according to author Daniel Coyle in his book *Tour de Force*. When his opponents began making fun of him, he offered to buy dinner to anyone who could keep up with him in the race. No one did, and Landis won the race by more than 10 minutes.

In 1995, Landis moved to southern California, expecting to find a more hospitable, year-around place to train and race. He soon developed a reputation for strength, endurance, and tenacity, finishing one race even after his tires had been completely worn away, riding only on the wheels' rims. Impressed by that type of reputation, seven-time Tour de France winner Lance Armstrong recruited Landis to ride with his team in 2002. Landis aided Armstrong in his 2002, 2003, and 2004 wins, and then went on to finish ninth himself in the 2005 race.

When his suspension expired on January 30, 2009, he returned to professional cycling again, with relatively modest success. He joined the OUCH Pro Cycling Team (now the UnitedHealthcare Pro Cycling Team) and finished 23rd in a field of 84 riders at his first competition, the Tour of California. He later moved to the Bahati Foundation Cycling Team which, over time and apparently partly because of its connection with Landis, began to fall apart. His career came to an unfortunate conclusion when he entered the 2010 Cascade Cycling Classic as the sole representative of the Bahati team, failing to complete the event. In January 2011, he finally announced his retirement from the sport he loved so much. In an interview with *Cycling News*, he said, "I've spent five years trying to get back to a place that I can never really go back to, and it's causing more stress than is worth it. . . . I've been riding my bike a lot, trying to figure out life, which is the same reason I did it to start with, so I've come full circle" ("Landis Retires from Cycling, Effective Immediately," 2011). In 2016, Landis set out on an entirely new career when he opened a cannabis retail business in Colorado, Floyd's of Leadville.

Reference

"Landis Retires from Cycling, Effective Immediately." 2011. *Cycling News*. http://www.cyclingnews.com/news/landis-retires-from-cycling-effective-immediately/. Accessed on October 6, 2017.

Ernst Laqueur (1880–1947)

The 1930s was a decade of great progress in understanding the chemical structure and physiological activity of sex hormones. The first sex hormone ever discovered, estrone, was identified by German chemist Adolf Butenandt in 1929; Butenandt also isolated the first male sex hormone, androsterone, only two years later. These breakthroughs were of enormous significance because they provided researchers for the first time with a mechanism for understanding the process of sexualization in terms of concrete chemical compounds that could be studied, characterized, synthesized, and produced commercially.

This new information was of immense interest to a few large pharmaceutical companies: Organon, located in Oss, Netherlands; Ciba, headquartered in Basel, Switzerland; Schering, in Berlin, Germany; and Syntex, in Mexico. With the announcement of new discoveries about sex hormones, these companies began to pour financial and personnel resources into bringing hormone products to the commercial market. Among the most successful of the companies, in terms of research break-throughs, was Organon. The company was founded in 1923 by Laqueur; Sall van Zwanenberg, owner of the Zwanenberg Slaughterhouse; and Dr. Jacques van Oss, a business consultant. Butenandt's research on sex hormones, as well as that of many other scientists, was supported by Organon. In perhaps its biggest commercial breakthrough, the company began producing its first product, insulin, in 1923. The discovery and synthesis of testosterone, the primary male sex hormone, were both the result of research by Organon-based researchers, primarily Karoly Gyula David, Elizabeth Dingemanse, Janos Freud, and Laqueur. In May 1935, this research team announced the discovery and characterization of testosterone in a now classic publication, "On Crystalline Male Hormone from Testicles (Testosterone)" (David, et al., 1935).

Ernst Laqueur was born in Obernigk, near Breslau, Germany, on July 8, 1880, to Seigfried and Anna Levy Laqueur. He grew up in a prosperous Jewish family and attended school in Breslau. That region is now part of southwestern Poland. After high school, Laqueur attended both the University of Breslau and the University of Heidelberg, where he studied medicine. In 1905, he was awarded his medical degree by the former institution. In spite of his Jewish background, Laqueur felt a greater affinity to his German nationality than to his religious affiliation and, in 1906, he, his wife, and their young daughter converted to the Evangelical religion. He is said to have taken this step to express his concern for a unified Germany in which religion would not be a decisive factor.

Between 1906 and 1910, Laqueur worked as an instructor and research assistant in physiology and pharmacology at the universities of Heidelberg, Königsberg, and Halle. In 1910, he was appointed professor of physiology at Halle, and two years later took a similar post at the University of Gröningen. When World War I broke out, Laqueur enlisted in the German army, where he served as a physician and instructor at the Army Gas School in Berlin. He also conducted research on gas warfare and treatment for gas poisoning at the Kaiser-Wilhelm Academy in Berlin.

After the war, Laqueur was offered an appointment as professor of pharmacology and physiology at the Flemish- and German-sponsored University of Ghent, in Belgium. He never took that position, however, as he was almost simultaneously convicted of treason in absentia by the new Belgian government that took over the university after the war. In any case, Laqueur had become ill with typhoid and returned directly to Germany at the war's conclusion. He remained there until he accepted an appointment as an assistant to the highly regarded Dutch physician and medical researcher Isidore Snapper, in Amsterdam in 1919. Only a year later, he received his own appointment, as professor of pharmacology at the University of Amsterdam.

With the rise of National Socialism (Nazism) in Germany in the 1930s, Laqueur decided to give up his German citizenship and become a Dutch citizen. When World War II first reached Holland in November 1940, he, along with all other Jewish professors, was removed from his office at the University of Amsterdam. The company he helped to found, Organon, was also sold to the German firm of Schering. Nonetheless, because he was originally a German citizen and he had served in the German army during World War I, he escaped many of the worst excesses experienced by other Jews in the Netherlands during the way. This "special treatment" resulted in some unpleasant feelings toward him after the war, and he never returned to full active participation in either the academic or the commercial world.

He did, however, continue to receive a number of honors and awards in recognition of his research accomplishments. In 1946, for example, he was invited to give the prestigious Harvey Lecture at the UCLA. He followed this event with a tour of North and South America, during which he became quite ill and was hospitalized for an extended period in Argentina. He returned home to a continuing dispute with administrators at Organon, which was never resolved before he died while on vacation in Gletsch Furka, Switzerland, on August 19, 1947.

Reference

David, K., E. Dingemanse, J. Freud, and Ernst Laqueur. 1935. Über Krystallinisches Männliches Hormon aus Hoden (Testosteron), Wirksamer als aus Harn oder aus Cholesterin Bereitetes Androsteron. *Biological Chemistry.* 233(5–6): 281–283. Published online: 2009-10-15 | DOI: https://doi.org/10.1515/bchm2.1935.233.5-6.281.

George J. Mitchell (1933–)

Mitchell was appointed in March 2006 by Major League Baseball commissioner Bud Selig to conduct an investigation of the use of illegal AAS by Major League Baseball players. The announcement followed closely upon the publication of a book, *Game of Shadows*, by *San Francisco Chronicle* reporters Mark Fainaru-Wada and Lance Williams. That book discussed in detail the distribution of illegal steroids by the San Francisco Bay area firm BALCO to a number of professional athletes, most prominently San Francisco Giants player Barry Bonds. The book was issued just prior to the season in which Bonds was expected to—and did—set a new Major League Baseball home run record for a single season.

George John Mitchell, Jr., was born in Waterville, Maine, on August 20, 1933, to George John Mitchell, Sr., a custodian at Colby College, and Mary Saad Mitchell, a textile worker. Mitchell helped put himself through secondary school by working as a janitor, like his father, before entering Bowdoin College, in Brunswick, Maine. He graduated with his bachelor's degree from Bowdoin in 1954 and enlisted in the U.S. Army, where he rose to the rank of first lieutenant. After leaving the army, he returned to Georgetown University, in Washington, D.C., from which he received his law degree in 1960. His first postgraduation job was with the U.S. Department of Justice, where he worked as a trial lawyer in the Antitrust Division. He left that position in 1962 to take a job as executive assistant to Senator Edmund S. Muskie (D-ME). He left that post in 1965 to take a job at the law firm of Jensen, Baird, Gardner and Henry, in Portland, Maine. He served with the firm for a dozen years, during which time he also remained active in politics. He ran for governor of the state in 1974, but lost the election to Republican James Longley. In 1977, President Jimmy Carter named Mitchell U.S. attorney for the State of Maine.

In 1980, Mitchell's political career took a turn when he was appointed by Governor Joseph Brennan to take the seat of former senator Edmund Muskie, who had been appointed secretary of state by President Carter. He then won reelection to that seat in 1982, and again in 1988. During his last term in the Senate, he served as majority leader from 1989 to 1995. He left the Senate at the end of his second term and declined a nomination by President Bill Clinton to a seat on the U.S. Supreme Court.

Mitchell's retirement did not, by any means, mean the end of his political career. In November 1995, President Clinton named Mitchell a special advisor on economic initiatives for Ireland. Mitchell produced a detailed report, calling for a number of steps that might lead to the end of the very long conflict between Great Britain and Ireland over the fate of Northern Island. Mitchell's work on the Irish problem eventually earned him a number of honors and awards, including the Presidential Medal of Freedom (the highest civilian honor that the U.S. government can give); the Philadelphia Liberty Medal; the Truman Institute Peace Prize; and the United Nations (UNESCO) Peace Prize.

In 2000, President Clinton asked Mitchell to take on another international issue, the conflict between Israel and the Palestinian Authority. He served as chair of the Sharm el-Sheikh International Fact-Finding Committee, whose goal it was to develop a pathway for the peace process between the two entities. The process ultimately failed (as have all other peace efforts in the region), but Mitchell again won accolades from both sides for his efforts on behalf of the process.

Mitchell's work on behalf of Major League Baseball in 2006–2007 was conducted in spite of the decision by the Player's Union not to cooperate fully in his investigation. He is said to have interviewed only two players in person, although he and his staff eventually collected more than 115,000 pages of documents from more than 700 witnesses, including 60 former major league players. Key witnesses in the investigation were Kirk Radomski, a former Mets clubhouse attendant, and Brian McNamee, a former trainer for Roger Clemens, one of the finest pitchers in Major League Baseball history. The complete Mitchell report can be viewed online at http://files.mlb.com/mitchrpt.pdf.

In 2009, Mitchell was called upon once more, this time by President Barack Obama, to serve as an intermediary in a contentious international issue, again the disagreements between Israel and the Palestinian Authority. Mitchell flew back and forth between Washington and the Middle East for two years, attempting to make some progress between the positions held by the two sides, again without success. In May 2011, he resigned that post and returned to private business.

In addition to his public service, Mitchell has continued to work in the private legal field. After leaving the Senate, he joined the Washington law firm of Verner, Liipfert, Bernhard, McPherson and Hand, where he was later chosen chairman. He has also been senior counsel at the law firm of Preti, Flaherty, Beliveau, Pachios, Orlick & Haley in Portland and partner and chairman of the Global Board of DLA Piper, US LLP, a global law firm. Mitchell is the author of four books on his life experiences: *Men of Zeal: A Candid Inside Story of the Iran-Contra Hearings* (with William Cohen, 1988); *World on Fire: Saving an Endangered Earth* (1991); *Not For America Alone: The Triumph of Democracy and the Fall of Communism* (1997); and *Making Peace* (1999).

National Institute on Drug Abuse

The origins of the National Institute on Drug Abuse (NIDA) date to 1935 when the U.S. Public Health Service established a research facility on drug abuse in Lexington, Kentucky. In 1948, that facility was officially renamed the Addiction Research Center. Research on drug abuse was facilitated at the site of the original facility, called Narco, which was adjacent to a prison that held drug offenders and was run cooperatively with the Federal Bureau of Prisons. The federal government's interest in drug abuse was expanded in 1971 when President Richard M. Nixon established the Special Action Office of Drug Abuse Prevention within the White Office. A year later, the Special Action Office initiated two programs: the Drug Abuse Warning Network (DAWN) and the National Household Survey on Drug Abuse (NHSDA), both of which continue today. DAWN is a public health surveillance system that monitors emergency department drug-related admissions. It is now a part of the Substance Abuse and Mental Health Services Administration (SAMHSA). The NHSDA is now known as the National Survey on Drug Use and Health and is also located in SAMHSA. Its function is to provide national and state-level data on the use of illegal drugs, tobacco, alcohol, and mental health to researchers and the general public.

The NIDA itself was created by the act of Congress in 1974 for the purpose of promoting research, treatment, prevention, training, services, and data collection on the nature and extent of drug abuse. In general, the activities of the NIDA can be classified into one of two major categories: the conduct and support of research on a variety of issues related to drug abuse and dissemination of this information for the purposes of future research and to improve programs of prevention and treatment of drug abuse as well as to inform decisions by state, local, and the federal governments on drug abuse policies and practices. The agency's organizational charts reflect the way in which these activities are organized. Three of the main NIDA offices deal with extramural affairs (funding of outside research), science policy and communications, and management. The agency also consists of a number of divisions that deal with intramural research (research within the agency); basic neuroscience and behavioral research; clinical research and behavioral research; epidemiology, services, and prevention research; and pharmacotherapies and medical consequences of drug abuse. Special programs, working groups, consortia, and interest groups focus on more specific topics, such as HIV/AIDS; childhood and adolescence issues; community epidemiology; women and sex/gender differences; nicotine and tobacco; neurosciences; and genetic issues.

The direction of NIDA activities over the period 2016–2020 has been laid out in the agency's Strategic Plan. That report describes in detail the elements of the agency's four-pronged program over the coming five years:

- Identify the biological, environmental, behavioral, and social causes and consequences of drug use and addiction across the lifespan.
- Develop new and improved strategies to prevent drug use and its consequences.
- Develop new and improved treatments to help people with substance use disorders achieve and maintain a meaningful and sustained recovery.
- Increase the public health impact of NIDA's research and programs.

The publication is available online at https://www.drugabuse .gov/sites/default/files/2016-2020nidastrategicplan.pdf.

As indicated here, dissemination of information is a major focus of the work carried out by the NIDA. Its publications include educational curricula, facts sheets, guidelines and manuals, journals, administrative and legal documents, posters, presentations, promotional materials, and reports. These

publications can be reviewed on the agency's website at http://
www.drugabuse.gov/publications by audience (students, teachers, parents, researchers, and health and medical professionals), by drug of abuse (e.g., alcohol, amphetamines, club drugs,
LSD, marijuana, and steroids), by drug topic (such as addiction science, comorbidity, criminal justice, drugged driving,
medical consequences, and relapse and recovery), by series
(among which are Addiction Science and Clinical Practice,
Brain Power, DrugFacts, Mind over Matter, and Research Reports), and by type.

The NIDA website also provides links to a number of resources for additional information about the subject of drug
abuse and about the agency itself, including the sections NIDA
in the News and NIDA Notes as well as sections on meetings
and events related to drug abuse topics, news releases, podcasts
of NIDA-related programs, and electronic newsletters. The
website is also available in a Spanish language edition.

Dick Pound (1942–)

Pound is described in his biography in the Canada's Sports
Hall of Fame as the "ultimate champion" of the concept of
purity in sport. For most of his adult life, Pound has cam-
paigned to reduce or eliminate the influence of performance-
enhancing substances and practices that supposedly provide an
unfair advantage for their users over athletes who do not rely
on such substances and practices. In 1999, he helped found
the WADA, of which he became the organization's first president. He served in that post until 2007, when he chose not
to run for an additional term at the agency. In 2014, Pound
was appointed by WADA to head a commission to investigate allegations of widespread cheating by Russian athletes
at the 2014 Sochi Winter Olympics. In the committee's report, issued on November 9, 2015, its authors concluded
that some nations had developed programs that were based
on "an embedded and institutionalized process designed to

secure winning at any cost." (The full report can be viewed at https://www.wada-ama.org/sites/default/files/resources/files/ wada_independent_commission_report_1_en.pdf.)

Richard William Duncan Pound (almost universally known as "Dick Pound") was born in St. Catharines, Ontario, on March 22, 1942. He spent his childhood in a number of cities and towns ranging from Ocean Falls, British Columbia, to La Tuque and Trois-Rivieres, Quebec. After graduating from Mount Royal High School in Montreál, he matriculated at McGill University, where he went on to become a star in swimming. He set school records in every freestyle event and won three Canadian intercollegiate gold medals in each of his freshman, sophomore, and senior years. At one point in his career, he held every freestyle swimming record up to a distance of 220 meters. He won the Canadian freestyle championship four times, in 1958, 1960, 1961, and 1962, and the Canadian butterfly championship in 1961. He swam on the Canadian team in the 1960 Olympic Games in Rome, where he finished sixth in the 100-meter freestyle and was fourth in the 4×400 meter relay. In addition to his swimming accomplishments, Pound was a first-class squash player, winning the Canadian intercollegiate championship twice. He was also a proficient golf and tennis player.

Pound received his bachelor of commerce and his bachelor of law degrees from McGill in 1962 and 1967 and his bachelor of arts degree from Sir George Williams University in 1963. He was licensed as a chartered accountant in 1964 and as a lawyer in 1968. Over the next decade, Pound worked as a chartered accountant and an attorney in Quebec and Ontario. He eventually reached the peak of both professions when he was named Queen's counsel in 1991 and fellow of the Order of Chartered Accountants, Quebec, in 2000. He currently works in the tax group of the law firm of Stikeman Elliott in Montréal, where his primary areas of practice are tax litigation and negotiations with tax authorities on behalf of clients, in addition to general tax advisory work and commercial arbitration.

Pound has retained his association with McGill throughout his adult life, serving as lecturer and adjunct faculty member, governor, member of a number of administrative committees, and chancellor of the university from 1999 to 2009.

For all of his accomplishments in the field of law, Pound is almost certainly best known for his role with the IOC and other amateur sports organizations. In 1978, he was elected a member of the IOC with special responsibility for negotiating sponsoring and television deals. He remained an active member of the committee for the next three decades, serving as chair of the Centennial Coin Programme, Centennial Working Group, Marketing Coordination Committee, and Olympic Games Study Commission, among other responsibilities. In all, he served a total of 18 years on the IOC, during 8 of which he was also vice president of the organization.

In 1999, as mentioned earlier, Pound was involved in the creation of the WADA, of which he was chosen the organization's first president. He held that post until his retirement in 2007, although he continues to serve on the organization's Foundation board. During his tenure, Pound became known for his very strong stands against the use of performance-enhancing substances and practices in sports, often making comments that were regarded as incendiary or provocative. One of his best-known ongoing feuds was with American cyclist Lance Armstrong, who objected to Pound's assertion in 2004 that "the public knows that the riders in the Tour de France and the others are doping." That feud reached new heights in 2005 when Armstrong apparently tested positive for erythropoietin and Pound demanded that his gold medal for the Tour de France that year be rescinded. Pound also had harsh comments about the use of performance-enhancing substances in other circumstances involving another cyclist, Floyd Landis; drug-using practices in the National Hockey League and the Austrian cross-country and Nordic ski teams; doping among professional golfers; and the growth of drug use in professional sports in general and American Major League

Baseball in particular. In an interview for the WADA magazine *Play True*, Pound laid out his basic beliefs about the use of performance-enhancing substances in sports:

> Those who do not honour their promises, who cheat, undermine the entire ethical construct of sport. In many cases, it is also dangerous cheating. Either way, this cheating has no place in sport and must be confronted, not condoned or ignored.

Pound has received many awards and honors during his long career in the law and amateur sports. These include the Scarlet Key Honour Society and the Carswell Company Prize at McGill; 10 honorary doctorates, from the United States Sports Academy, University of Windsor, University of Western Ontario, Laurentian University, Beijing Sports University, Lakehead University, Loughborough University, L'Université du Québec, Concordia University, and McGill; Officer of the Order of Canada; Officer of the National Order of Quebec; Gold and Silver Star of the Order of the Sacred Treasure, Government of Japan; and Laureus Spirit of Sport Award, WADA.

Grigory Rodchenkov (1958–)

Rodchenkov's name became widely known in July 2013, when he revealed to British journalist Nick Harris details of the long-standing practice of Russian sports officials of using drugs to improve the performance of athletes in a number of international competitions. Rodchenkov's claims became the basis of an ever-widening investigation carried out by the WADA that eventually led to the banning of hundreds of Russian athletes at the 2016 Summer Olympics in Rio, as well as similar actions by specialized sporting groups in their events.

Grigory Mikhailovich Rodchenkov was born in Moscow on October 24, 1958. As a young man, he competed in track and field and was awarded the title of "master of sports" by the Soviet government. He attended Moscow State University, from which he received his doctoral degree in chemistry, with a specialization in analytical chemistry. After graduation, he was hired to work at the Moscow Anti-Doping Center, where he was employed from 1985 to 1994. He then took a position with the Moscow office of Hewlett-Packard, as distributor of its Interlab analytical equipment. In 1998, Rodchenkov moved to Calgary, Canada, where he again worked at an anti-doping laboratory. He then returned to Moscow, where he became head of the Department of Chromatography for the Laverna Corporation.

In 2005, Rodchenkov was offered the position of director of the Russian Anti-Doping Center in Moscow by Nikolay Durmanov, head of the Russian Olympic Anti-Doping Committee. In 2014, he was responsible for anti-doping activities at the Winter Olympics in Sochi. As a reward for his outstanding service in this event, Russian president Vladimir Putin awarded him the prestigious Order of Friendship. He remained director of anti-doping programs in Russia until 2015, by which time he decided it was no longer safe for him to remain in Russia because of his doping allegations against Russian athletes. He then moved to Los Angeles, where he became involved in the production of a film about doping at the Sochi Games, called *Icarus*. He has also been spending his time in Los Angeles, according to *The New York Times*, "gardening, making borscht and writing in his diary." (For a complete account of the Rodchenkov allegations and their consequences for all involved, see https://www.nytimes.com/2016/05/13/sports/russia-doping-sochi-olympics-2014.html?_r=0.)

Leopold Ruzicka (1887–1976)

Ruzicka was a major participant in the attempt to identify the biochemical responsible for producing male secondary sexual characteristics in the 1930s. That research had a very long history, based on centuries-old knowledge that some substance, secreted by males in their urine, was responsible for the development of male sexual characteristics, such as body hair and a deep voice, as well as the ability to produce sperm. A number of breakthroughs in the late 19th and early 20th centuries culminated in the 1931 discovery by Adolf Butenandt of the hormone he called androsterone. Researchers knew, however, that an even more powerful substance responsible for male sexual characteristics remained undiscovered, and the race was on to find that substance. In the short period between May 27 and August 24, 1935, three separate groups of researchers reported the discovery and chemical structure of that substance, testosterone. One of those teams was led by Croatian biochemist Leopold Ruzicka, who later was awarded a share of the 1939 Nobel Prize in Chemistry (with Butenandt) for his research on polymethylenes and higher terpenes, chemical structures of which steroids are made.

Ruzicka was born Lavoslav Stjepan Ruzicka on September 13, 1887, in Vukovar, Hungary (then part of the Austro-Hungarian Empire, and now part of Croatia), to Stjepan Ruzicka, a cooper, and Ljubica Sever Ruzicka. After the death of his father in 1891, Ruzicka returned with his mother to her birthplace in Osijek, where he attended primary school and classical gymnasium (high school). Although Ruzicka was not particularly interested in the science courses offered at Osijek, he took an interest in chemistry largely because he was intrigued by the nature of natural products, an interest that motivated most of his research throughout the rest of his life.

After graduation from Osijek, Ruzicka matriculated at the Technische Hochschule (technical high school) at Karlsruhe, where he took his first formal courses in chemistry. He proved to be well adapted to the subject and finished his courses in less than two years. His instructor at Karlsruhe was the famous German chemist Hermann Staudinger, who was only 26 at the time. Working together, Ruzicka and Staudinger essentially created the field of plant product chemistry, focusing their research at first on the structure and action of a group of compounds now known as pyrethrins, the major component of many insecticides. It was this line of research that led eventually to the primary focus of Ruzicka's research throughout his life. As part of that research, he and his colleagues submitted one of the classic papers in the history of steroid chemistry, "On the Artificial Preparation of the Testicular Hormone Testosterone (Androsten-3-one-17-ol)," to the journal *Helvetica Chimica Acta* on August 31, 1935.

In 1912, Staudinger was offered a position at the newly created Eidgenössische Technische Hochschule (Swiss Federal Institute of Technology, generally known simply as ETH), now one of the most prestigious scientific research institutes in the world. Ruzicka followed his mentor to ETH, where he took up a long-standing position in the field of organic chemistry. Some of his earliest works there were supported by the oldest perfume manufacturer in the world, Haarman & Reimer, of Holzminden, Germany. The firm obviously saw potential benefits in the line of research being pursued by Ruzicka at ETH, and this type of support was continued from other perfume and chemical firms throughout Ruzicka's career. Ruzicka left ETH in 1926 for a three-year stint at the University of Utrecht, in the Netherlands, after which he returned to Switzerland and ETH, where he spent the rest of his career. His decision to return to ETH was motivated both by the stronger chemical industry in Switzerland and by the offer of directorship of the institute. Ruzicka remained at ETH until his retirement in 1957.

In addition to his research, teaching, and administrative responsibilities, Ruzicka was especially interested in Dutch and Flemish art. His collection was at one time regarded as one of the finest collections of such works in the world. He is said to have remarked that his devotion to art actually reduced the amount of time and energy he was able to devote to chemical research. Ruzicka died in Mammern, Switzerland, on September 26, 1976.

During his lifetime, Ruzicka was awarded honorary doctorates from eight different institutions: four in science, two in medicine, one in natural science, and one in law. He also received seven prizes and medals and was elected to 24 honorary memberships in chemical, biochemical, and other scientific societies around the world. In 1957, the ETH established the Ruzicka Prize for outstanding work in the field of chemistry conducted by a young researcher.

Arnold Schwarzenegger (1947–)

Schwarzenegger is an Austrian-born former bodybuilder, actor, businessman, and 38th governor of the state of California. Before he became active in politics in the early part of the 21st century, he was probably best known at first for his bodybuilding accomplishments, having won the Mr. Olympia bodybuilding contest seven times, the first in 1967 when he was 20 years old. He was then acknowledged as having almost the perfect build for a bodybuilder, with a massive chest, arms, and legs. Even today, bodybuilding magazines and blogs point to Schwarzenegger as a sort of Mr. Perfect.

After retiring from bodybuilding competitions, Schwarzenegger turned to movie acting, and starred in a number of feature films that include *Hercules in New York* (under the name Arnold Strong); *Stay Hungry* (for which he won a Golden Globe in 1976); *Pumping Iron* (a bodybuilding film from 1977); *Conan the Barbarian* (1982) and *Conan the Destroyer* (1984); *The Terminator* (1984), *Terminator 2: Judgment Day* (1991), *Terminator 3: Rise of the Machines* (2003), *Terminator Salvation* (2009), and *Terminator Genisys* (2015); *Red Sonja* (1985); *Twins* (1988); *Total Recall* (1990); *Kindergarten Cop* (1990); *Junior* (1994); and *Eraser* (1996).

Beginning in the 1990s, Schwarzenegger was subjected to almost constant questioning about the possibility that he had used anabolic steroids to improve his muscle mass during his bodybuilding career. During his teenage years, it was very clear that he had developed from a well-built, but hardly extraordinary, young man into an adult with quite uncommon physical features. In response to such questioning, Schwarzenegger almost inevitably admitted to the use of anabolic steroids as something he had to do in order to compete. He points out that at the time he used steroids, it was not illegal to do so and virtually all bodybuilders took advantage of the contribution they made to improvement in body structure. He also notes that he used steroids only for short periods of time, usually in the build-up to a competition, and then ceased using them after the competition. (For Schwarzenegger's own words on this matter, see https://www.youtube.com/watch?v=ebRglq-CPsY.) In interviews on the topic, Schwarzenegger now makes it clear that he doesn't recommend the use of steroids among professional or amateur athletes. He insists, however, that athletes should continue to take advantage of any legal substances that will improve their own performances.

Arnold Alois Schwarzenegger was born in the village of Thal, Austria, on July 30, 1947, to Gustav Schwarzenegger, chief of police in Thal, and Aurelia Jadrny Schwarzenegger. He was an average student in primary and secondary school, with a special interest in soccer. He was introduced to weight training by his soccer coach and soon found that he preferred working out with barbells to kicking a soccer bell. His interest in bodybuilding was further encouraged by a number of films he saw that starred well-built male leads, such as Steve Reeves and Johnny Weissmuller. By the age of 14, he had decided to begin competing in bodybuilding competitions. He soon became absolutely committed to this pursuit, noting in later interviews that "[i]t would make me sick to miss a workout. . . . I knew I couldn't look at myself in the mirror the next morning if I didn't do it." As a result, he sometimes broke into the local gym, where he worked out even when it was closed, just so as not to disrupt his schedule.

In 1965, Schwarzenegger joined the Austrian army, fulfilling the national requirement of one year of military service. Although his job was as a tank driver, he found enough time to continue his bodybuilding activities, winning the Junior Mister

Europe title that year. A year later, after leaving the army, he added three more titles to his list: Mister Europe, Best Built Man in Europe, and International Powerlifting Championship. In 1967, he won the first of five Mr. Universe championships, which he later described as his "ticket to America." A year later, he finally realized a lifelong dream of moving to the United States, where he made a meager living selling nutritional supplements and competing in bodybuilding contests. His hope of becoming a famous movie star was thwarted at first because of his thick accent. In fact, his voice had to be dubbed in after completion of the filming of his first movie, *Hercules in New York*, because he could not be understood in the original takes.

Schwarzenegger has been a lifelong Republican. He has said that he made that decision shortly after arriving in the United States, listening to a debate between presidential candidates Hubert Humphrey and Richard Nixon. He liked what Nixon had to say and said that if he (Nixon) was a Republican, then so was he (Schwarzenegger). Until after the turn of the century, however, Schwarzenegger's participation in political activities was quite limited. For example, he served on President George H. W. Bush's President's Council on Physical Fitness and Sports. He never, however, sought political office until 2003, when he announced that he was running for governor of California. That race was necessitated by a recall election against then-governor Gray Davis, who lost his seat in the election. Schwarzenegger was chosen to replace Davis, winning 48.58 percent of the vote compared to 31.47 percent for Democratic candidate Cruz Bustamante and 13.41 percent for fellow Republican Tom McClintlock.

Schwarzenegger was reelected governor in 2006 with 55.9 percent of the vote, but declined to seek reelection in 2010. He announced instead that he was planning to return to his acting career, listing a number of scripts that he was then considering. That decision was put on hold in 2011 largely because of marital problems resulting from an affair that he had with the family housekeeper that had resulted in the birth of a child and divorce from his wife of 25 years, Maria. In September 2015, Schwarzenegger announced that he would become star of the *Celebrity Apprentice* television show, a program previously hosted by President Donald Trump.

The Taylor Hooton Foundation

The Taylor Hooton Foundation (THF) was founded in 2004 in honor of Taylor Hooton, who took his life on July 15, 2003, largely as the result of using anabolic steroids. The foundation is a 501(c)3 tax-exempt organization that was created when Taylor's parents, relatives, and friends began to understand the profound effect that performance-enhancing drugs can have on the lives of individuals who use those substances. The foundation makes the point that such drugs are used not only by amateur and professional athletes but also by many men and women and boys and girls who see the drugs as a way of improving their own self-image. For that reason, the foundation refers to the drugs as appearance- and performance-enhancing drugs. The foundation lists as its partners a number of sports organizations, including Major League Baseball, National Football League, National Hockey League, National Baseball Hall of Fame, Minor League Baseball, National Athletic Trainers' Association, Canadian Football League, and New York Yankees baseball team.

THF lists six core values on its website: its commitment as a (1) family-based organization that (2) provides parents, coaches, and other adult influencers with knowledge and tools and that honors (3) the values, integrity, ethics (character), leadership, and respect that help individuals (4) make the right choices with respect to a healthy lifestyle, which is, itself, (5) a good steward of funds, and that functions as a (6) volunteer-oriented organization.

The THF website provides useful information about all aspects of steroid abuse, along with a special section on the risks posed by the use of certain dietary supplements. It also provides an opportunity to read real-life stories from and about individuals who have experienced problems with steroid abuse, as well as a blog on which readers can comment about the problem. A list and description of special events associated with steroid abuse is also available.

A major feature of THF's educational program is a pair of multimedia "assembly programs" designed for high school and college students on steroid-abuse problems. The programs are called "chalk talks" and currently focus on appearance- and performance-enhancing drugs, in one case, and nutrition and supplement safety, in the other.

United States Anti-Doping Agency

Until the end of the 20th century, issues relating to the use of illegal substances among Olympic Games athletes from the United States were handled by the USOC itself, as one of its many responsibilities. During that time, a number of questions were raised both within the United States and in other parts of the world as to the effectiveness of the USOC in carrying out its drug-testing program. As a result, on June 15, 1999, USOC president William J. Hybl appointed a Select Task Force on Drug Externalization to determine if there was an alternative way of approaching drug abuse problems among U.S. athletes. That committee issued its report in December of the same year, recommending the creation of an entirely new agency, separate and distinct from the USOC, for the purpose of administering such a drug-testing program. The USADA was established as a result of that recommendation. The USADA began operations on October 1, 2000. A year later, the U.S. Congress adopted legislation that officially recognized the USADA as "the official anti-doping agency for Olympic, Pan American and Paralympic sport in the United States" (now Public Law 107-67, section 644). The USADA is now the official anti-doping agency for virtually all amateur athletics organizations in the United States, ranging from the American Archery Association, American Badminton Association, and American Canoe Association to USA Swimming, USA Track & Field, and USA Wrestling.

The USADA's mission statement focuses on three primary objectives, the first of which is maintaining the integrity of athletics and sports by preventing and deterring the types of activities (such as illegal drug use) that violate the principles of true sports. A second and related objective is working to instill the principles of fair play among all athletes. Finally, the mission statement recognizes the rights of individual athletes to participate in fair competitions and, with success, to be "recognized as true heroes."

The focus of USADA's efforts largely mirrors those of the WADA, whose list of prohibited substances and methods of testing and test interpretation USADA follows closely. The USADA website provides detailed information about the way in which athletes are sampled for drug use, the types of tests conducted, the substances for which they are tested, the way in which test results are interpreted and announced, and the penalties issued in connection with the use of prohibited substances. The USADA also places special emphasis in drug testing on topics such as the therapeutic use of certain otherwise prohibited substances, the role of nutritional supplements in athletics and sport competitions, and the use of specialized energy drinks in sports and their possible connection with drug testing. An important additional activity of the USADA involves research on prohibited substances and drug-testing programs. Over the past decade, the agency has spent well in excess of $2 million annually for research on these topics. It has also cooperated with professional sports agencies, such as Major League Baseball and the NFL National Football League, to promote additional research on prohibited substances and testing. In connection with these activities, the USADA annually sponsors the USADA Symposium on Anti-Doping Science, at which researchers present papers on their most recent studies on drug abuse in sports.

The USADA also conducts an active and extensive program of education about drug abuse in athletics and sports. That program includes print and electronic resources for athletes, parents, coaches, and others concerned about the use of illegal substances in sports. These materials include the "Athlete Handbook," a comprehensive general resource on drugs and drug testing in athletics; the "Athlete Pocket Guide," an abbreviated form of the "Handbook"; copies of the "USADA Protocol for Olympic and Paralympic Movement Testing," "United States Olympic Committee Anti-Doping Policies," "World Anti-Doping Agency (WADA) Code," "USADA Whereabouts Policy," and other WADA publications; *The Joy of Sports*, a general introduction to the subject of drugs and drug testing; *Journey—Struggling with Ethics in Sports*; the *USADA Outreach Education Brochure*; "What Sports Means in America"; and two educational curricula for 10–14- and 14–20-year-olds.

The USADA also provides extensive information to athletes themselves to educate them about the problems of illegal drug use and about drug testing. This outreach program includes information about forthcoming Olympic events, the WADA "Whereabouts" policy, exemptions for therapeutic uses of certain drugs, the Global Drugs Reference Online resource, retirement from sports, and athlete webinars. Some typical offerings in the latter category include webinars on athletes in the registered testing pool, athletes who are not in such a pool, the Florida Road Cycling Association race series, and a program for masters track-and-field athletes. The USADA website also provides useful links to other organizations interested in the issue of drug abuse in athletics and sports, such as the Foundation for Global Sports Development, Steroid Analysis, the Taylor Hooton Foundation, Bike Pure, and P. E. Central. Among the best overall sources of information about USADA is its annual report. For example, for the 2015 report, see http://www.usada.org/wp-content/uploads/2015_annual_report.pdf.

The World Anti-Doping Agency

The WADA was established in 1999 in response to growing international concerns about the use of illegal substances by athletes participating in the Olympic Games. Evidence collected in preceding years had made it clear that drug use was out of control, not only in the Olympic Games but also in a number of other amateur and professional sports. The event that precipitated the creation of the agency was a raid conducted in 1998 by French police during the annual Tour de France cycling race in which very large quantities of illegal drugs were discovered among competitors and at competition sites. This event motivated the IOC to call a special conference in Lausanne, Switzerland, in February 1999 to discuss the problem of illegal substance abuse in sports. That conference eventually adopted a document establishing the WADA, to be funded by the IOC. The Declaration of Lausanne stated eight major objectives of the new agency, among them being "to promote and coordinate at international level the fight against doping in sport in all its forms including through in and out of competition"; "to reinforce at international level ethical principles for the practice of doping-free sport and to help protect the health of the athletes"; and "to promote and coordinate research in the fight against doping in sport." The document also called for the new agency to develop a list of substances prohibited for use in international athletic competitions, to create standards for drug testing, and to develop programs for drug education and treatment. The WADA was originally funded entirely by the IOC, although its funding now comes from both the IOC and a number of governmental agencies around the world.

The World Anti-Doping Program, developed and promulgated by the WADA, consists of three major elements: the World Anti-Doping Code; International Standards; and Model Rules, Guidelines, and Protocol. The World Anti-Doping Code was adopted in 2004 prior to the opening of the 2004 Olympic Games in Athens. The code is a very long document that consists of sections dealing with a description of the actions that constitute a violation of the code; standards of proof for use of an illegal substance; a list of prohibited substances; methods of testing and analysis of samples; results management; rights to fair hearings and appeal processes; sanctions on individuals convicted of illegal substance use; rules of confidentiality; regulations for the doping of animals in sports competitions; programs for education and research; responsibilities of governmental and organizing agencies; and relevant definitions. Based on the first use of the code in the 2004 Games, the IOC authorized a review and revision of the code in 2007. Those revisions went into effect in 2009, and, as of early 2017, more than 660 governmental agencies had adopted the code for their own sports programs.

An essential key to the activities of the WADA is the prohibited list, a document that lists all substances that may not be used in athletic competition, along with certain prohibited methods, such as enhancement of oxygen transfer, gene doping, and various types of physical and chemical manipulation. Prohibited substances are subdivided into five major categories: anabolic agents, peptide hormones, growth factors and related substances, beta-2 agonists, hormone and metabolic modulators, and diuretics and other masking agents. The substances listed as prohibited are further subdivided into those that are prohibited during competitions and those that are prohibited both in and out of competition. The most recent edition of the prohibited list was released in January 2017 and is available online at https://www.wada-ama.org/sites/default/files/resources/files/2016-09-29_-_wada_prohibited_list_2017_eng_final.pdf.

The WADA International Standards program consists of five documents to provide detailed information on topics described and discussed in the Anti-Doping Code: the prohibited list, methods of testing, testing laboratories, therapeutic use exemptions, and protection of privacy and personal information. The WADA Model Rules document translates general principles contained in the World Anti-Doping Code and other documents into practical steps that national sport agencies can take to translate those principles into specific testing and interpretation activities. The WADA guidelines project consists of a number of specific documents dealing with topics such as blood sampling, alcohol testing, detection of doping with human growth hormone, education programs, laboratory testing results, and reporting and managing of specific testing results. The WADA protocol documents explain and clarify testing responsibilities among various anti-doping organizations and agencies.

Anti-doping testing is a complex and often controversial process that can have profound effects on international competitions. For example, the winners of two recent Tour de France competitions have been disqualified and stripped of their titles because of illegal substance use. In order to manage the testing process most efficiently, the WADA has created a program known as the Anti-Doping Administration & Management System (ADAMS). ADAMS is an online program that permits all stakeholders in the testing process to keep track of every detail involved in the testing of athletes in a major competition (https://www.wada-ama.org/en/adams).

In addition to its extensive online resources and references, the WADA provides a host of other publications and materials, including a corporate press kit, doping control forms, an outreach model, global statistics, a digital library, and a list of participating federations and organizations. Among its print publications are an annual report, the at-a-glance series on specific doping issues, an athlete guide, a leaflet on the dangers of doping, the doping code, and the *Play True* magazine, available in both print and electronic versions.

John Ziegler (ca. 1920–1983)

Ziegler was an American physician best known for introducing the use of anabolic steroids for performance enhancement to the United States in the 1950s. In 1954, he had traveled to Vienna as an advisor to the U.S. weight lifting team at the World Weight-lifting Championships. The story is told that Ziegler shared drinks one evening with a member of the Russian team, who asked him, "What are you giving your boys," by way of inquiring about U.S. training practices. When Ziegler asked the same question of his Russian counterpart, he learned for the first time that those team members were receiving injections of testosterone. It was these injections that were responsible for the amazing increase in body mass and strength that Russian athletes were demonstrating at the time, not only at the weight lifting competition but in other international events, such as the Olympic Games of 1956. Ziegler left Vienna convinced that he needed to try some comparable training regimen for members of the U.S. weight lifting community. He experimented by injecting himself, an American trainer named Bob Hoffman, and three team weight lifters with small amounts of testosterone. He was amazed at the success of the treatment in producing increased muscle mass and strength, but was troubled by the androgenic effects that were associated with the testosterone treatments. He made up his mind to search out or develop a new substance that had the muscle-building properties of testosterone without the substance's undesirable side effects.

Ziegler's interest in anabolic steroids came about just as Ciba Pharmaceuticals was developing a drug along the lines of the product he was looking for. That drug, methandrostenolone (trade names Averbol, Danabol, and Dianabol), was developed for the treatment of wasting in patients suffering from debilitating diseases and individuals suffering from severe burns. It proved to be hugely successful in helping such individuals regain body mass and strength. Ziegler immediately recognized the potential of the chemical for building body mass and strength in weight lifters and, perhaps, other athletes. He began to make the drug available to members of the weight lifting team and other athletes who asked for it. The problem was that the drug was so successful that many of those to whom he gave it began using it in massive quantities, up to 10 times the amount he had recommended.

Over the years, Dianabol became increasingly popular as an anabolic steroid, and Ziegler became increasingly disillusioned about the misuse his clients made of the drug. By the beginning of the 1970s, he had essentially washed his hands of steroid use by athletics. In a 1972 interview with *Science* reporter Nicholas Wade, he said that he had "lost interest in fooling with IQ's of that caliber. Now it's [steroid use] about as widespread among these idiots as marijuana." In another interview for the *Journal of Sports History*, he added that "I wish to God now I'd never done it. I'd like to go back and take that whole chapter out of my life."

Birth data for John Bosley Ziegler are not generally available, and his birth information is given as sometime around 1920 somewhere in the Midwest. He entered the premedical program at Gettysburg College in 1938, graduating with his bachelor's degree four years later. Instead of immediately continuing his studies, he joined the U.S. Marine Corps and fought in the Pacific during World War II. During his time there, he suffered serious battle wounds that required extensive restorative surgeries when he returned home. After recovering from those surgeries, he enrolled at the University of Maryland Medical School, from which he earned his MD. He completed his residency and internship at Marine Corps hospitals in Norfolk, Virginia, and Mobile, Alabama, continuing with a two-year residency in neurology at the Tulane University School of Medicine. At the time, he had hoped to become a brain surgeon, but found that he did not have the manual skills for the specialty. Instead, he returned to Olney, Maryland, in 1954, where he opened a private practice specializing in the treatment of handicapped and severely injured patients and carrying out research at the nearby Ciba facility.

After he became disenchanted with his experience with anabolic steroids, Ziegler settled into the routine of general practice in Olney, where he remained until his death from heart failure in November 1983. Reminiscences of his life focus on his "restless, imaginative intellect" that prompted him to study everything from "nuclear medicine to hypnosis." As a way of pursuing this range of interests, he held a weekly salon at his home to which were invited an astonishing array of guests, ranging from "White House staffers to Marine generals and astrophysicists" (as mentioned by Shaun Assael in *Steroid Nation* [ESPN Books, 2007]). For many in the athletic and sports field, Ziegler will always be remembered as "Doctor Dianabol." To others who knew other sides of him, he will be remembered as "Doc Ziegler," or, more simply, "Montana Jack" or "Tex," because of his tendency to dress up as a Westerner and his reputation as a "hell-raiser" around Olney.

Introduction

This chapter provides some relevant data and documents dealing with the development of anabolic androgenic steroids (AAS), their use in medical and nonmedical settings, and regulations and court cases involving AAS. The Data section provides basic information on current and historical trends in AAS use and arrests in the United States and other parts of the world. The Documents section which follows is arranged in chronological order and includes excerpts from important committee and commission reports; from bills, acts, and laws; and from important legal cases.

Data

Table 5.1 Percentage of High School Students Who Ever Took Steroids without a Doctor's Prescription,* by Race/Ethnicity and Grade

Category	Female		Male		Total	
Race/Ethnicity	Percentage	CI**	Percentage	CI	Percentage	CI
White	1.8	1.2–2.7	3.6	2.8–4.6	2.7	2.1–3.4
Black	3.6	1.8–7.1	4.8	2.6–8.7	4.5	2.5–7.7
Hispanic	3.9	2.8–5.4	4.1	2.9–5.8	4.1	3.1–5.4

(continued)

High school wrestling and football star Zach Greenwald works out in the weight room at Paulsboro high school in Paulsboro, NJ, March 3, 2009. Greenwald says he doesn't use steroids and likes the testing program in New Jersey. (AP Photo/Mel Evans)

Table 5.1 *(continued)*

Grade	Percentage	CI	Percentage	CI	Percentage	CI
9th	3.4	2.3–5.0	3.5	2.6–4.9	3.6	2.8–4.6
10th	3.4	2.1–5.5	4.4	3.0–6.4	3.9	2.7–5.6
11th	2.0	1.4–2.8	2.8	2.0–3.9	2.7	2.0–3.6
12th	1.6	0.9–2.6	4.8	3.2–7.1	3.3	2.4–4.5
Total	2.7	2.1–3.5	4.0	3.1–5.1	3.5	2.8–4.3

*Pills or shots one or more times during life.

**95% confidence level (range of results of 95% confidence)

Source: Kann, Laura, et al. 2016, June 10. "Youth Risk Behavior Surveillance—United States 2015." *Morbidity and Mortality Weekly Report*. Table 63, page 113. Available online at https://www.cdc.gov/healthyyouth/data/yrbs/pdf/2015/ss6506_updated.pdf. Accessed on February 22, 2017.

Table 5.2   Perceived Harmfulness of Steroids among 12th Grade U.S. Students, 1989–2015* (Percentages)

1989	1990	1991	1992	1993	1994
63.8	69.9	65.6	70.7	69.1	66.1

1995	1996	1997	1998	1999	2000
66.4	67.6	67.2	68.1	62.1	57.9

2001	2002	2003	2004	2005	2006
58.9	57.1	55.0	55.7	56.8	60.2

2007	2008	2009	2010	2011	2012
57.4	60.8	60.2	59.2	61.1	58.6

2013	2014	2015
54.2	54.6	54.4

*Question: "How much do you think people risk harming themselves (physically or in other ways) if they take steroids?" (Asked of 8th and 10th graders only in 1991–1994.)

Source: Johnston, Lloyd D., et al. 2016. "Monitoring the Future: National Survey Results on Drug Use, 1975–2015: Overview, Key Findings on Adolescent Drug Use." Ann Arbor: Institute for Social Research, The University of Michigan. Tables 11, pages 87–88. http://www.monitoringthefuture.org/pubs/monographs/mtf-overview2015.pdf. Accessed on February 22, 2017.

Table 5.3. Disapproval of Steroid Use, among 12th Grade U.S. Students, 1990–2015* (Percentages)

1990	1991	1992	1993	1994	1995
90.8	90.5	92.1	92.1	91.9	91.0
1996	1997	1998	1999	2000	2001
91.7	91.4	90.8	88.9	88.8	86.4
2002	2003	2004	2005	2006	2007
86.8	86.0	87.9	88.8	89.4	89.2
2008	2009	2010	2011	2012	2013
90.9	90.3	89.8	89.7	90.4	88.2
2014	2015				
87.5	87.8				

*Question: "Do you disapprove of people (who are 18 or older) doing each of the following?" [taking steroids] (Asked of 8th and 10th graders only in 1991–1994.).

Source: Johnston, Lloyd D., et al. 2016. "Monitoring the Future: National Survey Results on Drug Use, 1975–2015: Overview, Key Findings on Adolescent Drug Use." Ann Arbor: Institute for Social Research, The University of Michigan. Table 14, pages 92–93 http://www.monitoringthefuture.org/pubs/monographs/mtf-overview2015.pdf. Accessed on February 22, 2017.

Table 5.4. Availability of Steroids, According to U.S. 12th Graders, 1991–2015 (Percentage of Respondents Indicating Availability)*

1991	1992	1993	1994	1995	1996
46.7	46.8	44.8	42.9	45.5	40.3
1997	1998	1999	2000	2001	2002
41.7	44.5	44.6	44.8	44.4	45.5
2003	2004	2005	2006	2007	2008
40.7	42.6	39.7	41.1	40.1	35.2

(continued)

Table 5.4 *(continued)*

2009	2010	2011	2012	2013	2014	2015
15.2	14.2	13.3	12.5	12.9	11.8	11.8

*Question: "How difficult do you think it would be for you to get [steroids], if you wanted some?"

Source: Johnston, Lloyd D., et al. 2016. "Monitoring the Future: National Survey Results on Drug Use, 1975–2015: Overview, Key Findings on Adolescent Drug Use." Ann Arbor: Institute for Social Research, The University of Michigan. Table 17, pages 96–97. http://www.monitoringthefuture.org/pubs/monographs/mtf-overview2015.pdf. Accessed on February 22, 2017.

Table 5.5 Total Anti-Doping Rule Violations, All Sports, 2013

Sport	Number of Tests	Number of ADRV	Percentage ADRV*
Summer Sports			
Aquatics	11,585	49	0.42
Archery	87	2	2.30
Athletics	24,942	235	0.94
Badminton	1,264	1	0.08
Basketball	5,546	21	0.40
Boxing	3,558	33	0.93
Canoe/Kayak	4,024	21	0.55
Cycling	22,252	153	0.69
Duathlon	151	1	0.66
Equestrian	566	6	1.06
Fencing	1,980	4	0.20
Field Hockey	1,452	1	0.07
Football (Soccer)	28,002	74	0.26
Golf	483	1	0.20
Gymnastics	2,142	2	0.09
Handball	3,231	9	0.28
Judo	4,476	40	0.89
Modern Pentathlon	555	2	0.36
Rowing	4,343	10	0.23
Rugby	6,126	50	0.82
Sailing	631	0	0.00

Summer Sports			
Shooting	2,350	11	0.47
Table Tennis	1,035	7	0.68
Taekwondo	1,588	10	0.63
Tennis	3,476	8	0.23
Triathlon	3,495	12	0.34
Volleyball	4,375	16	0.36
Weight lifting	8,533	248	2.91
Wrestling	8,533	92	1.08
Winter Sports			
Biathlon	2,338	7	0.30
Bobsleigh	1,372	0	0.00
Curling	537	1	0.19
Ice Hockey	3,488	17	0.49
Luge	477	1	0.21
Skating	4,655	6	0.13
Skiing	6,439	5	0.08

*Calculated by author from data provided in source report.

Source: 2015 Anti-Doping Test Figures. 2015. World Anti-Doping Agency. Table 2, pages 31–40. https://www.wada-ama.org/sites/default/files/resources/files/2015_wada_anti-doping_testing_figures_report_0.pdf. Accessed on February 23, 2017. (This section of the report includes breakdowns within sports, such as figure skating and speed skating.)

Documents

Drug Misuse: Anabolic Steroids and Human Growth Hormone (1989)

In 1989, the General Accounting Office conducted a study, at the request of Senator Joseph Biden (D-DE) on the use of anabolic steroids by amateur and professional athletes in the United States. The study reported not only on the statistics of anabolic androgenic steroid use but also on the health effects related to the use of such substances. The major statistical findings reported were as follows.

A national-based study found that 6.6 percent of male 12th graders use or have used anabolic steroids. According to the authors of the study, if this use rate is applied to the national population of males enrolled in secondary schools, it suggests that between 250,000 and 500,000 adolescents in the country use or have used these drugs. In four other studies, while not nationally representative, a similar or higher rate of anabolic steroid use among males was found, with study estimates ranging from 5 percent to 11.1 percent. In three of the four studies, anabolic steroid use was found to be much lower among females, ranging from 1 percent to 2.5 percent. . . .

The most frequent reasons cited for using steroids were (1) to increase strength, size, and speed and (2) to improve athletic performance. In the Arkansas study, 64 percent of steroid users reported that they wanted to increase strength, 50 percent wanted to increase size, and 27 percent wanted to improve physical appearance. In the national study of 12th graders, the largest percentage of users (47 percent) reported that their main reason for using the drug was to improve athletic performance. Another 27 percent of users reported "appearance" as the main reason for using anabolic steroids. . . .

We identified only five studies on the extent of steroid use among college students. Two studies on general drug use in a representative sample of the general student body from five universities were carried out over a 15-year period, 1970–84. The first study reported results for 1970 and 1973; the second, for 1970, 1976, 1980, and 1984. In the general student body of the five schools, data for 1970 and 1973 showed that 0 to 2 percent of students had ever used steroids. When data from this study were examined for athletes only, 15 percent of athletes reported using anabolic steroids in 1970. This rate increased to 20 percent for 1976, 1980, and 1984. In 1984, only 1 percent of nonathletes in the study reported steroid use.

The third and fourth studies examined steroid use by sport. In the third study, which was conducted in 1980 and focused on intercollegiate swimmers at six universities, 6 percent of male swimmers reported steroid use. No female swimmers reported use. In the fourth study, involving 2,048 intercollegiate athletes conducted in the fall of 1984 at 11 universities, the national prevalence rate was found to be 4 percent for steroid use in athletes for eight different sports. The highest rate of use was found among male football players (9 percent), followed by male basketball, track, and tennis athletes (each 4 percent); 1 percent of female swimmers reported steroid use.

The fifth study, published in 1988, provided information on 1,010 male students at three universities. Results from this study also support a higher rate of steroid use among athletes than among nonathletes. Of varsity athletes at two of the three schools in the study, 17 percent reported steroid use. This rate is significantly higher than the 2 percent of all males who reported using steroids in the total survey sample of the three schools.

Source: United States General Accounting Office. 1989, August. *Drug Misuse: Anabolic Steroids and Human Growth Hormone*. Washington, DC: United States General Accounting Office.

Anabolic Steroid Control Act of 1990

In 1990, the U.S. Congress passed and President George H. W. Bush signed a law adding anabolic steroids to the list of substances under the Controlled Substances Act. The main features of the act are as follows.

Section 1 provides a short title for the Act.

Sec. 2. Anabolic Steroid Penalties

(a) COACHES AND OTHERS PERSUADING OR INDUCING USE—Section 404 of the Controlled Substances Act (21 U.S.C. 844) is amended by inserting after subsection (a) the following:

'(b)(1) Whoever, being a physical trainer or adviser to an individual, endeavors to persuade or induce that individual to possess or use anabolic steroids in violation of subsection (a), shall be fined under title 18, United States Code, or imprisoned not more than 2 years, or both. If such individual has not attained the age of 18 years, the maximum imprisonment shall be 5 years.

'(2) As used in this subsection, the term 'physical trainer or adviser' means any professional or amateur coach, manager, trainer, instructor, or other such person, who provides any athletic or physical instruction, training, advice, assistance, or other such service to any person.'.

(b) ADDITION OF ANABOLIC STEROIDS TO SCHEDULE III—Schedule III of section 202(c) of the Controlled Substances Act (21 U.S.C. 812(c)) is amended by adding at the end the following:

'(e) Anabolic steroids.'.

(c) DEFINITION OF ANABOLIC STEROID—Section 102 of the Controlled Substances Act (21 U.S.C. 802) is amended by adding at the end the following:

'(41) The term 'anabolic steroid' means any drug or hormonal substance that promotes muscle growth in a manner pharmacologically similar to testosterone, and includes-

[The act then names 23 specific chemicals and their derivatives to be considered as "anabolic steroids" under this act.]

Sec. 3. Penalty for Distribution of Human Growth Hormone

Subsection (e) of section 303 of the Federal Food, Drug, and Cosmetic Act (21 U.S.C. 333) is amended—

(1)   by striking 'anabolic steroid' each place it appears and inserting 'human growth hormone'; and

(2)   by adding at the end the following:

'(3)   As used in this subsection, the term 'human growth hormone' means somatrem, somatropin, or an analogue of either of them.'.

Source: H.R.4658—Anabolic Steroids Control Act of 1990. Congress.gov. https://www.congress.gov/bill/101st-congress/house-bill/4658/text. Accessed on February 25, 2017.

H.R.3866—Anabolic Steroid Control Act of 2004

In 2004, the U.S. Congress passed and President George W. Bush signed a modification of the 1990 anabolic steroid legislation mentioned earlier. The primary change included in this legislation was the addition of more than 40 anabolic steroid chemicals to the list from the original legislation. The law also had a few other minor sections, as indicated here.

Section 1 provides a short title for the act.

Sec. 2. Increased Penalties for Anabolic Steroid Offenses Near Sports Facilities

(a)   IN GENERAL—Part D of the Controlled Substances Act is amended by adding at the end the following:

Anabolic Steroid Offenses Near Sports Facilities

SEC. 424. (a) Whoever violates section 401(a)(1) or section 416 by manufacturing, distributing, or possessing with intent to distribute, an anabolic steroid near or at a sports facility is subject to twice the maximum term of imprisonment, maximum fine, and maximum term of supervised release otherwise provided by section 401 for that offense.

[The term sports facility *is then defined.*

Section 3 then directs the United States Sentencing Commission to consider appropriate sentences for individuals convicted of violating the provisions of this law.

Section 4 lists the new steroids to be included under Schedule III of the Controlled Substances Act.]

Sec. 5. Reporting Requirement

Not later than 2 years after the date of the enactment of this Act, the Secretary of Health and Human Services, in consultation with the Attorney General, shall prepare and submit a report to the Judiciary Committee of the House and Senate, and to the Committee on Energy and Commerce of the House, evaluating the health risks associated with dietary supplements not scheduled under the amendments made by this Act which contain substances similar to those added to the list of controlled substances under those amendments. The report shall include recommendations on whether such substances should be regulated as anabolic steroids.

Source: H.R.3866—Anabolic Steroid Control Act of 2004. Congress.gov. https://www.congress.gov/bill/108th-congress/house-bill/3866. Accessed on February 24, 2017.

Anabolic Steroids Are Easily Purchased without a Prescription and Present Significant Challenges to Law Enforcement Officials (2005)

In 2005, Representatives Henry Waxman (D-CA) and Tom Davis (R-VA) asked the U.S. Government Accountability Office (GAO) to collect information as to whether illegal anabolic steroids could be purchased in the United States, to identify the common sources of these drugs, and to discover the primary challenges posed in investigating, prosecuting, and deterring individuals involved in the illegal anabolic steroid business. The following are the primary findings of GAO's research.

Summary

Our investigators easily obtained anabolic steroids without a prescription through the Internet. After conducting Internet searches, they found hundreds of Web sites offering anabolic steroids commonly used by athletes and bodybuilders for sale. The investigators then used an e-mail account in a fictitious name to place 22 orders. From these orders, we received 10 shipments of anabolic steroids; all were shipped from foreign countries. We also received 4 shipments from within the United States but the substances they contained, though marketed as anabolic steroids or other "muscle building" products, were not anabolic steroids according to the FDA. We are referring the evidence concerning our purchases to DEA and to FDA for appropriate action.

The officials we spoke with told us that most anabolic steroids sold illegally in the United States come from abroad, and that the Internet is the most widely used means of buying and selling anabolic steroids illegally. They also reported that, because of the foreign origin of the steroids and the widespread use of the Internet in steroid trafficking, extensive time and resources are usually required to investigate and prosecute steroid cases. Further, the sheer volume of all types of imports from abroad presents significant challenges in efforts to prevent anabolic steroids from illegally entering the United States. Additionally, some officials noted the relatively low sentences that result from application of the federal sentencing guidelines to persons convicted of illegal steroid trafficking.

[The GAO report then provided details about the ease with which illegal anabolic steroids can be purchased in the United Sates, some of which are reprinted here:]

The 10 orders of anabolic steroids we received were obtained through Web sites that openly and boldly offer anabolic steroids for sale. Some of the Web sites offer a variety of pharmaceutical drugs, while others sell anabolic steroids exclusively. They typically offer "private and confidential" sales of "discretely shipped" anabolic steroids that will "shape your body the way . . . you want it to look." . . .

There is a readily available supply of steroids worldwide because, in most countries, anabolic steroids can be sold legally without a prescription. Thus, many foreign distributors do not violate the laws of their own country when they sell these substances to people in the United States. As a result, U.S. law enforcement agencies have difficulty in obtaining assistance from their foreign counterparts in investigations of such distributors.

Law enforcement officials also identified smuggling of anabolic steroids across international borders into the United

States as an important part of the illegal distribution network and described how smugglers typically operate. . . .

The Internet is a primary vehicle for buying and selling anabolic steroids illegally. Internet Web sites, usually foreign based, advertise steroids for sale. Customers access these sites, inquire about purchases, and place orders. Sellers typically require advance payment through Western Union, PayPal, money orders, or credit cards. After receiving payment, sellers ship the steroids through international mail or an express carrier . . .

The Internet also provides an easy means for sellers to market to young people. Moreover, according to some of the law enforcement officials we spoke to, sales of steroids and other synthetic drugs are used by some sellers as a "gateway" to sales of narcotics, such as cocaine. Typically, in such cases, the seller uses an initial series of steroid or designer drug transactions to gauge whether the buyer is a legitimate customer and is not an undercover law enforcement investigator. After the seller has gained assurances that the customer is legitimate through the initial steroid sales, narcotics are offered for sale.

To prosecute illegal steroid dealers, law enforcement officials must identify them and gather evidence of their trafficking activity. However, anabolic steroid dealers can capitalize on the anonymity afforded by the Internet to thwart efforts to identify them. . . .

Law enforcement officials told us that although extensive time and resources are required to locate, charge, and convict criminal anabolic steroid dealers, the penalties under the Federal Sentencing Guidelines faced by persons convicted of such offenses do not reflect the seriousness of their crimes or provide adequate deterrence. Drug quantity is a principal factor in determining offense level and sentence for drug offenses under the sentencing guidelines . . . an offender responsible for selling 40,000 pills of a Schedule III substance other than an anabolic steroid, such as ketamine, would face a sentence of 33 to 41 months under the drug quantity rules of the sentencing guidelines. On the other hand, an offender convicted of selling 40,000 pills of an anabolic steroid would face a sentence of 0 to 6 months under those rules.

Source: United States Government Accountability Office. "GAO-06-243R Anabolic Steroids." Available online at http://www.gao.gov/new.items/d06243r.pdf. Accessed on February 24, 2017.

Clean Sports Act of 2005

For almost two decades, the U.S. Congress has been concerned about the use of anabolic and androgenic steroids by professional athletes. Individually and collectively, members of Congress have prodded professional baseball, football, basketball, and hockey leagues to "get their act together" and develop effective anti-doping policies. When these entities have been slow to do so, Congress has threatened federal action against the leagues to enforce stronger drug-testing policies. One such effort was the Clean Sports Act of 2005, sponsored by Senators John McCain and Ted Stevens in the Senate and Congressmen Tom Davis and Henry Waxman in the House. The following is Senator McCain's description of the legislation (which was introduced into the Congress, but was never passed).

The purpose of this bill is to protect the integrity of professional sports and, more importantly, the health and safety of our Nation's youth, who, for better or for worse, see professional athletes as role models. The legislation would achieve that goal by establishing minimum standards for the testing of steroids and other performance-enhancing substances by major professional sports leagues. By adhering to—and hopefully exceeding—these minimum standards, the Nation's major professional sports leagues would send a strong signal to the public that performance-enhancing drugs have no legitimate role in American sports.

This bill would prohibit our country's major professional sports leagues—the National Football League, Major League Baseball, the National Basketball Association, and the National Hockey League—from operating if they do not meet the minimum testing requirements set forth therein. Those standards would be comprised of five key components: the independence of the entity or entities that perform the leagues' drug tests; testing for a comprehensive list of doping substances and methods; a strong system of unannounced testing; significant penalties that discourage the use of performance-enhancing drugs; and a fair and effective adjudication process for athletes accused of doping. These elements are crucial components of any credible performance-enhancing drug testing policy.

More specifically, the bill would require all major professional sports leagues to have an independent third party administer their performance-enhancing drug tests. The legislation would further require that samples provided by athletes be tested by laboratories approved by the United States Anti-Doping Agency—USADA—and for substances banned by USADA. In addition, the bill would require not fewer than three unannounced tests during a league's season of play, and at least two unannounced tests during the off season. Under this legislation, if a player were to test positive for a banned performance-enhancing substance, that player would be suspended for 2 years for the first violation and banned for life for a second violation. Finally, if any player were to test positive, the professional sports league would be obligated to ensure that the player would have substantial due process rights including the opportunity for a hearing and right to counsel.

[McCain then explains how federal policy would be carried out.]

The need for reforming the drug testing policies of professional sports is clear. However, I introduce this legislation reluctantly. Over a year ago, I stated publicly that the failure of professional sports—and in particular Major League Baseball—to commit to addressing the issue of doping straight on and immediately would motivate Congress to search for legislative remedies. Despite my clear warning and the significant attention that Congress has given to this stain on professional sports, baseball, and other professional leagues have refused to do the right thing. . . .

I remain hopeful that professional sports will reform their drug testing policies on their own—a modest proposal in the eyes of reasonable people. However, the introduction of this bill demonstrates the continued seriousness with which Congress views this issue. It should be seen as a renewed incentive for the leagues to clean up their sports on their own without Government interference.

Source: Congressional Record—Senate. May 24, 2005, S5852. Available online at http://www.gpo.gov/fdsys/pkg/CREC-2005-05-24/pdf/CREC-2005-05-24-pt1-PgS5852.pdf. Accessed on February 24, 2017.

Mitchell Report (2007)

On March 30, 2006, Major League Baseball commissioner Bud Selig, concerned about the growing evidence of illegal substance abuse in Major League Baseball, asked former senator George J. Mitchell to head an investigation of drug abuse in professional baseball. Mitchell offered his report to Commissioner Selig on December 13, 2007. He later summarized the result of his research and his recommendations at a meeting of the U.S. House of Representatives Committee on Energy and Commerce on February 27, 2008. Some important features of Mitchell's testimony are reprinted here.

During the period discussed in my report, the use of steroids in Major League Baseball was widespread, in violation of federal law and baseball policy. Club officials routinely discussed the possibility of substance use when evaluating players. The response by baseball was slow to develop and was initially ineffective. The Players Association had for many years opposed a mandatory random drug testing program, but they agreed to the adoption of such a program in 2002, after which the response gained momentum. . . .

Everyone involved in baseball over the past two decades—Commissioners, club officials, the Players Association, and players—shares to some extent in the responsibility for the steroids era. There was a collective failure to recognize the problem as it emerged and to deal with it early on. As a result, an environment developed in which illegal use became widespread. . . .

The adoption of the recommendations set forth in my report will be a first step . . . and I will now summarize them. . . .

First, there must be an enhanced capacity to conduct investigations based on non-testing evidence. Some illegal substances are difficult or virtually impossible to detect. . . .

The Commissioner has accepted my recommendation to create a Department of Investigations, led by a senior executive, to respond promptly and aggressively to allegations of the illegal use or possession of performance enhancing substances. To do its job effectively, this department must establish credibility and cooperate closely with law enforcement agencies. I recommended that the Commissioner strengthen pre-existing efforts to keep illegal substances out of major league clubhouses by logging and tracking packages shipped to players at major league ballparks, conducting background checks and random drug tests on clubhouse employees, and adopting policies to ensure that allegations of a player's possession or use of performance enhancing substances are reported promptly to the Department of Investigations. . . .

Second, improved educational programs about the dangers of substance use are critical to any effort to deter use. Over the last several years, the Commissioner's Office and the Players Association have made an increased effort to provide players and club personnel with educational materials on performance enhancing substances. Several suggestions for improvement in this effort are set forth in my report.

Third, although it is clear that even the best drug testing program is, by itself, not sufficient, drug testing remains an important element of a comprehensive approach to combat illegal use. The current program was agreed to in 2006 and will remain in effect until 2011. Any changes to the program therefore must be negotiated and agreed to by the clubs and the Players Association. In my report, I set forth the principles that presently characterize a state-of-the-art drug testing program, and I urged the clubs and the Players Association to incorporate them into baseball's program when they next deal with this issue.

Source: "Drugs in Sports: Compromising the Health of Athletes and Undermining the Integrity of Competition." Hearing before the Subcommittee on Commerce, Trade, and Consumer Protection of the Committee on Energy and Commerce. House of Representatives. One Hundred Tenth Congress, Second Session, February 27, 2008. Available online at http://www.gpo.gov/fdsys/pkg/CHRG-110hhrg49522/pdf/CHRG-110hhrg49522.pdf. Accessed on February 25, 2017.

Effectiveness of Federal Anabolic Steroid Prevention Programs (2007)

In 2007, Representatives Henry Waxman (D-CA) and Tom Davis (R-VA) asked the U.S. GAO to conduct a study to determine the effectiveness of federal programs designed to reduce illegal steroid use by young American adults. The GAO provided a report on their study in October 2007, focusing primarily on two federally funded programs: Athletes Training and Learning to Avoid Steroids (ATLAS) and Athletes Targeting Healthy Exercise & Nutrition Alternatives (ATHENA). Following are the general conclusions GAO drew about these programs.

The GAO first attempted to identify factors that might be associated with illegal steroid use. It concluded that:

Almost half of the studies we reviewed identified certain risk factors and behaviors linked to the abuse of anabolic steroids among teenagers. . . . Several studies found that the use of alcohol and other drugs—such as tobacco, marijuana, and cocaine—is associated with the abuse of anabolic steroids among teenagers, including teenage athletes and non-athletes. . . . Several studies we reviewed found no difference between athletes and non-athletes in their abuse of anabolic steroids. . . . A few studies we reviewed found a positive correlation between anabolic steroid abuse and risky sexual behaviors such as early initiation of sexual activity and an increased number of sexual partners. Some studies found that aggressive behaviors such as fighting were related to anabolic steroid abuse by both males and females.

[Overall, the researchers concluded that:]

The cause-and-effect relationships between anabolic steroid abuse and other risky behaviors, such as violence, have not been determined.

[The researchers then investigated the success of federally funded programs to reduce steroid abuse:]

According to experts, available research does not establish the extent to which the ATLAS and ATHENA programs are effective over time in preventing anabolic steroid abuse among teenage athletes. Experts acknowledge that both programs appear promising in their ability to prevent the abuse of anabolic steroids among teenage athletes immediately following participants' completion of the programs. Assessment of the effectiveness of the ATLAS program 1 year later, however, found that the lower incidence of anabolic steroid use was not sustained, although participants continued to report reduced intentions to use anabolic steroids. The long-term effectiveness of the ATHENA program has not been reported.

[The GAO report concluded with a brief summary of information about the long-term health effects of steroid use on adolescents:]

According to experts, there are several gaps in research on the health effects of teenage abuse of anabolic steroids. Experts report that while there is some research that has examined the health effects of anabolic steroid abuse among adults—for example, the harmful effects on the cardiovascular, hormonal, and immune systems—there is a lack of research on these effects among teenagers. There is also a lack of research on the long-term health effects of initiating anabolic steroid abuse during the teenage years. Some health effects of steroid abuse among adults, such as adverse effects on the hormonal system, have been shown to be reversible when the adults have stopped abusing anabolic steroids. Experts point out, however, that it is not known whether this reversibility holds true for teenagers as well. While some experts suggest that anabolic steroid abuse may do more lasting harm to teenagers, due to the complex physical changes unique to adolescence, according to other experts there is no conclusive evidence of potentially permanent health effects. Experts also report that the extent of the psychological effects of anabolic steroid abuse and, in particular, of withdrawal from steroid abuse, is unclear due to limited research.

Source: "Anabolic Steroid Abuse: Federal Efforts to Prevent and Reduce Anabolic Steroid Abuse among Teenagers." [Washington, DC]: United States Government Accountability Office. October 2007. Available online at http://www.gao.gov/new.items/d0815.pdf. Accessed on February 25, 2017.

United States of America v. Marion Jones (2007)

In October 2006, Olympic gold and bronze medal winner Marion Jones pleaded guilty to lying about the use of steroids in preparation for athletic competitions. In preparation for her sentencing for this crime, prosecutors submitted a memorandum reviewing the primary elements of the case and their recommendation for her sentencing. The main points of that memorandum are as follows. (The judge accepted these recommendations in announcing Jones's sentence.)

Prosecutors reviewed Jones's statements in two trials, one before the U.S. District Court for Northern California and the other before the U.S. District Court for Southern New York. In each instance, they reviewed the facts presented at the trials and then drew the following conclusions.

Northern California Case

The defendant's use of performance-enhancing drugs encompassed numerous drugs (THG, EPO, Human Growth Hormone) and delivery systems (sublingual drops, subcutaneous injections) over a substantial course of time. Her use of these substances was goal-oriented, that is, it was designed to further her athletic accomplishments and financial career. Her false statements to the IRS-CI agent were focused, hoping not only to deflect the attention of the investigation away from herself, but also to secure the gains achieved by her use of the performance-enhancing substances in the first place. The false statements to the IRS-CI agent were the culmination of a long series of public denials by the defendant, often accompanied by baseless attacks on those accusing her, regarding her use of these substances.

The context of the defendant's use of performance-enhancing substances, as detailed in the documents seized from BALCO, shows a concentrated, organized, long-term effort to use these substances for her personal gain, a scenario wholly inconsistent with anything other than her denials being calculated lies to agents who were investigating that same conduct.

[Southern New York case:]

Jones was very nearly a witness for the Government in the criminal trial before your Honor. It is difficult to articulate how catastrophic would have been her perjurious testimony had the Government not fortuitously learned, at the eleventh hour, of the falsity of her statements. The defendant's false statements derailed the Government's investigative efforts and were highly material to its criminal investigation.

[The government then set forth its recommendations for sentencing:]

For the reasons set forth above, the Court should impose a sentence within sentencing range of 0 to 6 months' imprisonment stipulated to by the parties.

Source: United States District Court, Southern District of New York. *United States of America v. Marion Jones.* "Government's Sentencing Memorandum." Available online at http://assets.espn.go.com/media/pdf/071221/jonessentencingmemo.pdf. Accessed on February 25, 2017.

Mandatory Steroid Testing for High School Students in New Jersey (2007)

Some individuals concerned about the dangers posed by steroid abuse among young people have argued for mandatory testing of all high school athletes. In 2007, New Jersey became the first state to adopt such a program. Two other states—Illinois and Texas—later adopted similar laws, the latter of which reversed its decision in 2015. All three states experienced some common problems with their programs, perhaps the most important being cost. New Jersey, for example, spent $400,000 in the first four years of testing and found only one student who tested positive. Still, concerns about steroid abuse among high school athletes are such that the campaign for mandatory testing continues in a number of states. The New Jersey law reads as follows (extraneous citations are omitted).

18A:40A-22 Findings, declarations relative to substance abuse testing policies in public school districts.

1. The Legislature finds and declares that there are many school districts within the State with a growing problem of drug abuse among their students. The Legislature further finds that federal and State courts have held that it may be appropriate for school districts to combat this problem through the random drug testing of students

participating in extracurricular activities, including inter-scholastic athletics, and students who possess school park-ing permits. The Legislature also finds that a random drug testing program may have a positive effect on attaining the important objectives of deterring drug use and provid-ing a means for the early detection of students with drug problems so that counseling and rehabilitative treatment may be offered.

18A:40A-23 Adoption of policy for random testing of cer-tain students.

2. A board of education may adopt a policy, pursuant to rules and regulations adopted by the State Board of Education in consultation with the Department of Human Services, which are consistent with the New Jersey Constitution and the federal Constitution, for the random testing of the dis-trict's students in grades 9–12 who participate in extracur-ricular activities, including interscholastic athletics, or who possess school parking permits, for the use of controlled dangerous substances as defined in N.J.S.2C:35-2 and ana-bolic steroids. The testing shall be conducted by the school physician, school nurse or a physician, laboratory or health care facility designated by the board of education and the cost shall be paid by the board. Any disciplinary action taken against a student who tests positive for drug use or who refuses to consent to testing shall be limited to the stu-dent's suspension from or prohibition against participation in extracurricular activities, or revocation of the student's parking permits.

18A:40A-24 Public hearing prior to adoption of drug test-ing policy.

3. Each board of education shall hold a public hearing prior to the adoption of its drug testing policy. The policy shall be in written form and shall be distributed to students and their parents or guardians at the beginning of each school

year. The policy shall include, but need not be limited to, the following:

a. notice that the consent of the student and his parent or guardian for random student drug testing is required for the student to participate in extracurricular activities and to possess a school parking permit;

b. the procedures for collecting and testing specimens;

c. the manner in which students shall be randomly selected for drug testing;

d. the procedures for a student or his parent or guardian to challenge a positive test result;

e. the standards for ensuring the confidentiality of test results;

f. the specific disciplinary action to be imposed upon a student who tests positive for drug use or refuses to consent to testing;

g. the guidelines for the referral of a student who tests positive for drug use to drug counseling or rehabilitative treatment; and

h. the scope of authorized disclosure of test results

Source: New Jersey State Statutes. Title 18A: Education. Available online at ftp://www.njleg.state.nj.us/20042005/AL 05/209_.PDF. Accessed on February 25, 2017.

Anabolic Steroid Ban on Horse Racing in Kentucky (2008)

The discussion on the use of anabolic steroids as performance-enhancing substances in athletics has focused on humans in this book. The fact is that anabolic steroids have also been used on other animals involved in sports competitions, such as greyhounds and thoroughbred horses, quarter horses, and other breeds of horses. To a perhaps surprising degree, the use of anabolic steroids and other performance-enhancing drugs has largely been ignored in nonhuman competitors. In 2008, the Kentucky Horse Racing Commission changed that situation for at least one state by adopting new bans on the use of anabolic steroids in horses that are raced in the state. A description of the new regulations was included in the commission's 2008–2009 biennial report, as summarized here.

On Aug. 25, 2008, the KHRC approved the EDRC's [Equine Drug Research Council] recommendations to ban anabolic steroids for Thoroughbred and Standardbred racing and requested that Governor Beshear adopt the changes in state law through an emergency regulation.

Under the amendment to the drug regulation, anabolic steroids cannot be administered to a horse that is in competition. In addition, the presence of any naturally occurring anabolic steroid in a racehorse that is above natural levels will constitute a violation of the drug rule. The rule set forth naturally occurring physiological levels for boldenone, nandrolone, and testosterone which can be given for therapeutic reasons, but only under certain conditions.

The proposed regulation stated that a horse would be ineligible to race in Kentucky until at least 60 days after administration of a therapeutic anabolic steroid.

In addition, the EDRC recommended strengthening the penalties for detection of anabolic steroids and the KHRC acted on the recommendation by placing all anabolic steroids in the Class B Category when assessing penalties. A violation involving a Class B medication may carry a penalty of up to 60 days suspension. Under the previous drug rule, those steroids were treated as Class C medications, carrying a penalty of up to 10 days suspension.

The KHRC also approved the following EDRC recommendations relating to anabolic steroids to:

- Establish a 90-day grace period which started Sept. 5, 2008 in conjunction with Gov. Beshear signing the anabolic steroid ban into law, noting the KHRC would begin sending notices of positives to trainers and owners after the first 30 days of the grace period.

- Provide the capability for persons who claim a horse to be able to request that the horse be tested for anabolic steroids at the time the claim form is filed with the racetrack. The claimant will bear the cost of the test, but if the test results are positive, the claimant may void the claim.

- Provide the capability for trainers who ship horses to Kentucky shortly before the race to either follow the reporting requirements set forth in the regulation, certify that the horse has not received anabolic steroids in the last 60 days, or if the trainer cannot certify that the horse has not had anabolic steroids because they recently took the horse under their care, then the trainer must acknowledge and accept responsibility if a positive test result is returned for anabolic steroids.

Source: Kentucky Horse Racing Commission. 2008/2009 Biennial Report. Lexington, KY: Kentucky Horse Racing Commission. Available online at http://www.khrc.ky.gov/reports/Biennial%20Report%202008-2009.pdf. Accessed on February 25, 2017. Used by permission of the Kentucky Horse Racing Commission.

UCI v. Alberto Contador Velasco & RFEC and *Wada v. Alberto Contador Velasco & RFEC* (2012)

Alberto Contador is a Spanish professional cyclist, widely regarded as one of the most skilled cyclists of his era. He is one of only five riders to have won all three major cycling competitions, the Tour de France, Giro d'Italia, and Vuelta a España. After his 2010 Tour de France win, he tested positive for the banned anabolic steroid clenbuterol. Contador disputed that finding, claiming that the positive tests for his A and B samples were a consequence of having eaten contaminated steak. The alternative theory proposed by regulators was that Contador had consumed a nutritional supplement that contained clenbuterol as a contaminant. The World Anti-Doping Agency (WADA) specifically warns athletes against taking nutritional supplements whose composition they do not positively know. After a 17-month period of legal wrangling, the Court of Arbitration for Sport in Lausanne, Switzerland, finally ruled that the original tests were accurate, that Contador had ingested a prohibited substance (clenbuterol) in a nutritional supplement, and that he be stripped of his 2010 victory and banned from professional cycling for a period of two years. The essence of the court's decision is as follows.

Findings of the Panel

[The Panel first considers whether the nutritional supplement theory is possible, and concludes that it is. It then moves on to the question of:]

(7) Is The Meat Contamination Theory More Likely to Have Occurred Than the Supplement Theory?

485. As has been shown above, the Panel has to assess the likelihood of different scenarios that—when looked at individually—are all somewhat remote for different reasons.

486. However, since it is uncontested that the Athlete did test positive for clenbuterol, and having in mind that both the meat contamination theory and the blood transfusion theory are equally unlikely, the Panel is called upon to determine whether it considers it more likely, in light of the evidence adduced, that the clenbuterol entered the Athlete's system through ingesting a contaminated food supplement. Furthermore, for the reasons already indicated, if the Panel is unable to assess which of the possible alternatives of ingestion is more likely, the Athlete will bear the burden of proof according to the applicable rules.

487. Considering that the Athlete took supplements in considerable amounts, that it is incontestable that supplements may be contaminated, that athletes have frequently tested positive in the past because of contaminated food supplements, that in the past an athlete has also tested positive for a food supplement contaminated with clenbuterol, and that the Panel considers it very unlikely that the piece of meat ingested by him was contaminated with clenbuterol, it finds that, in light of all the evidence on record, the Athlete's positive test for clenbuterol is more likely to have been caused by the ingestion of a contaminated food supplement than by a blood transfusion or the ingestion of contaminated meat. This does not mean that the Panel is convinced beyond reasonable doubt that this scenario of ingestion of a contaminated food supplement actually happened. This is not required by the UCI ADR or by the WADC, which refer the Panel only to the balance of probabilities as the applicable standard of the burden of proof. In weighing the evidence on the balance of probabilities and coming to a decision on such basis, the Panel has to take into consideration and weigh all of the evidence admitted on record, irrespective of which party advanced which scenario(s) and what party adduced which parts of the evidence.

488. That said, the Panel finds it important to clarify that, by considering and weighing the evidence in the foregoing manner and deciding on such basis, the Panel in no manner shifted the burden of proof away from the Athlete as explained above (see supra §§ 243–265). The burden of proof only allocates the risk if a fact or a scenario can not be established on a balance of probabilities. However, this is not the case here.

489. Consequently, the Athlete is found to have committed an anti-doping violation as defined by Article 21 UCI ADR, and it remains to be examined what the applicable sanction is.

XII. The Sanctions

490. It is undisputed that it is the first time the Athlete is found guilty of an anti-doping rule violation.

491. As already mentioned, Article 293 UCI ADR reads as follows:

The period of Ineligibility imposed for a first anti-doping rule violation under article 21.1 (Presence of a Prohibited Substance or its Metabolites or Markers), article 21.2 (Use or Attempted Use of a Prohibited Substance or Prohibited Method) or article 21.6 (Possession of a Prohibited Substance or Prohibited Method) shall be 2 (two) years' Ineligibility unless the conditions for eliminating or reducing the period of Ineligibility as provided in articles 295 to 304 or the conditions for increasing the period of Ineligibility as provided in article 305 are met [typography as in original].

492. Pursuant to this provision, the period of ineligibility shall be two years. Accordingly, there is no discretion for the hearing body to reduce the period of ineligibility due to reasons of proportionality.

493. As none of the conditions for eliminating or reducing the period of ineligibility as provided in Articles 295 to 304 UCI ADR are applicable—in particular because the exact contaminated supplement is unknown and the circumstances surrounding its ingestion are equally unknown—the period of ineligibility shall be two years.

Source: "Arbitral Award Delivered by Court of Arbitration for Sport." https://www.wada-ama.org/sites/default/files/resources/files/cas-2011-a-2384-contador.pdf. Accessed on February 25, 2017. Used with the permission of the World Anti-Doping Agency (WADA) and may not be reproduced or otherwise cited without the express permission of WADA.

Designer Anabolic Steroid Control Act of 2014

The U.S. Congress seems to be involved in a seemingly never-ending battle to stay one step ahead of researchers and users who attempt to find new steroid analogs that can be used for performance- and/

or appearance-enhancing purposes. Most recently, the Congress considered bills in 2010, 2012, and 2014 for expanding the list of prohibited designer anabolic steroids and increasing the penalties for the production and distribution of such drugs. The 2014 bill finally passed and was signed by President Barack Obama on December 18, 2014, becoming Public Law 113–260. Its major sections are as follows.

After listing about two dozen specific drugs to be added to the Controlled Substances Act of 1970, this act made the following provisions for their control.

(C)(i) Subject to clause (ii), a drug or hormonal substance (other than estrogens, progestins, corticosteroids, and dehydroepiandrosterone) that is not listed in subparagraph (A) and is derived from, or has a chemical structure substantially similar to, 1 or more anabolic steroids listed in subparagraph (A) shall be considered to be an anabolic steroid for purposes of this Act if—

  (I) the drug or substance has been created or manufactured with the intent of producing a drug or other substance that either—

      (aa) promotes muscle growth; or

      (bb) otherwise causes a pharmacological effect similar to that of testosterone; or

  (II) the drug or substance has been, or is intended to be, marketed or otherwise promoted in any manner suggesting that consuming it will promote muscle growth or any other pharmacological effect similar to that of testosterone.

  (ii) A substance shall not be considered to be a drug or hormonal substance for purposes of this subparagraph if it—

(I)   is—

    (aa)   an herb or other botanical;

    (bb)   a concentrate, metabolite, or extract of, or a constituent isolated directly from, an herb or other botanical; or

    (cc)   a combination of 2 or more substances described in item (aa) or (bb);

        (II)   is a dietary ingredient for purposes of the Federal Food, Drug, and Cosmetic Act (21 U.S.C. 301 et seq.); and

        (III)   is not anabolic or androgenic.

(iii) In accordance with section 515(a), any person claiming the benefit of an exemption or exception under clause (ii) shall bear the burden of going forward with the evidence with respect to such exemption or exception.

(b) CLASSIFICATION AUTHORITY.—Section 201 of the Controlled Substances Act (21 U.S.C. 811) is amended by adding at the end the following:

(i)   TEMPORARY AND PERMANENT SCHEDULING OF RECENTLY EMERGED ANABOLIC STEROIDS.—

    (1)   The Attorney General may issue a temporary order adding a drug or other substance to the definition of anabolic steroids if the Attorney General finds that—

    (A)   the drug or other substance satisfies the criteria for being considered an anabolic steroid under section 102(41) but is not listed in that section or by regulation of the Attorney General as being an anabolic steroid; and

    (B)   adding such drug or other substance to the definition of anabolic steroids will assist in preventing abuse or misuse of the drug or other substance.

(2) An order issued under paragraph (1) shall not take effect until 30 days after the date of the publication by the Attorney General of a notice in the Federal Register of the intention to issue such order and the grounds upon which such order is to be issued. The order shall expire not later than 24 months after the date it becomes effective, except that the Attorney General may, during the pendency of proceedings under paragraph (6), extend the temporary scheduling order for up to 6 months.

(3) The Attorney General shall transmit notice of an order proposed to be issued under paragraph (1) to the Secretary of Health and Human Services. In issuing an order under paragraph (1), the Attorney General shall take into consideration any comments submitted by the Secretary in response to a notice transmitted pursuant to this paragraph.

(4) A temporary scheduling order issued under paragraph (1) shall be vacated upon the issuance of a permanent scheduling order under paragraph (6).

(5) An order issued under paragraph (1) is not subject to judicial review.

(6) The Attorney General may, by rule, issue a permanent order adding a drug or other substance to the definition of anabolic steroids if such drug or other substance satisfies the criteria for being considered an anabolic steroid under section 102(41). Such rulemaking may be commenced simultaneously with the issuance of the temporary order issued under paragraph (1).

Source: Public Law 113–260. https://www.congress.gov/113/plaws/publ260/PLAW-113publ260.pdf. Accessed on February 13, 2017.

World Anti-Doping Program (2015)

In 2004, the WADA adopted the World Anti-Doping Code, a document that enshrines the purposes and mechanisms by which the agency carries out its efforts to maintain fair practices in the conduct of international athletic events. The purpose, scope, and organization of the WADA anti-doping program are described in the introduction to the code, as follows.

The purposes of the World Anti-Doping Code and the World Anti-Doping Program which supports it are:

> To protect the Athletes' fundamental right to participate in doping-free sport and thus promote health, fairness and equality for Athletes worldwide, and

> To ensure harmonized, coordinated and effective anti-doping programs at the international and national level with regard to detection, deterrence and prevention of doping.

The Code

The *Code* is the fundamental and universal document upon which the World Anti-Doping Program in sport is based.

The purpose of the *Code* is to advance the anti-doping effort through universal harmonization of core anti-doping elements.

It is intended to be specific enough to achieve complete harmonization on issues where uniformity is required, yet general enough in other areas to permit flexibility on how agreed-upon anti-doping principles are implemented. The *Code* has been drafted giving consideration to the principles of proportionality and human rights.

The World Anti-Doping Program

The World Anti-Doping Program encompasses all of the elements needed in order to ensure optimal harmonization and best practice in international and national anti-doping programs. The main elements are:

Level 1: The *Code*
Level 2: *International Standards*
Level 3: Models of Best Practice and Guidelines

International Standards

International Standards for different technical and operational areas within the anti-doping program have been and will be developed in consultation with the *Signatories* and governments and approved by *WADA*. The purpose of the *International Standards* is harmonization among *Anti-Doping Organizations* responsible for specific technical and operational parts of anti-doping programs. Adherence to the *International Standards* is mandatory for compliance with the Code. The *International Standards* may be revised from time to time by the *WADA* Executive Committee after reasonable consultation with the *Signatories*, governments and other relevant stakeholders. *International Standards* and all revisions will be published on the *WADA* website and shall become effective on the date specified in the *International Standard* or revision.

Models of Best Practice and Guidelines

Models of best practice and guidelines based on the *Code* and *International Standards* have been and will be developed to provide solutions in different areas of anti-doping. The models and guidelines will be recommended by *WADA* and made available to *Signatories* and other relevant stakeholders, but will not be mandatory. In addition to providing models of anti-doping documentation, *WADA* will also make some training assistance available to the *Signatories*.

Fundamental Rationale for the World Anti-Doping Code

Anti-doping programs seek to preserve what is intrinsically valuable about sport. This intrinsic value is often referred to as "the spirit of sport." It is the essence of Olympism, the pursuit of human excellence through the dedicated perfection of each person's natural talents. It is how we play true. The spirit of sport is the celebration of the human spirit, body and mind, and is reflected in values we find in and through sport, including:

Ethics, fair play and honesty

Health

Excellence in performance

Character and education

Fun and joy

Teamwork

Dedication and commitment

Respect for rules and laws

Respect for self and other Participants

Courage

Community and solidarity

Doping is fundamentally contrary to the spirit of sport.

To fight doping by promoting the spirit of sport, the *Code* requires each *Anti-Doping Organization* to develop and implement education and prevention programs for *Athletes*, including youth, and *Athlete Support Personnel*.

Source: World Anti-Doping Code 2015. World Anti-Doping Agency. https://www.wada-ama.org/sites/default/files/resources/files/wada-2015-world-anti-doping-code.pdf. Accessed on February 25, 2017. Used with the permission of the World Anti-Doping Agency (WADA) and may not be reproduced or otherwise cited without the express permission of WADA.

McLaren's Independent Investigation Reports (2016)

On May 18, 2016, the WADA hired Canadian attorney Richard H. McLaren to investigate allegations that doping had been conducted extensively by agents of the Russian government at the 2014 Winter Olympics in Sochi, Russia, and, perhaps, on other occasions. McLaren presented the results of his investigations in two reports, the first filed on July 18, 2016, and the second on December 9, 2016. The major conclusions from each report are presented here.

First report:

Key Findings

1. The Moscow Laboratory operated, for the protection of doped Russian athletes, within a State-dictated failsafe system, described in the report as the Disappearing Positive Methodology.

2. The Sochi Laboratory operated a unique sample swapping methodology to enable doped Russian athletes to compete at the Games.

3. The Ministry of Sport directed, controlled and oversaw the manipulation of athlete's analytical results or sample swapping, with the active participation and assistance of the FSB, CSP, and both Moscow and Sochi Laboratories.

Second report:

Key Highlights of 2nd Report
Institutionalised Doping Conspiracy and Cover Up

1. An institutional conspiracy existed across summer and winter sports athletes who participated with Russian officials within the Ministry of Sport and its infrastructure, such as the RUSADA, CSP and the Moscow Laboratory, along with the FSB for the purposes of manipulating doping controls. The summer and winter sports athletes were

not acting individually but within an organised infrastructure as reported on in the 1st Report.

2. This systematic and centralised cover up and manipulation of the doping control process evolved and was refined over the course of its use at London 2012 Summer Games, Universiade Games 2013, Moscow IAAF World Championships 2013, and the Winter Games in Sochi in 2014. The evolution of the infrastructure was also spawned in response to WADA regulatory changes and surprise interventions.

3. The swapping of Russian athletes' urine samples further confirmed in this 2nd Report as occurring at Sochi, did not stop at the close of the Winter Olympics. The sample swapping technique used at Sochi became a regular monthly practice of the Moscow Laboratory in dealing with elite summer and winter athletes. Further DNA and salt testing confirms the technique, while others relied on DPM.

4. The key findings of the 1st Report remain unchanged. The forensic testing, which is based on immutable facts, is conclusive. The evidence does not depend on verbal testimony to draw a conclusion. Rather, it tests the physical evidence and a conclusion is drawn from those results. The results of the forensic and laboratory analysis initiated by the IP establish that the conspiracy was perpetrated between 2011 and 2015.

The Athlete Part of Conspiracy and Cover Up

5. Over 1000 Russian athletes competing in summer, winter and Paralympic sport, can be identified as being involved in or benefiting from manipulations to conceal positive doping tests. Based on the information reported to International Federations through the IP to WADA there are 600 (84%) summer athletes and 95 (16%) winter athletes.

London Summer Olympic Games

6. Fifteen Russian athlete medal winners were identified out of the 78 on the London Washout Lists. Ten of these athletes have now had their medals stripped.

IAAF Moscow World Championships

7. Following the 2013 IAAF Moscow World Championships, 4 athletics athletes' samples were swapped. Additional target testing is in progress.

Sochi Winter Olympic Games

8. Sample swapping is established by 2 female ice hockey players' samples with male DNA.

9. Tampering with original sample established by 2 [sport] athletes, winners of four Sochi Olympic Gold medals, and a female Silver medal winner in [sport] with physiologically impossible salt readings.

10. Twelve medal winning athletes (including the above 3) from 44 examined samples had scratches and marks on the inside of the caps of their B sample bottles, indicating tampering.

11. Six winners of 21 Paralympic medals are found to have had their urine samples tampered with at Sochi.

Sources: "WADA Investigation of Sochi Allegations." https://www.wada-ama.org/sites/default/files/resources/files/20160718_ip_report_newfinal.pdf; https://www.wada-ama.org/sites/default/files/resources/files/mclaren_report_part_ii_2.pdf. Accessed on February 25, 2017. Used with the permission of the World Anti-Doping Agency (WADA) and may not be reproduced or otherwise cited without the express permission of WADA.

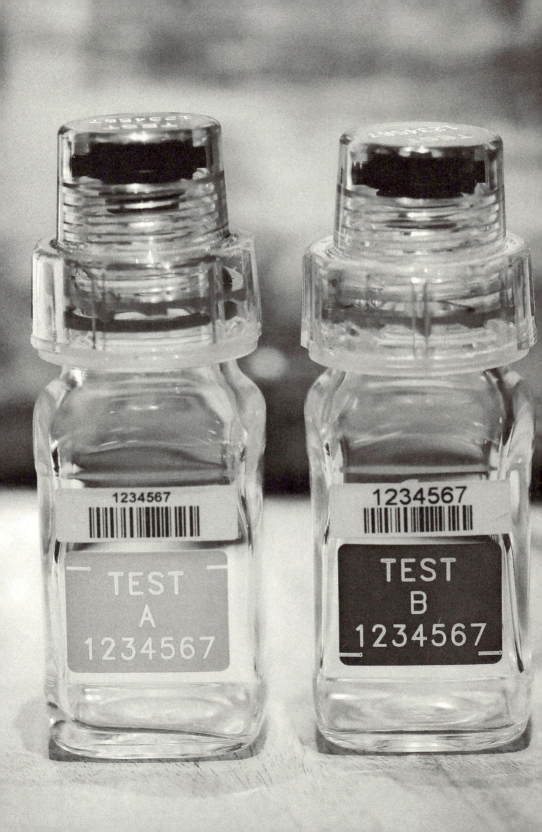

Introduction

Sex and gender are topics of major interest both to professionals in the field and to everyday individuals. Untold numbers of books, articles, book chapters, reports, and web pages have been devoted to a discussion of one or more aspects of these topics. This bibliography provides only a sampling of some of the most recent of these items, as well as some publications of historical interest. In some cases, an item has appeared both in print and on the Internet, in which case it is so designated in the print listing.

Books

Alexander, Hansen. 2017. *The Life and Trials of Roger Clemens: Baseball's Rocket Man and the Questionable Case against Him.* Jefferson, NC: McFarland & Company.

> One of the most widely discussed case studies in the use of anabolic steroids in sports involved one of Major League Baseball's most successful pitchers, Roger Clements. This book follows accusations of steroid use against Clements,

---

A and B sample bottles from the Berlinger Special BEREG-Kit for human urine doping testing, 2016. World Anti-Doping Agency investigator Richard McLaren found that FSB agents tampered with samples during the 2014 Sochi Winter Olympics, leaving no sign of scratches or marks to untrained eyes. (AP Photo/Matt Dunham)

his denial of those charges, and the ultimate outcome of the controversy.

Assael, Shaun. 2007. *Steroid Nation: Juiced Home Run Totals, Anti-Aging Miracles, and a Hercules in Every High School: The Secret History of America's True Drug Addiction.* New York: ESPN Books.
    In a well-written narrative style, the author reviews the origins and development of steroid abuse problems in the nation's major professional sports, as well as in a range of amateur venues.

Baoutina, Anna. 2011. "Performance Enhancement by Gene Doping." In Claude Bouchard and Eric P. Hoffman, eds. *Genetic and Molecular Aspects of Sport Performance.* Chichester: Wiley-Blackwell, 373–382.
    This book chapter provides a good general introduction to the practice of gene doping, a procedure by which gene transfer is conducted in an effort to improve an individual's athletic performance.

Beamish, Rob. 2011. *Steroids: A New Look at Performance-Enhancing Drugs.* Santa Barbara, CA: Praeger.
    The author reviews the history of the use of anabolic steroids in sports and athletics and discusses the current status of that issue.

Clark, Dan. 2011. *Gladiator: A True Story of 'Roids, Rage, and Redemption.* New York: Scribner.
    The author, commonly known as "Nitro" on the *American Gladiators* television program, tells of his experiences with the use of androgenic anabolic steroids.

Conte, Victor, and Nathan Jendrick. 2008. *BALCO: The Straight Dope on Steroids, Barry Bonds, Marion Jones, & What We Can Do to Save Sports.* New York: Skyhorse.
    The authors review some important cases involving the use of steroids by Barry Bonds, Marion Jones, and other

elite athletes and suggest some steps that must be taken to reduce or eliminate the use of androgenic anabolic steroids by professional athletes.

Dennis, Mike, and Jonathan Grix. 2012. *Sport under Communism: Behind the East German "Miracle."* New York: Palgrave Macmillan.

The authors analyze the reasons that sports teams and individuals from East Germany were among the most successful in the world over a three-decade period at the end of the 20th century.

Fouché, Rayyon. 2017. *Game Changer: The Technoscientific Revolution in Sports.* Baltimore: Johns Hopkins University Press.

The author argues that science and technology have dramatically altered the elements of sports competition in recent years. He discusses the role of drugs and supplements, along with other technologies, in this regard.

Goldberg, Ray. 2012. *Taking Sides. Clashing Views in Drugs and Society.* 10th ed. New York: McGraw-Hill.

The author reviews all sides of the debate over the use of performance-enhancing drugs in sports in a "debate-style format." His goal is to "stimulate student interest and develop critical thinking skills."

Grace, Fergal, and Julien Baker, eds. 2012. *Perspectives on Anabolic Androgenic Steroids (AAS) and Doping in Sport and Health.* Hauppauge, NY: Nova Science Publishers.

This book provides essays on the use of androgenic anabolic steroids in sports and athletics from the standpoint of sports medicine research, medical practice, behavioral science, molecular physiology, sociology, and the ethics of sports doping.

Griffiths, Scott. 2016. *Steroids and the Growing Crisis of Male Body Image: Get Big or Die Trying.* London: Routledge.

The author reviews the growing use of steroids by individuals for the use of improving body image, in contrast to the goal of improving athletic performance. Various chapters deal with aspects of the topic, such as the history of steroids, the stigma and stereotypes surrounding their use, the role of steroids in eating disorders, muscle dysmorphia, the association between steroid use and perceptions of masculinity, and possible interventions to help men who are dissatisfied with their body image and/or have considered using steroids.

Hall, Matthew, Sarah Grogan, and Brendan Gough, eds. 2016. *Chemically Modified Bodies: The Use of Diverse Substances for Appearance Enhancement*. London: Palgrave Macmillan.

This excellent collection of essays discusses the whole range of the use of chemical substances, such as anabolic steroids, to deal with an individual's problems of body image. Various chapters discuss topics such as muscle dysphoria and anabolic steroid use, the use of drugs by female adolescents to change their body appearance, and the use of both legal and illegal substances in dealing with body image issues.

Hamidi, Mehrdad, Mohammad-Ali Shahbazi, and Hajar Ashrafi. 2012. *Drug Abuse in Sport: Doping*. New York: Nova Science Publishers.

The authors provide an excellent review of the history of efforts by sportsmen and sportswomen to enhance their performances with drugs and other substances. They also review the current status of the use of illegal substances in amateur and professional athletics.

Hunt, Thomas M. 2011. *Drug Games: The International Olympic Committee and the Politics of Doping, 1960/2008*. Austin: University of Texas Press.

The author reviews the history of illegal drug use by participants in the Olympic Games dating from at least

1960. He discusses the issues involved in getting sports organizations to recognize the extent of the problem and the responses developed to athletic drug abuse.

Johnson, Mark. 2016. *Spitting in the Soup: Inside the Dirty Game of Doping in Sports*. Boulder, CO: VeloPress.
   Johnson reviews the history of doping in sports from the earliest days for which information is available to the status of doping in today's world.

Kashatus, William C. 2017. *Suicide Squeeze: Taylor Hooton, Rob Garibaldi, and the Fight against Teenage Steroid Abuse*. Philadelphia: Temple University Press.
   The author uses these stories as take-off points from which to discuss efforts to develop prevention and treatment programs for dealing with this problem.

Latta, Sara L. 2015. *Investigate Steroids and Performance Drugs*. Berkeley Heights, NJ: Enslow Publishers.
   This book provides a good general introduction to the topics of steroids and performance-enhancing drugs for young adults.

Lenehan, Pat, and Tony Miller. 2004. *Anabolic Steroids: A Guide for Users and Professionals*. Manchester, UK: Lifeline Publications. http://lx.iriss.org.uk/sites/default/files/resources/Anabolic%20steroids.pdf. Accessed on February 26, 2017.
   This somewhat dated book is a superb resource for a great deal of basic and practical information on the nature and use of anabolic steroids. The technical information is provided in a very readable format and would appear to be intended for both professionals in the field of medicine and individuals who might be involved in the use, prevention, and/or treatment of steroids for therapeutic and recreational purposes.

Llewellyn, William. 2011. *Anabolics*. 10th ed. Jupiter, FL: Molecular Nutrition.

One of the best-known, most widely used, and highly respected reference books in the field of anabolic steroids, this manual provides extensive introductory information about anabolic steroids and related substances, including their chemical structure and function and physiological actions and side effects. The major part of the book is devoted to a thorough review of nearly 200 anabolic substances.

Mazanov, Jason. 2017. *Managing Drugs in Sport*. London; New York: Routledge, Taylor & Francis Group.

The chapters in this book deal with an array of topics, such as the role of drugs in sports, the evolution of drug control in sports, policies relating to the management of drug use in sports, business ethics and drug control programs, managing drug risks in sports, and marketing and management of integrity.

McClusky, Mark. 2014. *Faster, Higher, Stronger: How Sports Science Is Creating a New Generation of Superathletes, and What We Can Learn from Them*. New York: Hudson Street Press.

McClusky notes that the basic nature of sports has changed significantly in recent decades and can now be considered as a working relationship between athlete and scientist through which the former achieves the greatest possible success possible in his or her sport.

McNamee, Mike, and Verner Møller, eds. 2011. *Doping and Anti-Doping Policy in Sport: Ethical, Legal and Social Perspectives*. Abingdon, UK; New York: Routledge.

The papers in this volume were presented at the third annual conference of the Network of Humanistic Doping Research, held at Aarhus University in August 2009. They cover topics such as the burden of proof in endogenous substance cases, some implications of imperfect testing procedures, privacy rights and doping procedures, the ethics of testing citizens in recreational gyms, and steroid issues in the court of public opinion.

McVeigh, R., ed. 2013. *Anabolic Steroids and Other Performance and Image-Enhancing Drugs*. New York: Wiley-Blackwell.
This collection of essays covers an historical perspective, a global review of use prevalence, profiles of individuals who use such drugs, how performance-enhancing drugs work, health effects of performance-enhancing drugs, and some country-by-country case studies, and others.

Mottram, David R., and Neil Chester, eds. 2010. *Drugs in Sport*. 5th ed. Abingdon, Oxon: Routledge/Taylor & Francis Group.
This collection of essays covers virtually every aspect of the use of drugs in sports, including an introduction to the regulation of drug use in sports, prohibited substances and procedures in sports, substances and procedures that are allowed in athletics, and the extent of doping in sports.

Nieschlag, Eberhard, Hermann M. Behre, and Susan Nieschlag, eds. 2012. *Testosterone: Action, Deficiency, Substitution*. 4th ed. Cambridge, UK; New York: Cambridge University Press.
This standard text provides detailed information on all aspects of testosterone, from its chemical properties and synthesis to its biological effects and side effects.

O'Leary, John, ed. 2001. *Drugs and Doping in Sports: Socio-Legal Perspectives*. London: Cavendish Publishing. http://www.imd.inder.cu/adjuntos/article/407/Drugs%20and%20Doping%20in%20Sports.pdf. Accessed on February 27, 2017.
The essays in this book cover a range of topics related to doping and anti-doping efforts in sports, including challenges of anti-doping programs to an athlete's reputation, the fundamental rights of an athlete in anti-doping programs, drug testing in amateur athletics in the United

States, and some views of international elite athletes about drug use and drug testing.

Roach, Randy. 2011. *Muscle, Smoke & Mirrors*. Vol. 2. Bloomington, IN: AuthorHouse.
This book is the second volume of a long and detailed history of the sport of bodybuilding, with strong emphasis on the role that the use of illegal drugs has had in changing the direction and very nature of the sport.

Roberts, Paul K., ed. 2010. *Steroid Use and Abuse*. New York: Nova Biomedical Books.
The papers in this anthology provide an overview of the chemical and physiological properties of androgenic anabolic steroids, as well as a discussion of their licit and illicit uses.

Rosen, Daniel M. 2008. *Dope: A History of Performance Enhancement in Sports from the Nineteenth Century to Today*. Westport, CT: Praeger.
This book's seven chapters are divided into the time periods from 1860 to 1959, 1960 to 1969, 1970 to 1979, 1980 to 1989, 1990 to 1999, and 2000 to 2008, with an outlook for the future.

Thieme, Detlef, and Peter Hemmersbach, eds. 2010. *Doping in Sports*. Heidelberg; New York: Springer.
This book is part of Springer's *Experimental Pharmacology* series dealing with the technical aspects of most major performance-enhancing drugs, including all of the important anabolic androgenic steroids.

Waddington, Ivan, and Andy Smith. 2009. *An Introduction to Drugs in Sport: Addicted to Winning?* Abingdon; New York: Routledge.
The authors review the complex relationships between drug use and amateur and professional sports, with special

attention to topics such as sports law, policy, and administration; case studies in football and cycling; the role of sports federations, such as the World Anti-Doping Association; and the relevance of the profession of sports medicine.

Walsh, David. 2017. *From Russia with Drugs* [e-book]. New York: Simon & Schuster. http://www.simonandschuster.com/books/From-Russia-With-Drugs/David-Walsh/9781471158179. Accessed on October 6, 2017.

Walsh presents the complete story of the uncovering of widespread, officially sanctioned doping among Russian athletes over the past half century.

Wilson, Wayne, and Ed Derse, eds. 2001. *Doping in Elite Sport: The Politics of Drugs in the Olympic Movement*. Champaign, IL: Human Kinetics.

The papers in this volume are subdivided into three major categories: the science of doping; the history, ethics, and social context of doping; and the politics of doping. The last of these sections includes papers on the relatively little-discussed aspect of doping of considerable interest and importance.

Articles

American College of Sports Medicine. 1987. "Position Stand on the Use of Anabolic-Androgenic Steroids in Sports." *Medicine and Science in Sports and Exercise*. 19(5): 534–539.

The statement explains the benefits and risks associated with the use of anabolic steroids in sports, as determined by the American College of Sports Medicine. This position statement has apparently not been updated since its original publication.

Amos, Anne, and Saul Fridman. 2009. "Drugs in Sport: The Legal Issues." *Sport in Society: Cultures, Commerce, Media, Politics*. 12(3): 356–374.

The authors point out that drug testing has now become an integral part of most sports competition, but that some fundamental legal questions remain to be answered about the basis and interpretation of such tests.

Baumann, Gerhard P. 2012. "Growth Hormone Doping in Sports: A Critical Review of Use and Detection Strategies." *Endocrine Reviews*. 33(2): 155–186.
This paper covers a wide range of technical issues relating to the chemical nature and detection of human growth hormone, along with a discussion of its use by athletes in sports competition and efforts to ban the product by anti-doping agencies.

Birzniece, V. 2015. "Doping in Sport: Effects, Harm and Misconceptions." *Internal Medicine Journal*. 45(3): 239–248.
This review article notes that doping in sports is even more common and more of a problem in recreational sports than in professional sports, but that it receives much less attention than does the problem of drug testing in the latter. It summarizes the main groups of doping agents used by athletes, with the main focus on their effects on athletic performance and adverse effects.

Brinkmann, Albert O. 2011. "Molecular Mechanisms of Androgen Action—A Historical Perspective." *Methods in Molecular Biology*. 776: 3–24.
The author provides a technical review of the discovery and development of testosterone and other androgenic anabolic steroids.

Cadwallader, Amy B., et al. 2010. "The Abuse of Diuretics as Performance-Enhancing Drugs and Masking Agents in Sport Doping: Pharmacology, Toxicology and Analysis." *British Journal of Pharmacology*. 161(1): 1–16. https://www.ncbi.nlm.nih.gov/pmc/articles/PMC2962812/. Accessed on February 27, 2017.

The values of using diuretics in athletic competition are widely recognized in the sporting community and are now banned by all anti-doping agencies. This article reviews the chemical and physiological character of these products and explains their use and risks in sports.

Callaway, Ewen. 2011. "Sports Doping: Racing Just to Keep Up." *Nature*. 475(7356): 283–285. http://www.nature.com/news/2011/110715/full/475283a.html. Accessed on February 18, 2017.

This article reviews some of the challenges associated with the testing of elite athletes for use of illicit drugs and the development of a biological passport as a way of dealing with this problem.

Clement, Christen L., et al. 2012. "Nonprescription Steroids on the Internet." *Substance Use & Misuse*. 47(3): 329–341.

In a study of popular websites between March 2006 and June 2006, the authors found that prescription androgenic anabolic steroids were readily available without prescription on most websites, with only about 5 percent of such websites providing accurate information about health risks associated with the use of these substances.

Cohen, Jason, et al. 2007. "A League of Their Own: Demographics, Motivations and Patterns of Use of 1,955 Male Adult Non-Medical Anabolic Steroid Users in the United States." *Journal of the International Society of Sports Nutrition*. 4(12). DOI: 10.1186/1550-2783-4-12. Available online at http://jissn.biomedcentral.com/articles/10.1186/1550-2783-4-12. Accessed on February 27, 2017.

The authors report on a study in which users of androgenic anabolic steroids recruited from Internet sites that sell the drugs report on their own history of steroid use. They find that most individuals did not begin using steroids during adolescence, nor is their use particularly associated with athletics, but is motivated by desires to improve one's body in order to improve one's self-image.

Cordaro, F. G., S. Lombardo, and M. Cosentino. 2011. "Selling Androgenic Anabolic Steroids by the Pound: Identification and Analysis of Popular Websites on the Internet." *Scandinavian Journal of Medicine & Science in Sports.* 21(6): 247–259.

The authors report on their study of 30 websites from which anabolic androgenic steroids are available for sale. They report that such websites cite manufacturers of drugs, some of which appear not to exist, but fail to mention risks associated with the drugs. The vast majority of products (97.9 percent) are advertised as "medicines" and about a third as "supplements."

D'Angelo, Carlos, and Claudio Tamburrini. 2010. "Addict to Win? A Different Approach to Doping." *Journal of Medical Ethics.* 36(11): 700–707.

The authors suggest a third alternative in the debate between those who wish to use testing to detect illegal use of drugs in sports and those who prefer to allow such use. They recommend an approach that involves personalized prevention and treatment programs that will reduce the use of illicit drugs in sporting events.

De Lessio, Joe. 2015, March 31. "Genetic Doping Is the Next Frontier in Cheating in Sports." *New York Magazine.* http://nymag.com/next/2015/03/genetic-doping-is-the-next-frontier-of-cheating.html. Accessed on February 26, 2017.

The author provides a good introduction to the process of genetic doping and outlines the ways in which it might revolutionize the process of doping in sports and, in fact, the field of athletics itself.

Dimopoulou, Christina, et al. 2016. "EMAS Position Statement: Testosterone Replacement Therapy in the Aging Male?" *Maturitas.* 84: 94–99.

This article summarizes the position of the European Menopause Andropause Society on the risks and advantages of using testosterone therapy on men with low testosterone levels. It provides a good overview of current information on the use of testosterone for therapeutic uses.

Dotson, Jennifer L., and Robert T. Brown. 2007. "The History of the Development of Anabolic-Androgenic Steroids." *Pediatric Clinics of North America*. 54(4): 761–769.
  This article traces the history of anabolic androgenic use and abuse from their earliest discovery to the approximate date of the article.

Eisenberg, Marla E., Melanie Wall, and Dianne Neumark-Sztainer. 2012. "Muscle-Enhancing Behaviors among Adolescent Girls and Boys." *Pediatrics*. 130(6): 1019–1026. https://pediatrics.aappublications.org/content/pediatrics/early/2012/11/14/peds.2012-0095.full.pdf. Accessed on February 17, 2017.
  This study of 2,793 adolescents from 20 urban middle and high schools found that the use of performance-enhancing drugs was substantially higher than had previously been reported, leading the authors to conclude that the practice "is cause for concern."

Gilbert, Bil. 1969. "Problems in a Turned-On World"; "Something Extra on the Ball"; and "High Time to Make Some Rules." *Sports Illustrated*. June 23, June 30, July 7, 1969. http://www.si.com/vault/issue/43044/72/2, http://www.si.com/vault/issue/43032/36/2, and http://www.si.com/vault/issue/43009/32/2. Accessed on February 21, 2017.
  This series of three articles on doping in sports is of classic importance because it is one of the first (if not *the* first) times that the issue was brought to the attention of the general public in a widely popular sports magazine.

Goldberg, Ryan, Bill Finley, and Lucas Marquardt. 2013. "A Painful Truth." *TDN Magazine*. In six parts: May 2, 2013; May 9, 2013; May 16, 2013; May 29, 2013; June 15, 2013; and June 22, 2013. Links to the six articles are available online at http://www.teamvalor.com/news/june2013/tdnseries.pdf. Accessed on February 22, 2017.

> This superb collection of articles reviews the long-standing problem of doping in horse racing, with specific titles including "A History of Drugs in Racing"; "War on Drugs? Vet Records and State Rules Say No"; "The International Difference"; "Behind Closed Doors: A Look Inside U.S. Testing Labs"; "As the Science Gets Better, Catching the Cheats Becomes Easier"; and "Race Horse Is Not a Diagnosis."

Hallgren, M., et al. 2015. "Anti-Social Behaviors Associated with Anabolic-Androgenic Steroid Use among Male Adolescents." *European Addiction Research*. 21(6): 321–326.

> The authors note that androgenic anabolic steroid use is generally regarded as "more benign" than other types of drug abuse. They review published data over a period of eight years to test that hypothesis. They find that the hypothesis appears not to be correct and that, in fact, "risk ratios for virtually all measured anti-social behaviors were significantly higher among AAS users compared to non-AAS illicit drug users and to drug non-users."

Harmer, P. A. 2010. "Anabolic-Androgenic Steroid Use among Young Male and Female Athletes: Is the Game to Blame?" *British Journal of Sports Medicine*. 44(1): 26–31.

> Harmer suggests that estimates of steroid abuse by adolescent athletes are inflated and that, in fact, young adults may be driven to the use of steroids not primarily because of athletic concerns but because of other factors in their lives and their surround social milieu.

Heuberger, Jules A.A.C., et al. 2013. "Erythropoietin Doping in Cycling: Lack of Evidence for Efficacy and a Negative Risk-Benefit." *British Journal of Clinical Pharmacology.* 75(6): 1406–1421. https://www.ncbi.nlm.nih.gov/pubmed/23216370. Accessed on February 20, 2017.

> The authors of this paper report that they found no scientific evidence for the claim that erythropoietin improves a cyclist's athletic performance. Its use, therefore, should provide no advantage to a user in a sports competition. The article is of interest also because of the response it drew from experts in the field with a somewhat different view. See, for example, Eric van Breda, Jos Benders, and Harm Kuipers. 2014. "Little Soldiers in Their Cardboard Cells." *British Journal of Clinical Pharmacology.* 77(3): 580–581. DOI: 10.1111/bcp.12187 PMCID: PMC4371541. https://www.ncbi.nlm.nih.gov/pmc/articles/PMC4371541/. Accessed on February 20, 2071.

Hoberman, John M., and Charles E. Yesalis. 1995. "The History of Synthetic Testosterone." *Scientific American.* 272(2): 76–81.

> This article describes some of the most important steps in the discovery of testosterone and its artificial synthesis.

Jampel, Jonathan D., et al. 2016. "Self-Perceived Weight and Anabolic Steroid Misuse among US Adolescent Boys." *Journal of Adolescent Health.* 58(46): 397–402.

> The study reported in this paper explores the ways in which boys' perceptions of their weight status affect future steroid use for dealing with that issue.

Kanayama, Gen, James I. Hudson, and Harrison G. Pope. 2010. "Illicit Anabolic-Androgenic Steroid Use." *Hormones and Behavior.* 58(1): 111–121. http://www.uky.edu/~sbarron/psy459/discussions/discussion3.pdf. Accessed on February 15, 2017.

The authors offer an overview of the illicit use of androgenic anabolic steroids, including a history of their development, current magnitude of the problem, adverse medical and behavioral effects of the drugs, and issues of dependence and addiction.

Kanayama, Gen, and Harrison G. Pope, Jr. 2012. "Illicit Use of Androgens and Other Hormones: Recent Advances." *Current Opinion in Endocrinology, Diabetes, and Obesity*. 19(3): 211–219.

The authors report on a thorough review of literature on the misuse of androgenic anabolic steroids. They conclude that it "is becoming increasingly important to understand the origins and consequences of androgen dependence as a potentially major issue for public health."

Kersey, Robert D., et al. 2012. "National Athletic Trainers' Association Position Statement: Anabolic-Androgenic Steroids." *Journal of Athletic Training*. 47(5): 567–588.

This position statement brings together the best available information on androgenic anabolic steroids, with the objective of providing a basis for advising athletes by trainers, educators, and other health professionals.

Leme de Souza, Guilherme, and Jorge Hallak. 2011. "Anabolic Steroids and Male Infertility: A Comprehensive Review." *BJU International*. 108(11): 1869–1865.

The authors review a number of studies that deal with the effects of anabolic steroid use and abuse on male fertility.

Mauerberg-de Castro, Eliane, Debra Frances Campbell, and Carolina Paioli Tavares. 2016. "The Global Reality of the Paralympic Movement: Challenges and Opportunities in Disability Sports." *Motriz: Revista de Educação Física*. 22(3): 111–123. http://www.scielo.br/scielo.php?script=sci_arttext& pid=S1980-65742016000300111. Accessed on February 19, 2017.

The authors note that disabled athletes are confronted with challenges and opportunities in the field of doping similar to those faced by their non-disabled colleagues. They review some specific instances of cheating among disabled athletes in past competitions.

Morente-Sánchez, Jaime, and Mikel Zabala. 2013. "Doping in Sport: A Review of Elite Athletes' Attitudes, Beliefs, and Knowledge." *Sports Medicine*. 43(6): 395–411. http://www .pilarmartinescudero.com/bibliografia_dopaje/australianos/ac titudesdopajeZabala.pdf. Accessed on February 15, 2017.

The authors note that there have been relatively few studies on the attitudes, beliefs, and knowledge of athletes themselves about the use of illegal substances in sports. The purpose of this study, then, is to collect information that is available on those topics. They summarize the results of 30 peer-reviewed studies and find that, while today's athletes are better informed about doping regulations, most are still poorly informed about the use and effects of dietary supplements and performance-enhancing drugs in general.

Parkinson, A. B., and N. A. Evans. 2006. "Anabolic Androgenic Steroids: A Survey of 500 Users." *Medicine and Science in Sports and Exercise*. 38: 644–651.

Concerned about their perceived lack of information about the effects of steroid taking among adult men, these researchers conducted an online survey of 500 volunteers, among whom three quarters were neither bodybuilders nor athletes. They found that their respondents used anabolic steroids primarily for cosmetic reasons, and in doses significantly larger than had been found in previous surveys.

Placentino, Daria, et al. 2015. "Anabolic-Androgenic Steroid Use and Psychopathology in Athletes. A Systematic Review."

Current Neuropharmacology. 13(1): 101–121. https://www
.ncbi.nlm.nih.gov/pmc/articles/PMC4462035/. Accessed on
February 25, 2017.

> The authors review all existing qualifying research reports
> on the effects of the ingestion of anabolic steroids on an
> individual's psychological profile and behavior. They con-
> clude that there is strong evidence that the use of steroids
> is associated with a variety of such behaviors, including
> increased aggressiveness, mood destabilization, eating be-
> havior abnormalities, and psychosis. The effect of previ-
> ous existing psychological disorders in these behaviors,
> however, is not yet fully understood.

Pope, Harrison G., Gen Kanayama, and James I. Hudson.
2012. "Risk Factors for Illicit Anabolic-Androgenic Steroid
Use in Male Weightlifters: A Cross-Sectional Cohort Study."
Biological Psychiatry. 71(3): 254–261.

> The authors investigate factors that may be associated
> with the use of anabolic steroids by a selected group of
> weight lifters and find that two factors are of particular
> significance: body image and conduct disorder.

Sagoe, Dominic, et al. 2015. "Polypharmacy among Anabolic-
Androgenic Steroid Users: A Descriptive Metasynthesis." *Substance Abuse Treatment, Prevention, and Policy.* 10(1): 1–19.

> The term *polypharmacy* refers to the practice of using
> two or more drugs at the same time. This study claims
> to be the first such research that attempts to summa-
> rize the effects of such practices among individuals who
> include anabolic steroids in their drug regimen. The
> study is very detailed and comprehensive and provides
> invaluable information about the health consequences
> of using various combinations of drugs, both legal and
> illegal.

Saugy, M., et al. 2006. "Human Growth Hormone Doping in
Sport." *British Journal of Sports Medicine.* 40 (Suppl 1): i35–i39.

DOI: 10.1136/bjsm.2006.027573 PMCID: PMC2657499. https://www.ncbi.nlm.nih.gov/pmc/articles/PMC2657499/. Accessed on February 20, 2017.

This article provides a good introduction to the properties of human growth hormone, understandable to the general public, along with a review of its therapeutic uses and its potential applications as a dopant in sports and other athletic pursuits.

Savulescu, J., B. Foddy, and M. Clayton. 2004. "Why We Should Allow Performance Enhancing Drugs in Sport." *British Journal of Sports Medicine*. 38(6): 666–670. http://bjsm .bmj.com/content/38/6/666.full. Accessed on February 26, 2017.

The lead author of this article is one of the best-known and most outspoken authorities on the importance of removing bans on the use of performance-enhancing drugs in sports. The authors offer a detailed and thoughtful analysis of this problem and the reasons for their position on the issue.

Shoskes, Daniel A., Lawrence S. Hakim, et al. 2016. *Testosterone Replacement Therapy Translational Andrology and Urology*. 5(6).

The entire issue of this journal is devoted to a group of papers on the "current state of the art and global perspective" on uses of testosterone for therapeutic purposes.

Sottas, Pierre-Edouard, et al. 2011. "The Athlete Biological Passport." *Clinical Chemistry*. 57(7): 969–976.

This article explains the need for a "biological passport," the characteristic features of such a document, and the ways in which it provides a whole new avenue for dealing with the problem of doping among elite athletes.

Thomas, Johanna O., et al. 2010. "Elite Athletes' Perceptions of the Effects of Illicit Drug Use on Athletic Performance." *Clinical Journal of Sport Medicine*. 20(3): 189–192.

This study of 974 elite athletes in Australia found that participants were relatively well informed about the short-term mental and physical consequences of using performance-enhancing drugs but were less well informed and apparently less concerned about long-term effects.

Van de Kerkhof, Daan, et al. 2000. "Evaluation of Testosterone/Epitestosterone Ratio Influential Factors as Determined in Doping Analysis." *Journal of Analytical Toxicology*. 24(2): 102–101.

The authors explain the testosterone/epitestosterone test for illegal drug use and discuss some possible reasons for false positive results. The article is a good general technical introduction to the use of the testosterone/epitestosterone test.

Wendt, John T. 2015. "Horse Racing in the United States: A Call for a Harmonized Approach to Anti-Doping Regulation." *Journal of Legal Aspects of Sport*. 25(2): 176–188.

The author reviews recent developments in the doping of race horses in the United States and suggests that the problem has created "a crisis in the industry." He argues that a more unified set of rules about doping would be a step toward solving this problem.

Werner, T. C., and Caroline K. Hatton. 2011. "Performance-Enhancing Drugs in Sports: How Chemists Catch Users." *Journal of Chemical Education*. 88(1): 34–40. http://www.chem.wisc.edu/courses/343/Gellman/fall2010/Doping%20detection.pdf. Accessed on February 26, 2017.

This article is intended for teachers of chemistry at the high school and college levels. It is designed to show how general interest in the use of performance-enhancing drugs among students can be used to teach certain basic concepts in chemistry and their application to this topic.

Reports

Butler, Mark, ed. 2015. *IAAF World Championships Beijing 2015 Statistics Handbook.* Monaco: IAAF Communications Department. http://iaaf-ebooks.s3.amazonaws.com/2015/Beijing-2015-Statistics-Handbook/projet/IAAF-World-Championships-Beijing-2015.pdf. Accessed on February 20, 2017.

> Among the vast amount of data contained in this 832-page report is a listing of all known cases of athletes who failed doping tests at championship IAAF and Olympic events up to 2015.

Factsheet: The Fight against Doping and Promotion of Athletes' Health Update—September 2016. Lausanne: International Olympic Committee. https://stillmed.olympic.org/media/Document%20Library/OlympicOrg/Factsheets-Reference-Documents/Medical/Fight-against-Doping/Factsheet-The-Fight-against-Doping-and-Promotion-of-Athletes-Health.pdf#_ga=1.255298568.1868910684.1481307880. Accessed on February 20, 2017.

> This fact sheet summarizes available data on the number of drug tests conducted at all Summer and Winter Olympic Games from 1968 through the Winter Games of 2014. Somewhat ironically, the International Olympic Committee notes that "it is pleased that the strong anti-doping message and other efforts to combat the problem have acted as effective deterrents to ensure clean and fair competition for all athletes" at the very time that evidence of massive cheating over long periods of time by Russian and other national teams was being discovered and reported.

LaBotz, Michelle, and Bernard A. Griesemer. 2016. "Use of Performance-Enhancing Substances." *Pediatrics.* 138(1): e1–e12. http://pediatrics.aappublications.org/content/pediatrics/early/2016/06/24/peds.2016-1300.full.pdf. Accessed on February 17, 2017.

This report is provided by the American Academy of Pediatrics to provide "guidance for the clinician in rendering pediatric care." This report provides the latest information available on the use of performance-enhancing drugs by the pediatric population along with a description of the most commonly used performance-enhancing substances. One of the report's interesting conclusions is that the use of performance-enhancing substances seems to be spreading rapidly to the nonsport, nonathletic community, especially among children and young adults who are concerned about the adequacy of their own body image.

McLaren, Richard H. 2016. *WADA Investigation of Sochi Allegations* and *Independent Commission Report #2*. World Anti-Doping Agency. https://www.wada-ama.org/sites/default/files/resources/files/20160718_ip_report_newfinal.pdf and https://www.wada-ama.org/sites/default/files/resources/files/wada_independent_commission_report_2_2016_en_rev.pdf. Accessed on February 26, 2017.

These two reports by an "independent person" were commissioned by WADA in an effort to discover the accuracy of allegations of widespread cheating by Russian athletes at the 2014 Sochi Winter Olympics and other sporting venues. They include evidence of long-term and widespread illegal use of banned substances in a variety of sporting events by the Russians.

Pound, Richard W., Richard H. McLaren, and Günter Younger. 2015. *The Independent Commission Report #1*. World Anti-Doping Agency. https://www.wada-ama.org/sites/default/files/resources/files/wada_independent_commission_report_1_en.pdf. Accessed on February 26, 2017.

The Pound report is one of the key documents released in 2015 and 2016 on the nature and extent of formalized cheating by Russian athletes at the Sochi Winter Olympic Games of 2014 and other sporting events.

Report to WADA Executive Committee on Lack of Effective-ness of Testing Programs. 2013. Working Group Established Following Foundation Board Meeting of May 18, 2012. https://www.wada-ama.org/sites/default/files/resources/ files/2013-05-12-Lack-of-effectiveness-of-testing-WG-Re port-Final.pdf. Accessed on February 25, 2017.

This study was commissioned by WADA to determine the effectiveness of existing testing programs conducted by the agency. The report noted overall that "there are clearly many systemic, organizational and human reasons why the drug testing programs have been generally unsuccess-ful in detecting dopers/cheats." The commission offered a large number of recommendations for improvements by WADA, international sport organizations, national anti-doping agencies, governmental bodies, individual athletes and entourages, accredited laboratories, and major-event organizers.

2015 Anti-Doping Testing Figures. 2016. World Anti-Doping Agency. https://www.wada-ama.org/sites/default/files/resources/ files/2015_wada_anti-doping_testing_figures_report_0.pdf. Accessed on February 27, 2017.

WADA annually publishes a report on its anti-doping program, including data on virtually every imaginable aspect of this program. This 274-page report is the most recent document available at the time of this writing.

2013–2014 UIL Anabolic Steroid Testing Report. [n.d.] Univer-sity Interscholastic League. https://www.uiltexas.org/health/ info/2013-2014-uil-anabolicsteroid-testing-report. Accessed on February 17, 2017.

This report by the University Interscholastic League sum-marizes the results of anabolic steroid testing in second-ary schools in the state of Texas during the school year 2013–2014. Of the 2,633 tests conducted, two positive results were reported.

What Are Anabolic Steroids? 2006. National Institute on Drug Abuse. https://d14rmgtrwzf5a.cloudfront.net/sites/default/files/rrsteroids_0.pdf. Accessed on February 24, 2017.

This report is one in a series of research reports produced by the National Institute on Drug Abuse about the use and misuse, properties, and risks associated with various primarily illegal drugs. This publication covers topics such as the meaning of anabolic steroids and related compounds, the prevalence of steroid use in the United States, health effects of steroid use, treatments available for steroid abuse, and additional sources of information on the subject.

Internet

"All Athletes Definitely Not Going to Rio." 2016. z-news.xyz. http://z-news.xyz/all-athletics-definitely-not-going-to-rio/. Accessed on February 26, 2017.

This website attempts to provide news on a wide variety of topics taking place in Russia. It contains some of the most interesting perspectives on the results of WADA investigations on cheating in Russian sports with regard to the participation of Russian athletes in the 2016 Summer Olympics in Rio de Janeiro.

Allin, Jane. [2011]. "The Chemical Horse." The Horse Fund. http://horsefund.org/the-chemical-horse-part-1.php. Accessed on February 27, 2017.

This 10-part series provides one of the best generally available reviews of the history of doping in horse racing and the current status of the problem.

"Anabolic Steroid Abuse." 2006. National Institute on Drug Abuse. https://d14rmgtrwzf5a.cloudfront.net/sites/default/files/rrsteroids_0.pdf. Accessed on February 26, 2017.

This report provides an excellent general introduction to the issue of steroid abuse, with sections on the scope of steroid abuse in the United States, reasons that people abuse steroids, how steroids are misused, and the health consequences of misusing steroids.

"Anabolic Steroids." 2006. Substance Abuse and Mental Health Services Administration. http://162.99.3.213/products/manu als/advisory/pdfs/anabolicsteriods.pdf. Accessed on February 26, 2017.

This website is an electronic version of the SAMHSA *Substance Abuse Treatment Advisory* series, providing general information on the topic of steroid abuse, as well as some useful references and additional resources.

"Anabolic Steroids." 2014. Medline Plus. https://medlineplus .gov/anabolicsteroids.html. Accessed on February 26, 2017.

This website is a good resource for information about a variety of articles, websites, and other sources of information about anabolic steroids. "Anabolic Steroids Information." 2017. Anabolic Bible. http://www.anabolic-bible .org/ShowPage.aspx?callpage%20%EF%80%BD%20 Introduction. Accessed on February 26, 2017.

This website calls itself the "ultimate resource for information on anabolic steroids." It contains sections on the effects of anabolic steroids, the history of anabolic steroids and their use for medical and nonmedical purposes, the chemistry and pharmacology of steroids, and side effects of androgenic anabolic steroid use.

"Androgenic Anabolic Steroids." 2017. Rx List. http://www.rx list.com/anabolic-androgenic_steroids/drugs-condition.htm. February 15, 2017.

This website provides an excellent general introduction to the topic of androgenic anabolic steroids, including sections on how they are abused, how they affect the brain, how they affect mental health, and how widespread their abuse appears to be.

Antonovich, Michael. 2012. "The FIM's Assault on Performance Enhancing Drugs." Transworld Motorcross. http://motocross.transworld.net/1000124312/features/the-fims-assault-on-performance-enhancing-drugs/. Accessed on May 24, 2012.

> The author describes efforts by the FIM (Fédération Internationale de Motocyclisme), the ruling organization for motocross sports, to introduce drug testing into a sport that had previously not been overly concerned about the potential problems of steroid abuse.

Baker, Millard. 2017. "Banning Drugs in Sports: A Skeptical View by Norman Fost MD." Vimeo. https://vimeo.com/8526040. Accessed on February 17, 2017.

> This video is of considerable historical interest because it provides the views of one of the most famous critics of drug testing in elite sports, Norman Fost, professor of pediatrics and medical ethics at the University of Wisconsin at Madison.

Balko, Radley. 2008. "Should We Allow Performance Enhancing Drugs in Sports?" *Reason Magazine*. http://reason.com/archives/2008/01/23/should-we-allow-performance-en/singlepage. Accessed on February 26, 2017.

> This web page contains the text of a presentation made by Balko, senior editor of *Reason* magazine, in 2008, in which he claims that the debate over androgenic anabolic steroids is really about "paternalism and control" of sports agencies over the individuals who play for them.

"Blood Horse." 2017. http://www.bloodhorse.com/horse-racing/articles/tag/blood-doping. Accessed on February 27, 2017.

This website has a very large number of articles dealing with all aspects of doping of race horses, some quite esoteric subjects, but many topics of interest to the general public.

"A Closer Look: The Athlete Biological Passport." 2015. U.S. Anti-Doping Agency. http://www.usada.org/closer-look-athlete-biological-passport/. Accessed on February 17, 2017.

This web page provides an overview of the so-called biological passport now required of elite athletes, with answers to some common questions about its use. The page also has links to other sources, such as the World Anti-Doping Agency, with additional information on the biological passport.

Crisp, Stephen, Terry Sheehan, and John Hughes. 2008. "The Science of Doping Control." http://www.laboratoryequipment.com/article/2008/11/science-doping-control. Accessed on February 26, 2017.

This article, although somewhat dated, provides a good general introduction to the most common methods of drug detection used for sporting events. It focuses on gas chromatography and mass spectrometry and associated technologies.

Darkes, Jack. [n.d.] *Anabolic/Androgenic Steroid Use and Aggression—I: A Review of the Evidence, II: Does the Evidence Support a Causal Inference?* http://www.thinkmuscle.com/articles/darkes/aggression-01.htm and http://www.thinkmuscle.com/articles/darkes/aggression-02.htm. Accessed on February 26, 2017.

This excellent article reviews in great detail evidence concerning the possible effects of anabolic steroid use on a variety of psychological behaviors, such as irritation and rage. The article suggests that a possible cause-and-effect relationship between steroid use and these behaviors is very difficult to determine with certainty and that it probably may not exist.

Davis, Charles Patrick. 2016. "Steroid Drug Withdrawal." MedicineNet.com. http://www.medicinenet.com/steroid_with drawal/article.htm. Accessed on February 26, 2017.

An issue that is not frequently addressed in articles on anabolic steroids is the physical and psychological problems that may be associated with cessation of their use. This article fills that void with a thorough discussion of the signs and symptoms of the condition, methods of diagnosis, and treatments available.

Dimant, Eugen, and Christian Deutscher. 2015. "The Economics of Corruption in Sports: The Special Case of Doping." Harvard University Edmond J. Safra Center for Ethics. https:// poseidon01.ssrn.com/delivery.php?ID=06108102401311 5028066016116011099014032053053031010004101020099030127021026092072124054054025045018036026019065127091114118000018000070045050023002066097092015010093050076009017074068023007066102069124094103090112022016068116124067007010023027025095031&EXT=pdf. Accessed on February 19, 2017.

The authors take note of the significant role of cheating in both amateur and professional athletics, and point out that such behaviors have real and important economic consequences and motivations. They discuss those issues in this paper.

"Diuretics and Other Masking Agents." 2017. Technische Universitat Munchen. http://www.doping-prevention.com/lv/vielas-un-metodes/diuretics-and-other-masking-agents/diuretics-and-other-masking-agents.html. Accessed on February 27, 2017.

This website provides some good visual presentations on the nature of masking agents and their use in sports.

"Drugs and Testing." 2016. USLegal. https://sportslaw.uslegal
.com/drugs-and-testing/. Accessed on February 26, 2017.

This website outlines the basic legal issues involved in
current anti-doping programs in the United States. It
discusses, in particular, programs run by the National
Football League, the National Collegiate Athletic Association, and the International Olympic Committee.

Eber, Lorie. 2013. "Let's Stop the Pretense of Drug Testing of Professional Athletes." *Huffington Post.* http://www
.huffingtonpost.com/lorie-eber/performance-enhancing-
drugs_b_2736891.html. Accessed on February 19, 2017.

Eber offers some familiar arguments in opposition to required drug testing of elite athletes, such as the lack of
success in identifying cheaters and the problem in deciding as to which substances are to be banned and which
are not to be.

Fretz, Caley. 2015. "The Test That Caught Tom Danielson."
Velonews. http://www.velonews.com/2015/08/news/the-test-
that-caught-tom-danielson_381086. Accessed on February 27,
2017.

This article explains how the testosterone/epitestosterone
test is used for detecting illegal drug use, and how it was
employed in one specific case. *Also see* van de Kerkhof,
under Articles, for technical details.

Freudenrich, Craig, and Kevin P. Allen. 2017. "How
Performance-Enhancing Drugs Work." How Stuff Works Entertainment. http://entertainment.howstuffworks.com/athlet
ic-drug-test.htm. Accessed on February 26, 2017.

This general introduction to the use of performance-
enhancing substances includes sections on the reasons that athletes use such drugs, their effects on the
human body, various types of performance-enhancing

drugs, and testing athletes for doping. A good reference list is also provided.

Frounfelter, Gregory G., and Greg E. Bradley Popovich. 2000. "Ethical Considerations Regarding Anabolic-Androgenic Steroid Use." Professionalization of Exercise Physiology. https://www.asep.org/asep/asep/EthicalConsiderations.html. Accessed on February 26, 2017.

> The authors briefly review the chemistry and physiology of androgenic anabolic steroid use, but focus on moral issues related to such use, with special attention to the role of medical care providers.

Goldberg, Ryan. 2014. "Secret to Success: A Derby Win and Racing's Doping Addiction." *Pro Publica*. https://www.propublica.org/article/secret-to-success. Accessed on February 27, 2017.

> The author discusses one of the most famous cases of horse racing doping in history, although with a consideration of its impact on the sport itself.

Gwartney, Dan. 2011. "History of the Development of Anabolic Androgenic Steroids." *Muscular Development*. http://www.musculardevelopment.com/articles/chemical-enhancement/3224-history-of-the-development-of-anabolic-androgenic-steroids.html#.WIJexFUrKpp. Accessed on February 27, 2017.

> This article appears to have been inspired by a research article of the same title by Dotson and Brown (see under Articles) with some additional interesting information, observations, and commentary.

Herper, Matthew. 2011. "The Case for Performance-Enhancing Drugs in Sports." *Forbes*. http://www.forbes.com/sites/matthewherper/2011/05/20/the-case-for-performance-enhancing-drugs-in-sports/. Accessed on February 26, 2017.

The author explains why he favors the legalization of performance-enhancing drugs in athletics.

"History of Anabolic Steroids." 2017. Steroidal.com. https://www.steroidal.com/history-anabolic-steroids/. Accessed on February 26, 2017.

This website provides an extensive and detailed history of the discovery, development, use, and regulation of anabolic steroids in sports dating from ancient times to the present day.

Horwitz, Steven. 2017. "Performance Enhancing Drugs." Mom's Team. http://www.momsteam.com/team-of-experts/steven-horwitz-dc/performance-enhancing-drugs. Accessed on February 26, 2017.

This website contains three good articles on specific aspects of anabolic steroids, "Ten Signs of Steroid Abuse," "What Are Anabolic Steroids and How Do They Work?" and "Anabolic Steroids: Your Child's Road to the Gold or to the Grave?"

"How Do Anabolic Steroids Work?" 2011. YouTube. https://www.youtube.com/watch?v=osid6s-C0VA. Accessed on February 15, 2017.

This short video provides a simplified, easy-to-understand explanation of the physiological effects of anabolic steroids on the human body.

"Is Testosterone Replacement Therapy Right for You?" 2017. WebMD. http://www.webmd.com/men/guide/testosterone-replacement-therapy-is-it-right-for-you#1. Accessed on February 17, 2017.

This website offers a good general introduction to the practice of testosterone replacement therapy, the forms in which it is carried out, some benefits and risks, and possible issues in the use of the procedure for performance enhancement in sports.

Katz, Jeffrey. 2008. "Should We Accept Steroid Use in Sports?" npr. http://www.npr.org/2008/01/23/18299098/should-we-accept-steroid-use-in-sports http://www.npr.org/templates/story/story.php?storyId Accessed on February 26, 2017.

> Six experts on the topic of steroid use in sports argue the pros and cons (three on each side) about the morality and ethics of allowing athletes to use steroids.

King, Joseph. 2016. *The Big Book of Steroids*. Amazon.com. https://www.amazon.com/Big-Book-Steroids-Performance-Enhancing-ebook/dp/B01C3J0LB8/ref=sr_1_1?s=books&ie=UTF8&qid=1484848689&sr=1-1&keywords=performance+enhancing+drugs. Self-published. Accessed on October 6, 2017.

> This book discusses and explains the many applications of steroids in bodybuilding and other sports, including comments on physical, psychological, legal, and other aspects of their applications in these fields.

Kirkup, James. 2015. "Athlete Doping Crisis Is Just One More Reason to Allow Drugs in Sport." *The Telegraph*. http://www.telegraph.co.uk/sport/othersports/drugsinsport/11778747/Athletics-doping-crisis-is-just-another-reason-to-allow-drugs-in-sport.html. Accessed on February 16, 2017.

> Kirkup argues that "[s]port is already about who has the best resources, so let's just be honest and allow performance-enhancing drugs too."

Kishner, Stephen. 2015. "Anabolic Steroid Use and Abuse." *Medscape*. http://emedicine.medscape.com/article/128655-overview. Accessed on February 26, 2017.

> This highly respected Internet resource provides useful and technical information on the chemistry, physiology, and pharmacology of anabolic steroids, with an extended

discussion of topics such as the biopharmacology of testosterone, testosterone esters and derivatives, adverse effects, clinical uses, and steroid abuse. An extensive list of references is also provided.

Le Page, Michael. 2016. "Gene Doping in Sport Could Make the Olympics Fairer and Safer." *New Scientist*. https://www.newscientist.com/article/2100181-gene-doping-in-sport-could-make-the-olympics-fairer-and-safer/. Accessed on February 25, 2017.

The author explains the process of gene doping and argues that it is a process that is inevitable in athletics and that anti-doping agencies will have no way of monitoring or banning the procedure. He suggests, therefore, that it would be "far better for everyone" if we just accept them.

Lefler, Leah. 2017. "The Elixir of Life: A Brief History of Testosterone." http://leahlefler.hubpages.com/hub/The-Elixir-of-Life-A-Brief-History-of-Testosterone. Accessed on March 11, 2017.

The author discusses the period in history during which the Elixir of Life was widely popular, and then continues to comment on the current popularity, characteristics, and misuse of testosterone and related substances.

Masoliver, Dan. 2016. "Should Blood Doping Be Legal in Sports?" *Men's Health*. http://www.menshealth.co.uk/fitness/should-blood-doping-be-legal-in-sport. Accessed on February 16, 2017.

This article summarizes and repeats most of the major arguments for legalizing the use of certain forms of doping in sports. An interesting response to the article can be found in "Should Doping Be Legalised? The Olympic Drug Debate," listed later in this section.

McEwan, Iain J., and Albert O. Brinkmann. 2016. "Androgen Physiology: Receptor and Metabolic Disorders." *Endotext*.

https://www.ncbi.nlm.nih.gov/books/NBK279028/. Accessed on February 15, 2017.

This posting offers a technical and detailed explanation of the physiological changes that occur as a result of androgenic anabolic steroid ingestion. Additional details about the family of substances are also provided.

"Medical and Illicit Use of Anabolic Steroids." 2017. NetCE Continuing Education. http://www.netce.com/coursecontent .php?courseid. Accessed on February 26, 2017.

This website provides course materials for the topic named in its title. The course is part of the online educational program of NetCE Continuing Medical, whose purpose it is to provide course material on a wide variety of topics of interest and value to health care professionals.

Miller, Anna Medaris. 2016. "Before You Try Steroids to Build Muscle, Read This." *US News and World Report*. http://health .usnews.com/wellness/articles/2016-04-21/before-you-try-ste roids-to-build-muscle-read-this. Accessed on February 19, 2017.

Miller takes note of the trend toward the use of steroids for improving one's body image, and then reviews some of the risky side effects associated with this practice.

Mitchell, Kevin. 2016. "Maria Sharapova Receives Two-Year Ban for Failing Drug Test." *The Guardian*. https://www.the guardian.com/sport/2016/jun/08/maria-sharapova-banned-two-years-failing-drugs-test-meldonium. Accessed on February 16, 2017.

Five-time Grand Slam professional tennis player Maria Sharapova is banned from competition until January 26, 2018, for having taken a drug on the WADA list of banned substances. She claims that she has been taking the drug for 10 years because of a magnesium deficiency and did not know it was illegal to do so.

Mørkeberg, Jakob. 2013. "Blood Manipulation: Current Challenges from an Anti-Doping Perspective." American Society of Hematology Education Program. http://asheducationbook.he matologylibrary.org/content/2013/1/627.full.pdf. Accessed on February 27, 2017.

>This paper provides an excellent general introduction to the background and current status of the use of various types of blood manipulation as a way of improving athletic performance.

Nasr, Susan L. 2008. "How Gene Doping Works." HowStuff Works.com. http://science.howstuffworks.com/life/genetic/gene-doping.htm. Accessed on February 26, 2017.

>Nasr provides a good, understandable, general introduction to the topic of gene doping and how it can be used to improve a person's athletic performance.

Neil, B. 2013. "Doping in Sports—A Moral or Legal Issue?" *Tribe Sports.* http://community.tribesports.com/blog/doping-in-sport-a-moral-or-legal-issue. Accessed on February 27, 2017.

>The blogger discusses the question as to whether doping and anti-doping efforts in sports pose moral and/or legal questions. The article is of interest not only because of its own thoughtful analysis but also because of the number of good responses it produced from readers.

Ormsbee, Michael, and Matt Vukovich. 2005. "Performance Enhancing Drugs." IDEA Health and Fitness Association. http://www.ideafit.com/fitness-library/performance-enhancing-drugs. Accessed on February 26, 2017.

>In this somewhat dated but still very helpful article, the authors suggest that the use of anabolic steroids in the United States has become essentially a fait accompli, and that athletes now need to become aware of the health

effects that may be associated with their use. An extensive list of pre-2005 references is included in the article.

Pacelle, Wayne. 2015. "Horse Sense Needed to End Doping in Horse Racing." A Humane Nation. http://blog.humanesoci ety.org/wayne/2015/06/end-doping-in-horse-racing-industry .html. Accessed on February 26, 2017.

> The president and CEO of the Humane Society of the United States discusses the problem of doping in horse racing and suggests some legislative steps that can be taken to deal with this problem.

"Paulick Report." 2017. http://www.paulickreport.com/. Accessed on February 27, 2017.

> Arguably the best single source of information and commentary on issues related to the doping of race horses (and horse racing in general), the Paulick Report offers a number of articles on specific aspects of this issue, along with commentaries on the problems and solutions involved.

Paulson, Steve. 2015. "The Moral Argument for Doping in Sports." *Nautilus*. http://nautilus-web-602376506.us-east-1 .elb.amazonaws.com/blog/the-moral-argument-for-dop ing-in-sports. Accessed on February 17, 2017.

> This blog consists of an interview with Julian Savulescu, professor at the Uehrin Centre for Practical Ethics at the University of Oxford, in which Savulescu presents ethical arguments as to the reasons that doping should be allowed in elite sports. (Savulescu wrote an essay for Chapter 3 of the first edition of this book in 2013.)

Perez, A. J. 2010. "Cops' Use of Illegal Steroids a 'Big Problem.'" *AOL News*. http://www.911omissionreport.com/cop_ steroids.html. Accessed on February 26, 2017.

> This article explains how the special conditions under which police officers work may cause them to consider

the use of anabolic steroids to "beef up" as a way of dealing with those problems. The writer describes specific problems in Trenton, New Jersey, South Bend, Indiana, and Orlando, Florida, in which steroids were involved in inappropriate police actions.

"Performance Enhancing Anabolic Steroid Abuse in Women." 2011 [reaffirmed in 2015]. The American College of Obstetricians and Gynecologists. http://www.acog.org/ Resources-And-Publications/Committee-Opinions/Committee-on-Gynecologic-Practice/Performance-Enhancing-Anabolic-Steroid-Abuse-in-Women. Accessed on February 26, 2017.

This paper by the American College of Obstetricians and Gynecologists reviews the history of steroid use by women in sports and athletics, and for other purposes, with a general discussion of its physical, psychological, and other effects on women.

"Performance-Enhancing Drugs in Athletics: Research Roundup." 2015. *Journalist's Resource.* https://journalistsresource.org/studies/society/culture/athletic-academic-performance-enhancing-drugs-research-roundup. Accessed on February 19, 2017.

This web page provides a number of recommendations for journalists for resources on specific aspects of the issue of performance-enhancing drugs, such as economics, prevalence, health effects, and attitudes.

Pesta, Dominik H., et al. 2013. "The Effects of Caffeine, Nicotine, Ethanol, and Tetrahydrocannabinol on Exercise Performance." *Nutrition & Metabolism.* 10:71. DOI: 10.1186/1743-7075-10-71. http://nutritionandmetabolism.biomedcentral.com/articles/10.1186/1743-7075-10-71. Accessed on February 25, 2017.

The substances listed in the title of this article are among the most commonly ingested products worldwide. Three of the four are legal everywhere. The question is how, if at all, their ingestion affects a person's athletic performance, a question that the article attempts to answer.

"Play Healthy." 2015. Partnership for Drug-Free Kids. http://playhealthy.drugfree.org/. Accessed on February 25, 2017.

This website is maintained as a cooperative endeavor of the Partnership for Drug-Free Kids and Major League Baseball for the purpose of informing children and young adults about the risks associated with the use of performance-enhancing drugs. The site contains a useful section with detailed information about most of the major performance-enhancing drugs, including steroids, human growth hormone, stimulants, erythropoietin, diuretics, and human chorionic gonatropin.

Pope, Harrison G., Jr., Jag H. Khalsa, and Shalender Bhasin. 2016. "Body Image Disorders and Abuse of Anabolic-Androgenic Steroids among Men." *JAMA*. doi:10.1001/jama.2016.17441. http://jamanetwork.com/journals/jama/fullarticle/2592911. Accessed on December 15, 2016.

This paper summarizes much of what is known about the association of body image dysphoria and use of anabolic androgenic steroids, along with some suggestions as to steps that might be taken in order to deal with this issue.

"Position Statement on Anabolic Androgenic Steroids." 2014. National Federation of State High School Associations. http://www.nfhs.org/sports-resource-content/position-statement-on-anabolic-androgenic-steroids/. Accessed on February 25, 2017.

This position statement explains that the federation "strongly opposes the use of anabolic, androgenic steroids (AAS) and other performance-enhancing substances by high school athletes" because such use "violates legal, ethical and competitive equity standards, and imposes unacceptable long-term health risks."

Presto, Greg. 2010. "11 Questions about Performance-Enhancing Drugs." *Men's Health.* http://www.menshealth.com/health/performance-enhancing-drugs?fullpage true. Accessed on February 25, 2017.

The author raises some practical questions associated with the use of anabolic steroids by "athletes and average guys," such as when steroid use jumped from bodybuilding to mainstream sports, connections between steroid use and hand-eye coordination, and the risks associated with human growth hormone.

Price, Satchel. 2016. "Everything You Need to Know about the Doping Scandal Rocking the Russian National Team." *SB Nation.* http://www.sbnation.com/2016/7/22/12258488/russia-doping-scandal-suspensions-rio-olympics-2016. Accessed on February 20, 2017.

This web article provides an excellent general overview of the doping scandal preceding the 2016 Summer Olympic Games in Rio de Janeiro, with links to some of the most important documents and articles related to this situation.

"Prohibited List 2017." 2017. World Anti-Doping Agency. https://www.wada-ama.org/sites/default/files/resources/files/2016-09-29_-_wada_prohibited_list_2017_eng_final.pdf. Accessed on February 20, 2017.

This publication contains a list of all banned substances and procedures for elite athletes in most forms of competition worldwide. The list is updated on a regular basis.

"Resources." 2017. World Anti-Doping Agency. https://www.wada-ama.org/en/resources. Accessed on February 26, 2017.

The WADA website is a very rich source of documents on all aspects of doping and anti-doping topics. This page contains links to specific topics such as ADAMS (WADA's Anti-Doping Administration & Management System), the anti-doping community, athlete biological passports, athlete outreach, code compliance, data protection, the doping control process, education and awareness, finance, general anti-doping information, governance, laboratories, legal issues, the Play True program, research, science and medicine, social science, The Code, therapeutic use exemption, the Whereabouts program, and the World Anti-Doping program.

"Rio Paralympics 2016: Russian Athletes Banned after Doping Scandal." 2016. BBC. http://www.bbc.com/sport/disability-sport/37002582. Accessed on February 20, 2017.

The continuing fallout of WADA reports of cheating by Russian sporting groups led to the ban of all Russian competitors in the 2016 Rio Paralympic competition in September of that year. This article explains the circumstances of that ban, the basis for the decision made, and reaction by Russian officials and other interested parties.

Rosene, Peter. 2016. "Cheater, Cheater: Thoroughbred-Racing Regulations Walking the Fine Line between Therapy and Doping." *The Kentucky Journal of Agriculture Natural Resource Law.* http://www.kjeanrl.com/full-blog/2016/1/24/peterrosene blog. Accessed on February 27, 2017.

The author discusses the problems of finding the correct form of legislation to prevent doping of race horses without also banning legitimate medical treatment for the animals.

"S5 Diuretics and Other Masking Agents." 2017. anti-doping. ch. http://www.antidoping.ch/en/prevention/mobile-learning-programs/mobile-lesson-substances-and-methods/s5-diuretics-and-other. Accessed on February 27, 2017.

This website is a part of a set of lessons designed for young adults about doping-related issues. It provides a clear introduction to the nature of masking agents, the way in which such agents work on the body, and their possible use and abuse in various sports.

Sayer, Luke. 2016. "Possible Ways the Therapeutic Use Exemption Can Be Improved to Prevent Abuse." *Law in Sport.* http://www.lawinsport.com/articles/item/are-therapeutic-use-exemptions-open-to-abuse-and-how-can-they-be-improved. Accessed on February 26, 2017.

> This website describes claims by a group called Fancy Bears that therapeutic use exemptions have been commonly misused by elite athletes to gain the benefits of doping without penalty. The site provides a good introduction to the use of therapeutic use exemption substances and some recommendations for improving the use for which they were designed.

"Should Doping Be Legalised? The Olympic Drug Debate." 2016. *The Science of Sport.* https://sportsscientists.com/2016/08/doping-legalised-olympic-drug-debate/. Accessed on February 16, 2017.

> This article in support of the continuation of drug testing of elite athletes was written in response to an article in the British version of *Men's Health* (see Masoliver's article earlier in this section).

"Should Performance Enhancing Drugs (Such as Steroids) Be Accepted in Sports?" 2016. ProCon.org. http://sportsanddrugs.procon.org/. Accessed on February 27, 2017.

> This excellent website presents arguments both in favor of and against the banning of performance-enhancing drugs in sports and athletics. Specific sections of the website deal with topics such as core questions, top 10 pro-and-con arguments, an historical timeline, and comments from readers.

Shugarman, Alan E. 2017. "Muscle Building Supplement Guide." http://www.nutritionexpress.com/article index/authors/alan e shugarman ms rd/showarticle.aspx?articleid=793. Accessed on February 13, 2017.

> This article provides an overview of some of the most common drugs used by bodybuilders, weight lifters, and other strength and power athletes.

Shugarman, Alan E. 2017. "Nitric Oxide." http://www.nutri tionexpress.com/articleindex/authors/alaneshugarmanmsrd/ showarticle.aspx?articleid=784. Accessed on February 13, 2017.

> The author explains the use of nitric oxide for building muscle mass, as well as listing and describing some of the specific substances from which one can obtain nitric oxide from dietary sources.

Steadman, Ian. 2012. "How Sports Would Be Better with Doping." *Wired*. https://www.wired.com/2012/09/sports-and-dop ing/. Accessed on February 16, 2017.

> Steadman presents the interesting argument that permitting the use of illegal drugs by elite athletes may be the only way to maintain public interest in sporting events as other methods of improving performance become more and more efficient.

"Steroid Laws." 2017. Anabolics.com. http://www.anabolics .com/pages/Steroid-Laws#.WIo94FUrKpo. Accessed on February 26, 2017.

> This website provides some useful general information about the legal status of steroids and other performance-enhancing drugs, such as current laws in the United States, possession and distribution, controlled deliveries, seizures and entrapments, and the success of U.S. laws.

"Testing." 2017. U.S. Anti-Doping Agency. http://www.usada .org/testing/. Accessed on February 16, 2017.

> The U.S. Anti-Doping Agency website provides detailed information on all aspects of drug testing for elite athletes, including urine and blood collection, athlete's rights, disabled athletes, the Whereabouts program, arbitration procedures, test scheduling, sample collection, and results management.

"Testosterone Therapy: Potential Benefits and Risk as You Age." 2015. Mayo Clinic. http://www.mayoclinic.org/healthy-lifestyle/sexual-health/in-depth/testosterone-therapy/art-20045728.

>This website provides an overview of testosterone replacement therapy and its benefits and risks, especially for older men.

"UCI Opens Biological Passport Case against Sergio Henao." 2016. *Cycling News*. http://www.cyclingnews.com/news/uci-opens-biological-passport-case-against-sergio-henao/. Accessed on February 17, 2017.

>This article provides an insight into the way in which biological passports can be used to determine whether or not a person has violated anti-doping rules in a sporting competition. Henao was later cleared of any misconduct in this regard (see http://www.cyclingnews.com/news/sergio-henao-cleared-by-uci-over-biological-passport-case/).

Weislo, Laura. 2013. "Index of Lance Armstrong Doping Allegations over the Years." *Cycling News*. http://www.cyclingnews.com/features/index-of-lance-armstrong-doping-allegations-over-the-years/. Accessed on February 24, 2017.

>The many allegations that star cyclist Lance Armstrong used performance-enhancing substances in winning more Tour de France titles than any other cyclist in history constitute one of the most interesting and most devastating stories of doping in sports in modern history. The website lists well over 100 stories that appeared in *Cycling News* from July 1999 to January 2013.

Introduction

The discovery and general use of steroids dates only to the late 19th century. Yet, the roots of the steroid abuse story go back much farther in history. This chapter lists some of the most important events that have occurred throughout that history.

At least 6000 BCE   Humans learn of the demasculinizing effects of castration by trial and error, a bit of agricultural knowledge that survives for millennia without any theoretical basis.

776 BCE   Date of the first Olympic Games in Greece. Competitors at the Games are thought to have ingested the testicles of male animals to gain strength, speed, and endurance to aid them in their participation in the Games.

1760s   Scottish physician John Hunter studies the effects of transplanting testicular tissue from male chickens to female chickens and to demasculinized males (capons). He discovers that both females and capons develop male characteristics, such as growing a comb and displaying crowing behavior.

1840s   German physiologist Arnold Berthold conducts a series of experiments in which he found that castrated roosters had combs and wattles reduced in size, reduced aggressive

Juan Jose Cobo Acebo of Spain, seated, waits at the doping control bus after the 11th stage of the Tour de France cycling race between Lannemezan and Foix, in southern France, July 16, 2008. (AP Photo/Christophe Ena)

behavior toward other males, and reduced interest in hens. His experiments were among the first studies on endocrine-determined behavior in animals.

1889   At the age of 72, Mauritian-born physiologist Charles Édouard Brown-Séquard reports having injected himself with fluid taken from the testes of dogs and guinea pigs, after which he experiences a significant renewal of physical strength and mental abilities.

1896   Austrian physiologists Oskar Zoth and Fritz Pregel publish a paper describing their experiments in injecting themselves with testicular extracts from animals. They suggest the possibility that such procedures may be effective in increasing the skills needed by athletes in a variety of sports.

1902   English physiologists William Bayliss and Ernest Starling discover the action of the first hormone, secretin. The name *hormone*, meaning "I arouse to activity," is suggested to Starling by a colleague, William B. Hardy.

1918   Austrian physiologist Eugen Steinach performs the first "Steinach operation," a type of vasectomy that he believed would restore a man's sexual prowess and overall good health. The Steinach operation soon becomes widely popular throughout the Western world as a method of "rejuvenation" for men.

1920s–1930s   Russian-born French surgeon Serge Abrahamovitch Voronoff attempts to improve male sexual function by grafting tissue from monkey testicles into human male testicles. The procedure is very popular for a while, but soon falls into disuse and notoriety.

1928   The International Association of Athletics Federation adopts the world's first sports association drug policy, one that was virtually impossible to enforce because methods for testing for most drugs were not yet available.

1929   German chemist Adolf Butenandt isolates the first sex hormone, estrone, obtained from the urine of pregnant women. Two years later, he isolates the first male sex hormone, which he names androsterone (andro: "male," ster: "sterol," one: ketone family).

1930s   Swiss physician Paul Niehans develops the theory of cellular therapy, in which the healthy cells of an animal organ are transplanted into the unhealthy organ of a human to improve the functioning of the latter. Niehans specialized in such procedures to improve the sexual functioning of older men.

1934   Croatian biochemist Leopold Ružička synthesizes androsterone, an accomplishment that contributed to his receipt of a share of the 1939 Nobel Prize in Chemistry.

1935   Researchers at the Dutch pharmaceutical firm of Organon, led by Ernst Laqueur, announce the discovery of a crystalline substance with a physiological effect more pronounced than that of androsterone, which they call *testosterone*.

1935   Only a few months after the Organon discovery, research teams led by Butenandt and Ružička announce in two separate articles the first synthesis of testosterone from cholesterol. The development makes possible, at least in principle, the production of testosterone on a commercial scale.

1935   American medical researcher Charles D. Kochakian discovers that androsterone has anabolic as well as androgenic effects, establishing for the first time the possibility of using the substance for muscle- and tissue-building purposes.

1937   Clinical tests on the use of testosterone for the treatment of hypogonadism begin. At the same time, interest in the use of testosterone to improve masculine characteristics is already underway, often in a less rigorous and controlled manner.

1939   The Nobel Prize in Chemistry is divided equally between Adolf Friedrich Johann Butenandt "for his work on sex hormones" and Leopold Ru_i_ka "for his work on polymethylenes and higher terpenes" (compounds of which steroids and related compounds are produced).

1941   An 18-year-old trotting horse by the name of Holloway with a rapidly diminishing skill at racing is treated with testosterone injections. Over the following few months, he shows marked improvement in his racing skills and, at the age of 19, sets a new record for the one-mile distance of 2 minutes 10 seconds. Holloway is, thus, the first "athlete" for whom positive "doping" in a competitive event has been confirmed.

1945   American writer Paul de Kruif publishes *The Male Hormone*, a book in which the anabolic and androgenic effects of testosterone products are described. The book is probably the first widely available introduction to the topic for the general public worldwide.

Late 1940s   Testosterone injections are used for therapeutic purposes in undernourished survivors of German concentration camps at the conclusion of World War II.

Early 1950s   Sports teams in the Soviet Union and other Soviet bloc nations begin the use of anabolic and androgenic steroids (AAS) in training programs for many of their national athletic teams.

1954   The first results of the Soviet training programs with AAS use appear in the 1954 Olympic Games when Russian weight lifters sweep most medal awards in their divisions.

1954   U.S. Olympic trainer John Ziegler learns of the Soviet AAS use in training programs and obtains samples of drugs used by the Soviets from their makers, Ciba Pharmaceuticals.

1958   The U.S. Food and Drug Administration approves the use of a version of the AAS used by Soviet trainers that contains fewer androgenic effects and greater anabolic effects. Approval is granted for use with the elderly and burn victims, but it rapidly becomes popular among bodybuilders, weight lifters, and other athletes for off-label purposes. Produced by Ciba Pharmaceuticals, the drug is called Dianabol (chemically, methandrostenolone).

1966   The Fédération Internationale de Football Association (Federation of International Football Associations, or FIFA) and Union Cycliste Internationale (International Cycling Association) both adopt drug-testing policies.

1967 In response to concerns about the increasing use of drugs in athletic competitions, the International Olympic Committee (IOC) establishes the Medical Commission to study the problem of doping, develop methods for testing for the use of illegal substances, and develop alternative methods of helping athletes.

1968 The IOC conducts the first tests for illegal substances at the Summer and Winter Games in Mexico City and Grenoble, France, respectively. AAS drugs are not included because adequate tests for them are not yet available. There is one positive test in the Summer Games and none in the Winter Games.

1974 The German Democratic Republic ("East Germany") adopts official policies requiring the use of AAS in training programs for the nation's athletes.

1975 The IOC adds AAS to its list of banned drugs.

1976 The Olympic Games at Montréal are the first such competitions to include testing for AAS. At the Games, East German women win 11 of 13 individual gold medals, adding to the suspicion that they have been taking steroids in preparation for the contests.

1981 Steroid "guru" Daniel Duchaine publishes *The Original Underground Steroid Handbook for Men and Women*, describing the use of AAS for bodybuilding, weight lifting, and other activities, as well as a list of substances to be used for that purpose. He issued an expanded and updated version in 1988.

1983 Officials at the Pan American Games in Caracas institute unannounced drug testing. At least two dozen athletes from the United States and other nations withdraw from the Games before they begin. In addition, 23 medals are withdrawn after their winners test positive for prohibited drugs. Among those who lose their medals is weight lifter Jeff Michels, who is stripped of three gold medals.

1984 Former musician Victor Conte and colleagues found the Bay Area Laboratory Cooperative, better known as BALCO. Originally formed as a blood and urine analysis facility, the company is reputed to have become involved in supplying illegal supplements to a number of famous athletes, including Barry Bonds, Jason Giambi, Marion Jones, and Bill Romanowski.

1986   The National Collegiate Athletic Association adopts a drug-testing policy for all sports under its control. The policy includes anabolic steroids.

1987   The National Football League (NFL) begins testing players for AAS, the earliest such policy in American professional sports leagues.

1988   U.S. sprinter Ben Johnson is stripped of his world record gold-medal-winning victory in the Olympic 100-meter dash after testing positive for the AAS stanozolol.

1988   The U.S. Congress passes and President Ronald Reagan signs the Anti-Drug Abuse Act of 1988, which bans the sale of AAS for other than medical purposes. It also provides penalties for the sale of AAS within 100 feet of schools.

1988   The National Association for Stock Car Auto Racing announces a drug-testing policy based on "reasonable suspicion" that a drug is being used.

1990   The U.S. Congress adopts the Anabolic Steroid Control Act of 1990, which places anabolic steroids under Schedule III of the Controlled Substances Act.

1991   Major League Baseball (MLB) commissioner Fay Vincent issues a seven-page memorandum banning the use of certain illegal substances in the League. The substances for which athletes will be tested are amphetamines, cocaine, marijuana, opiates, and phenylcyclidine. AAS are not yet included in the list.

1991   Winfried Leopold, chief swimming coach of the East German Olympic swimming team, admits that the use of AAS has been an integral part of the nation's training program for more than two decades.

1992   Former professional football player Lyle Alzado dies of a rare form of brain cancer. He blamed his medical condition on AAS, which he had been using for more than 20 years. (No medical evidence, however, is currently available for a connection between the two.)

1997   MLB commissioner Bud Selig issues a memorandum banning drug use that is almost identical to the one issued by Fay Vincent six years earlier. Again, AAS are not included in the list of banned drugs.

1998   St. Louis Cardinals player Mark McGwire establishes a new MLB record by hitting 70 home runs. He later acknowledges that he has been using a steroid precursor chemical for some time. AAS are still not illegal in MLB.

1999   The World Conference on Doping in Sports is held in Lausanne, Switzerland. It adopts the Lausanne Declaration on Doping in Sport, which announces the forthcoming formation of an international anti-doping agency (now called the World Anti-Doping Agency ([WADA]).

1999   The National Basketball Association modifies its drug policy, first announced in 1983, to include anabolic androgenic steroids.

1999   The U.S. Major League Soccer organization announces a ban on the use of AAS.

2000   Upon recommendation of the United States Olympic Committee's Select Task Force on Externalization, the U.S. Anti-Doping Agency is created to "uphold the Olympic ideal of fair play, and to represent the interests of Olympic, Pan American Games, and Paralympic athletes."

Early 2000s   American chemist Patrick Arnold invents the first two synthetic AAS not listed on anti-doping schedules: norbolethone and tetrahydrogestrinone (also known as THG or "The Clear").

2001   MLB institutes its first random AAS drug-testing policy at the Minor League level. At this point, no Major League player may be tested for AAS.

2002   As part of its collective bargaining agreement, and at the insistence of the U.S. Senate, MLB institutes a random experimental testing program for AAS at the Major League level. No penalty may be assessed for anyone who tests positive for AAS drugs.

2003   MLB institutes a mandatory random drug-testing program for AAS for all Major and Minor League players.

2003   The WADA announced a new World Anti-Doping Code that lists substances banned in international competitions, provisions for testing for such substances, and related anti-doping issues. The Code is first put into use at the 2004 Olympic Games in Athens.

2004   The U.S. Congress passes the Anabolic Steroid Control Act of 2004, which updates and revises the earlier 1990 law placing steroids under Schedule III of the Controlled Substances Act. The Act lists 59 specific substances to be listed under the schedule.

2005   MLB adopts a schedule of penalties for players who test positive for drugs, beginning with a 10-day suspension without pay for the first positive test, a 30-day suspension for the second positive test, a 60-day suspension for the third positive test, and a one-year suspension for the fourth positive test.

2005   MLB player Jose Canseco releases a book, *Juiced: Wild Times, Rampant 'Roids, Smash Hits & How Baseball Got Big*, describing his own experiences with AAS and claiming that 85 percent of all MLB players regularly use AAS drugs.

2006   The National Hockey League institutes a drug-testing program, although it announces that it believes it has "no drug problem."

2006   MLB appoints former U.S. senator George Mitchell to head a committee studying the use of anabolic steroids in Major League Baseball.

2007   American cyclist Floyd Landis is stripped of his 2006 Tour de France championship for testing positive for elevated testosterone levels.

2007   The NFL expands and tightens its drug policy by adding certain substances to its prohibited list and expanding the number of players to be tested annually.

2007   The IOC strips runner Marion Jones of three gold medals and two bronze medals won in the 2000 Olympics because of her use of AAS.

2007   A federal grand jury in San Francisco indicts San Francisco Giants baseball player Barry Bonds for lying about the use of steroids.

2008   Runner Marion Jones is sentenced to six months in prison for her use of illegal AAS.

2008   Former MLB pitcher Roger Clemens and his trainer Brian MacNamee testify before the U.S. House of Representatives' Committee on Oversight and Government Reform that Clemens never used anabolic steroids.

2008   The State of Kentucky bans the use of AAS in horse racing in the state.

2009   The Belgium National Bodybuilding Championships are canceled when all 20 competitors flee the site of competition when anti-doping officials show up unannounced to do surprise steroid testing.

2010   Mark McGwire and Floyd Landis both admit that they used illegal AAS throughout their professional sports careers.

2010   A federal grand jury in Washington, D.C. indicts Roger Clemens for lying to a congressional committee about his use of illegal steroids during his career in MLB.

2011   A jury finds Barry Bonds guilty of obstruction of justice, but reaches no decision on three more serious counts against the former MLB player.

2012   The Court of Arbitration for Sport strips Spanish cyclist Alberto Contador of his 2010 Tour de France championship for testing positive for anabolic steroids.

2012   MLB pitcher Roger Clemens is found innocent of all charges of using illegal drugs during his career.

2012   American cyclist Tyler Hamilton is stripped of his gold medal in the 2004 Olympics Games after he admits that he had used illegal performance-enhancing drugs.

2014   A German documentary film called *Secret Doping—How Russia Makes Its Winners* reveals a long-term, concerted effort by the Russian government to provide performance-enhancing drugs to athletes in a variety of sports.

2014   In response to the above revelation, the WADA commissions an investigation to study these allegations. The investigation is led by former WADA president, Dick Pound. The commission issues its report on November 15, 2015, essentially confirming and extending the findings reported in the *Secret Doping* film.

2015   In a drug operation code named Operation Cyber Juice, the U.S. Drug Enforcement Agency arrests 90 people and shuts down 16 underground steroid facilities.

2016   Former director of the Russian Anti-Doping Agency, Grigory Rodchenkov, releases information about an ongoing, widespread, officially authorized program for the doping of Soviet and later Russian athletes. He specifically describes in some detail the process by which this program was implemented at the 2014 Winter Olympics in Sochi, Russia.

2016   In response to Rodchenkov's announcement, the WADA creates a second commission to investigate the claims regarding the doping of Russian athletes. The commission is headed by Canadian attorney Richard H. McLaren. The commission issues its report in two parts, released on July 18, 2016, and December 9, 2016. The report suggests that Rodchenkov's claims may be "only the tip of the iceberg" with regard to Russian doping of athletes.

2016 As a result of information provided in the McLaren report, 117 Russian athletes are banned from participating in the Summer Olympics held in Rio de Janeiro.

2017 Russian tennis star Maria Sharapova succeeds in having her 2-year ban for drug use reduced to 15 months. The original ban resulted when Sharapova tested positive for the prohibited drug meldonium in 2016.

2017 The International Olympic Committee barred Russia from competing in the 2018 Winter Olympic Games in PyeongChang, South Korea due to evidence of widespread doping practices. Individual athletes who tested cleanly were allowed to compete under the designation "Olympic Athletes from Russia" (OAR), carrying a neutral Olympic flag.

2018 The International Olympic Committee decided against allowing OAR athletes to carry the Russian flag at the closing ceremonies after two Russians tested positive for doping.

Introduction

Discussions of steroids may involve terminology that is unfamiliar to the average person. In some cases, the terms used are scientific, technical, or medical expressions, used most commonly by professionals in the field. In other cases, the terms may be part of the so-called street slang that users themselves employ in talking about the drugs they use, the paraphernalia associated with drugs, or the experiences associated with steroid use. This chapter lists and defines a few of the terms needed to understand explanations provided in this book.

AAS   A common acronym standing for "anabolic androgenic steroids."

addiction   A chronic condition in which a person's body has developed a dependence on some exogenous chemical, generally accompanied by physical changes in the brain.

anabolic   Having reference to a substance that builds new tissue.

anabolism   The metabolic process by which simple compounds, such as sugars and amino acids, are combined in the body to produce more complex compounds, such as carbohydrates and proteins.

analog (also **analogue**) A chemical compound that is structurally similar to some other compound. Testosterone analogs have chemical structures similar to those of testosterone itself.

androgenic Having reference to a substance that produces typical male secondary sexual characteristics.

androstenedione A naturally occurring hormone from which testosterone is formed in the body.

aromatization A chemical process by which excess testosterone in the body is converted into the female hormone estrogen.

atrophy The process by which the mass and strength of body tissue decrease, often as the result of lack of use or because of the use of an exogenous chemical.

basement drug A counterfeit drug.

blending The process of combining the use of steroids with the use of other drugs.

catabolism The metabolic process by which complex compounds in the body, such as carbohydrates and proteins, are broken down into simpler organic compounds, such as sugars and amino acids.

chemical analog *See* analog.

cycling The schedule on which an individual uses steroids.

cycloalkane An organic (carbon-containing) compound consisting of only carbon and hydrogen atoms joined to each other in a ring of carbon atoms.

designer drug/steroid A synthetic compound that is created in the laboratory to have physiological effects similar to those of some natural or other synthetic compounds.

diuretic Any substance that increases the output of urine from the body.

doping The process of using an illegal substance, such as steroids, in an athletic competition.

drug test A chemical analysis of some bodily fluid, usually blood or urine, to detect the presence of certain specified chemicals, such as illegal drugs.

endogenous   Created within the body.

epitestosterone   An isomer (structurally similar form) of testosterone produced naturally in the body, but with different physiological effects from testosterone.

ergogenic   Performance enhancing.

exogenous   Created outside of the body.

gonane   A grouping of four cycloalkane rings joined to each other forming the core of a steroid molecule.

gynecomastia   A process by which males develop unusually large mammary glands, resulting in the development of atypically large breasts.

hormone   A chemical substance (protein) produced in one part of the body that travels to another part of the body and produces a physiological effect at that site.

hypertrophy   The increase in the size or bulk of an organ or tissue.

lean mass   The mass of muscle in the body.

libido   Sex drive.

macrocycle   The elements that make up a year-long training program, usually including preparation, competition, and transition phases.

megadosing   The process of ingesting very large quantities of a substance, such as a steroid, often far beyond levels considered safe by the medical profession.

microcycle   The elements that make up a brief period in a training cycle, usually one week.

off-label use   Any use of a prescription pharmaceutical for which it was not originally and specifically approved.

organotherapy   Strictly, the treatment of a disease with extracts from the organs (usually the glands) of an animal. Also, the consumption of animal organs by athletes in an attempt to gain physical traits associated with those organs (such as the consumption of testicles to increase masculine traits of strength and endurance).

periodization   The process of arranging a training schedule into discrete segments so as to achieve some maximum effect. *Also see* macrocycle, microcycle.

plateau   A condition in which the continued use of AAS no longer has an increased effect on a person's body.

plyometrics   A type of athletic training designed to improve one's ability to move rapidly and powerfully.

prohormone   A chemical substance that is a precursor to a hormone produced in the body but that has little or no hormonal effects in and of itself.

pyramiding   The process by which the number of drugs taken or the quantity of one drug, or both, is gradually increased to some maximum point, followed by a gradually tapering off.

'roid rage   An uncontrollable and often unpredictable outburst of anger, frustration, combativeness, or other negative emotion brought about by the use of steroids.

shotgunning   The practice of taking steroid drugs according to some irregular schedule.

stacking   The process in which a person uses two or more AAS in combination with each other.

steroid   An organic (carbon-containing) compound consisting of a core of four cycloalkane rings joined to each other. In popular parlance, the term often refers to the specific category of anabolic steroids.

supraphysiological   Having to do with quantities of a substance greater than is normally found in the body.

tapering   The process of slowly reducing the amount of drugs taken over some given period of time.

T/E drug test   A common drug test used with athletes that measures the ratio of testosterone to epitestosterone in the body.

testosterone   A hormone secreted primarily by the testes, responsible for the development of male sex organs and secondary sexual characteristics, such as deepening of the voice, development of body hair, and increase in body and muscle mass.

virilization   The process by which a female begins to develop male sexual characteristics, often the result of using AAS.

withdrawal symptoms   The appearance of unusual or abnormal physical and/or psychological characteristics as the result of discontinuing the use of some chemical substance.

About the Author

David E. Newton holds an associate's degree in science from Grand Rapids (Michigan) Junior College, a B.A. in chemistry (with high distinction), an M.A. in education from the University of Michigan, and an EdD in science education from Harvard University. He is the author of more than 400 textbooks, encyclopedias, resource books, research manuals, laboratory manuals, trade books, and other educational materials. He taught mathematics, chemistry, and physical science in Grand Rapids, Michigan, for 13 years; was professor of chemistry and physics at Salem State College in Massachusetts for 15 years; and was adjunct professor in the College of Professional Studies at the University of San Francisco for 10 years.

The author's previous books for ABC-CLIO include *Global Warming* (1993), *Gay and Lesbian Rights—A Resource Handbook* (1994, 2009), *The Ozone Dilemma* (1995), *Violence and the Mass Media* (1996), *Environmental Justice* (1996, 2009), *Encyclopedia of Cryptology* (1997), *Social Issues in Science and Technology: An Encyclopedia* (1999), *DNA Technology* (2009), *Sexual Health* (2010), *The Animal Experimentation Debate* (2013), *Marijuana* (2013), *World Energy Crisis* (2013), *Steroids and Doping in Sports* (2014), *GMO Food* (2014), *Science and Political Controversy* (2014), *Wind Energy* (2015), *Fracking* (2015), *Solar Energy* (2015), *Youth Substance Abuse* (2016), and *Global Water Crisis* (2016). His other recent books include *Physics: Oryx Frontiers of Science Series* (2000); *Sick!* (four volumes) (2000); *Science, Technology, and Society: The Impact of Science in the 19th Century* (two volumes) (2001); *Encyclopedia of Fire* (2002); *Molecular Nanotechnology: Oryx Frontiers of Science Series* (2002); *Encyclopedia of Water* (2003); *Encyclopedia of Air* (2004); *The New Chemistry* (six volumes) (2007); *Nuclear Power* (2005); *Stem Cell Research* (2006); *Latinos in the Sciences, Math, and Professions* (2007); and *DNA Evidence and Forensic Science* (2008). He has also been an updating and consulting editor on a number of books and reference works, including *Chemical Compounds* (2005), *Chemical Elements* (2006), *Encyclopedia of Endangered Species* (2006), *World of Mathematics* (2006), *World of Chemistry* (2006), *World of Health* (2006), *UXL Encyclopedia of Science* (2007), *Alternative Medicine* (2008), *Grzimek's Animal Life Encyclopedia* (2009), *Community Health* (2009), *Genetic Medicine* (2009), *The Gale Encyclopedia of Medicine* (2010–2011), *The Gale Encyclopedia of Alternative Medicine* (2013), *Discoveries in Modern Science: Exploration, Invention, and Technology* (2013–2014), and *Science in Context* (2013–2014).